ONE HUNDRED
MILLION
ACRES

ONE HUNDRED MILLION ACRES

KIRKE KICKINGBIRD

&

KAREN DUCHENEAUX

WITH A FOREWORD BY *Vine Deloria, Jr.*

Macmillan Publishing Co., Inc.

New York

Collier Macmillan Publishers

London

Macmillan Publishing Co., Inc.
Collier-Macmillan Canada Ltd.

Library of Congress Catalog Card Number: 72-77650
First Printing 1973
Printed in the United States of America

Contents

Foreword

THE INDIAN brave is seated on his horse high on the distant hill, a speck on the horizon. In the valley below are the first wagons of what will be an endless stream of settlers on their way to a promised land. So goes the scenario of the winning of the West that most Americans recognize. But it was actually much different.

The irony of the present understanding of American Indian problems is that in attempting to break through into contemporary consciousness the Indian power movement found itself immediately deluged by the fantasies of an America that had all but forgotten that Indians existed. By the late nineteen sixties a number of books describing contemporary Indian problems had been written. A group of Indian activists had landed on and secured Alcatraz. The fishing-rights struggle of the rivers of the Pacific Northwest had boiled over into the newspapers. Each year, Indians told themselves, would be the "Year of the Indian."

But the media put an end to that dream rather quickly. The reading public was directed to *Bury My Heart at Wounded Knee*, a rehash of the wars of the 1860–90 period, which attempted to present the attitudes and outlooks of the various Indian leaders in their efforts to negotiate with the federal government. The book succeeded in its intention, but its reception indicated that it was much easier for white America to sympathize with phantoms of a bygone era than to confront the fact that the situation of the Indian had not improved in the intervening years.

Following closely on the heels of Dee Brown's phenomenal

best seller came a blatant hoax that was accepted as a true account. *The Memoirs of Chief Red Fox*, which turned out to be a plagiary of an obscure book written by an Indian agent sometime before World War II, was embraced by critics and readers alike for telling "what Indians were really like." No one thought to check the claim of Red Fox with his tribe, nor could anyone identify the educated Indians of the Red Power movement with the heroic poets of Dee Brown and Cash Asher.

The Red Fox fiasco was followed by a melodramatic scissors-and-paste job by T. C. McLuhan entitled *Touch the Wind*, in which the heartrendering surrender speeches were piled one on top of the other until the last century of life-and-death struggle for the American West became a convention of Indian poets standing on the hillside in the twilight reciting the wrongs of a mythical demon known as the "government."

With the concept of modern Indians thus completely buried under a collection of trivia and nostalgia, the media focused on Women's Liberation, satisfied that they had solved the problems of the American Indian community. So much for Indians, people thought, and promptly began another century of degradation, abuse and deprivation of the original inhabitants. Raymond Yellow Thunder, a fifty-one-year-old Sioux Indian from Pine Ridge, South Dakota, was beaten up, taken to an American Legion hall, stripped from the waist down, and made to dance before the assembled veterans of America's glorious past, the same people who decades earlier had fought to preserve the dignity of man from totalitarian aggression.

In the state of Washington three hundred state game wardens, Tacoma city police and miscellaneous law officers illegally entered Indian lands which were outside of their jurisdiction, and brutally beat and arrested a group of Indians who were camped there fishing under the provisions of the treaties of 1854 and 1855. A year later the governor of the state signed into a law a bill allowing the state of Washington to tax Indian reservations over which it had specifically been forbidden any jurisdiction whatsoever. Mumbling that he thought the state had a case, Daniel Evans initiated a series of costly suits brought by Indians when he signed into law the bill to tax Indians on those reservations over which the state of Washington had refused to accept civil and criminal jurisdiction fifteen years before.

In the state of Minnesota the Chippewa Indians won a case on fishing and hunting on public lands within the Leech Lake Reservation in the Land of Ten Thousand Lakes. The local whites who had gotten all excited about the students and blacks who refused to obey the laws of the land promptly set up a vigilante committee to fight any Indian who tried to exercise his right as decreed by the court. Laws were fine when they were applied against Indians, but heaven help the state that tried to recognize Indian rights which might possibly infringe upon the recreation pleasures of white sportsmen.

The last few years have been characterized by one common theme. Whites are damned sorry that all those Indians got killed at Sand Creek and Wounded Knee, but if any Indians think that things have changed they better look closely at the crowd gathering at the reservation boundary. The vigilantes are out in force and if they didn't finish the job at the Washita then they are prepared to do it now. And a century from now another Dee Brown can recount how terrible it all was—but that's progress. It had to be done if the West was to be settled and civilization brought to an untamed wilderness.

Repentance is not a common commodity in contemporary America even if it is brimming with red-blooded, God-fearing Americans who are only interested in securing the Constitutional rights of life, liberty and pursuit of happiness to American citizens and the blessings of democracy to the rest of the world.

Thus after a ten-year struggle to bring Indian people's problems to the attention of the American public, the net achievement can be said to have been a clever *Life* magazine story recounting how striking Indian art really is, a fairly well-to-do elderly white in Corpus Christi who had the satisfaction of hoaxing the American public and the launching of a thousand anthologies containing Chief Joseph's surrender speech.

This book will come as a shock to its readers. It is as contemporary as today's headlines. It is broad, sweeping in its scope and informative in a sense never encountered by the reading public. It gives an accurate account of the present state of Indian lands. No recopy job from the diary of an obscure Indian agent, no hokey retyping of Black Hawk's dinner speech to Abraham Lincoln at old Fort Armstrong and no startling discovery of the logistics of the Little Big Horn.

The complexities of Indian land titles are very much like the dialogue in Alice in Wonderland. Indian title means what the United States has wanted it to mean whenever the subject has come up. *One Hundred Million Acres* attempts to pin down the historical foundations of the recognition of ownership accorded the original inhabitants when they were first discovered by Columbus.

In spite of the rapid expansion and cancerous growth of the United States, Indian tribes still maintain a quasi-independent status vis-à-vis other nations of the globe in that they are in a state of expectant nationhood. One judge of the United States Supreme Court likened them to the Hebrews wandering in the Sinai wilderness—a nation among nations, disenfranchised in part but capable of becoming cognizable owners of land. This doctrine may strike a note of discord in modern conceptions of industrial superstates, but when it is seen in a world context which includes Ireland, the Basques of Spain, and the tribal-internecine rivalries in Africa and Indochina, it becomes a rather sophisticated doctrine.

Among the more surprising elements of Indian land tenure is the aspect of continual experimentation with property rights which has been visited upon the individual tribes by Congressional fiat. Rather than advocating a profound, logical and rigorous relationship of ward-guardian, or trustee-ward, the United States policy has fluctuated between the strictest enforcement of trust duties and the most lax and benign neglect worthy of a Moynihan tome.

Indian land titles therefore reflect more about what policy makers have considered a justifiable method of social engineering via the adjustment of property rights than any legal doctrine that could be recognized by a court of law in this country or any other within the European tradition of land tenure.

The most surprising doctrine, and one hearkening to the days of William the Conqueror effortlessly readjusting Saxon titles to his own convenience, is the idea that the United States "takes" Indian lands by implication. Several chapters in this book are devoted to an explanation of the various methods by which certain departments of the government have managed to walk off with thousands of acres of Indian lands. By merely finding conflicting Presidential orders setting aside certain public lands for certain purposes, government agencies have marched right on to Indian reservations and cut out the best lands for themselves. At other times, by maintaining that two erroneous surveys merged to create a valid boundary line, government officers have taken many acres from Indian reservations and either allowed cattlemen to move into the Indian lands or silently tucked the lands into their own pockets.

The whole conception of a trustee benefiting from his own error at the expense of his ward has a slightly un-American tinge to it. Yet few Americans realize that this method is the most popular device among bureaucrats who seek to expand their territorial empires at the expense of the taxpayer and the Indian tribes involved. To regain lands illegally taken from them Indian tribes today present the stiffest combination of legal argument combined with an aggressive media campaign and political action. The program has worked with the return of Taos Blue Lake in New Mexico and the Mount Adams area in Washington state. It is as recent as tomorrow's headlines.

One of the difficulties in presenting the Indian side of the story has been that the majority of Indian people live in the isolated and neglected regions of the American West. The news media are concentrated in New York City where Indians are a rare commodity—so rare that Chief Red Fox was actually considered an Indian by newspaper and television people. Since Indians are not constantly before the eyes and ears of eastern America, the assumption has been that no real problems existed except those deliberately conjured up by a demonic Bureau of Indian Affairs.

Within eastern America, from the polluted right bank of the Mississippi to the rocky and oil-covered coasts of Maine, live nearly 100,000 Indians in some eighty distinct communities. For the most part these people were living in such isolated parts of the East that the settlement of the Ohio and Mississippi valleys rushed right by them. They were so few that they presented no formidable military threat to the God-fearing settlers and they simply continued to live as they always had lived.

The civil rights movement awakened white America to the oppression of blacks in the South, primarily in the areas of public accommodations and school segregation. Part of the backlash of the civil rights movement has been that Indian communities in North and South Carolina, Louisiana and Mississippi which had previously maintained their own community institutions became subject to school consolidation and integration orders. Schools which had been operated by Indians for their own benefit became the first schools to receive any attention in the integration of black pupils. It is, when you stop to consider it, much easier to merge Indians and blacks together and call it an integrated school than to share such facilities between whites and blacks.

The result of the move to consolidate Indians with the rest of southern society, while studiously avoiding any admixture of black and white, has been to underline rather prominently the fact that a number of Indian communities still exist in the southeastern United States. Because of this sudden high profile, bureaucrats within Interior have been stirring in their chairs uneasily as they have been forced to realize that a considerable part of their trust responsibilities have been casually shirked off with respect to eastern Indian communities.

One Hundred Million Acres proposes that one fundamental federal policy be established for all dependent Indian communities. The actual needs of these communities are very small and identification of them serves only too well to remind people that the reserves of the West are badly overadministered in some respects, neglected almost wholly in others. A national federal policy with respect to the first Americans, as the politicians so fondly tag Indians, would set guidelines of community rights and define and limit the extent to which Indian communities *should* depend upon federal service support.

One Hundred Million Acres may be one of the most important books ever published on the subject of Indians. It represents the first effort by Indian people to present their side of a legal controversy. Prior to this volume, legal issues concerning Indian rights have been the subject of white scholars who have had an interest in Indian legal problems as an exotic offshoot of more basic legal questions. We have seen such ludicrous explanations of the legal history of Indians as that of Father Prucha who has seen Andrew Jackson as a benevolent friend of the Five Civilized Tribes and their Removal with its Trail of Tears as a happy scouting lark.

Critics have complained that when Indians have tried to

present their side of the story that the account has been "over-emotional" and an "overreaction" to the events of history. Perhaps if the critics had had bulldozers crushing their churches and historical places they would feel a twinge of resentment against the invaders of their communities also.

We hope this book can begin an era of understanding between Indian people and the American public. What happens to Indian lands and Indian rights is simply a microcosm of what is happening to the whole American society, indeed the world. The contained denial of legal rights to a weak minority is mirrored in the steadfast refusal of American politicians of both major parties to even the odds between the rich families and their corporate interests and the majority of American people. Perhaps with this book we can urge the reading public to leave the fantasy world of T. C. McLuhan and the whimsical hoax of Chief Red Fox and undertake a serious examination of the status of American Indians today.

The basic difference between the red man and his white brother has been one of fundamentally opposed world views and religious understandings. The white man has tended to see history as a series of good-hearted efforts to achieve the present happy state of industrial America. All previous civilizations are regarded as valid because they advanced or promoted some facet of present-day American understanding of the world. The red man has tended to avoid categorizing history as a sequence of events of more than regional significance. It has been inconsequential to him that Greece and Rome existed at all.

From this distinction in historical perception has come an inability by either party to cross over into the thought patterns of the opponent and make an argument which can be understood. That is the importance of this book. It is *not* an Indian presentation of the land question in terms acceptable to Indian people. That would involve a fundamental change in the ability of white men to perceive religious sensitivity in relation to creation and a creator.

Rather, this book is the first effort by Indian people, and, one might add, young, educated-into-western-logical-systems Indian people, to present a reasonable, documented and detailed argument for the recognition of land titles to Indians *within the thought system of western man.* If Indians arguing on Indian premises are not acceptable, the authors maintain, then Indians arguing on Anglo-Saxon legal premises should surely be acceptable.

Many psychologists have toyed with the idea that the white man can never sink his roots into the soil of North America because he has never approached either the land or its inhabitants as equals but as objects of scorn. Perhaps it is more important to understand the fear with which the Europeans approached the New World—a fear that has never relaxed itself even to this day.

Columbus had great difficulty with his sailors who were convinced that he was mad and that they all would perish when their ships sailed to the edge of the world and drifted off into space. So exotic was the New World they encountered that the first explorers looked for a land of magical cities and fountains qualitatively different than their familiar European geography. Cities of gold lived in men's minds and memories for centuries after the Spanish had conquered central America.

On the Atlantic coast, settlement was accomplished more by default than by intention. Given the choice between European gallows and transportation to an unknown world, many chose the gallows; probably an equal number counted themselves dead already and lengthened their lives by coming to North America. The fear of punishment and the certainty of eternal damnation in a fiery hell, when balanced against the unknown terrors of a world that appeared endless, transformed one type of fear into a determination to survive the unknown. By obliterating any trace of the original nature of the new land and its living creatures, they hoped to conquer their fear.

Certainly one cannot surmise that the good burghers of London, Amsterdam and York packed their material wealth and hastened to the New World to establish virtual replicas of London, Amsterdam and York on the Atlantic seacoast. Nor did pardoned men wish to reestablish their happy memories of England in the New World. The creation of towns bearing names of European counterparts was a desperate effort to provide some continuance of identity once the great sea voyage had cut off all possibility of maintaining a tradition rooted in European historical experiences.

It is probably this early fear that the wilderness would swallow them, as it had Sir Walter Raleigh's Lost Colony, that made the settlers so determined to tame the continent. Today in the decay of the cities, the vast migration westward by individuals and corporations, the mighty projects for turning western America into what Boston and New York could have been, or once were, one can see that this primeval fear of white America has not been conquered, only translated to face a new mode of existence.

The fundamental turning point in white America's failure to become a native of the continent will revolve around land-use problems. A recognition of the major Indian contention—the sacredness of land—as reflected in a legal affirmation of the rights of Indian communities to hold their lands as national entities exempted from the arbitrary decisions of state and federal governments, will mark the maturing of America as a society. At present we are told that it is "greening." After nearly four centuries we would hope so.

Having "greened," it is now time to mature.

VINE DELORIA, JR.

To the Reader

DURING THE PREPARATION of this book the United States Congress passed four pieces of legislation in September and October of 1972 which affected lands mentioned in this book. Public Law 92–480 (October 9, 1972) declared that the United States would hold in trust 13,077 acres of submarginal lands for the Stockbridge-Munsee Tribe. Public Law 92–488 (October 13, 1972) declared that 770 acres of land were to be held by the United States in trust for the Burns Paiutes of the Burns Indian Colony, Oregon (see the chapter entitled "Those Whom Even Time Forgot"). Public Law 92–470 (October 6, 1972) authorized the acquisition of a village site for the Payson Band of Yavapai Apaches not exceed 85 acres in the Tonto National Forest. This legislation also recognized the Payson Band as a tribe under the Indian Reorganization Act (see Tonto Apaches in "Those Whom Even Time Forgot"). Public Law 92–427 (September 21, 1972) declared that some 61,360 acres were to be held by the United States in trust for the Confederated Tribes of the Warm Springs Reservation (see the "Forest Service Strikes Again & Again . . .").

Acknowledgments

We would like to thank the Honorable Willie Hensley, an Eskimo and Alaskan state senator, for his aid in researching and drafting the chapter entitled "Snowball in Hell." Our thanks also to Harold E. Gross, Esq., Director of the Indian Legal Information Development Service for his aid in researching and drafting the chapter entitled "Submarginal Lands are Alive and . . . Well?"

Introduction

THE DESCENDANTS of the Pilgrim Fathers were all decked out in their finest costumes on Thanksgiving Day 1969, when, unlike their esteemed forebears, they were set upon by a group of angry Indians. Although it was wholly outside the New England tradition of the Pilgrims and Indians sitting down to consume turkey and dressing, the demonstration by the Indian students who constitute the Organization of Native American Students had a point. In the intervening centuries the Pilgrims had gotten out of hand.

The little old ladies—proper Bostonians from another, more peaceful era—were furious at the Indian intrusion into the ceremonies. A diminutive soul, decked in Puritan finery, dashed over to a gigantic Indian student who easily topped six feet. "You're ruining it," she shrieked. And then in curious demonstration of her grasp of American history, "Why don't you go back where you came from?"

It was natural, in a way, that an easterner should consider Indians an exotic commodity. After all, there had been no Indians in that part of the country for some time. The Pilgrim Fathers had seen to that. But the incident is illustrative of fundamental attitudes held by the majority of non-Indians in this country. They have been so busy with other things that they have forgotten where they came from and how the whole thing started.

This book is an effort to provide some of that hidden and forgotten data. The current interest in Indians has resulted in a spate of books with brilliant photographs of Indian chiefs, reams of poetic speeches, quaint sayings of the famous Indian leaders of yesteryear and a rush toward the nostalgia of the "good old days" when everyone knew exactly who the Indians were and what they were up to.

What has been buried—besides the many hearts at Wounded Knee—is the true nature of the settling of the North American continent. It was not really as romantic as most would like to think. By and large it was a series of tedious land transactions shored up by hundreds of memoranda by administrators making sure that the United States received the best possible interpretation of the treaties and transactions of the immediate past.

The major source of all Indian-white conflict and confrontation has been land. What is the fundamental position that land should occupy in a society or the economics of a society? Does it belong to whoever measures and fences it? Or is it an inalienable basis of a community's existence and therefore incapable of subdivision?

There is no denying that racial attitudes played an important part in the wars between white and Indian over ownership of parts of the continent. Indians in the South were the first people to be subjected to slavery. But the major subject under consideration from beginning to end has always been land. The economic consequences of rivalry between the use of the land for agriculture and its use for hunting triggered immense conflict. It still does today; in a great many states where Indians still maintain their rights to live by fishing, they reject oil refineries and factories on their lands.

Sitting Bull, the great medicine man of the Dakotas (generally known as the Sioux), clarified the puzzlement of Indians about the question of land. In 1883, while opposing government policies that would have allotted to individual Indians the tribal lands at the Standing Rock Reservation in North Dakota, Sitting Bull declared,

If a man loses anything and goes back and looks carefully for it he will find it; and that is what the Indians are doing now when they ask you to give them the things that were promised them in the past; and I do not consider that they should be treated like beasts, and that is the reason I have grown up with the feelings I have. I feel that my country has gotten a bad name; and I sit sometimes and wonder who it is that has given it a bad name.

As people have understood history it is Indians that have gotten a bad name. When they fought for their lands, their struggle was called an uprising, their victories recorded as massacres. Because whites could not understand the Indians' concept of land tenure, they derided the communal use of land as inefficient or, worse, thought that the Indians were trying to "get away with something." This attitude developed in the remote past and has to this day characterized the relationship between Indians and whites.

The world of the European prior to the discovery of the New World was relatively simple. It was flat, finite, and Christian. It had been created specifically for those who believed in the one true religion, and while other, non-Christian peoples did inhabit remote stretches of the known world, they existed primarily for the missionary activity.

While the New World was unknown in Europe except for vague legends of "lands to the west" derived from the experiences of the Vikings and tales of the travels of an Irish monk, no one was exactly sure what lay beyond the setting sun. Explorers were commissioned by kings, queens, and emperors of Europe to find new trade routes to the east and especially to India.

The discovery of the lands of the western hemisphere was a shock to most Europeans. No one had expected to find two immense continents sitting out there where the edge of the flat earth should have been nor a substantial number of people where no one had been thought to live.

In order to encourage exploration and the development of trade the doctrine was developed quite early that the European nation that discovered a land had exclusive rights to trade with it. This doctrine encouraged a dramatic race between exploring expeditions to "claim" lands on behalf of their respective sovereigns. It was not long before Europeans decided that their nations should not claim only trading privileges in an area but the land itself.

A debate ensued in Europe between those who classified the inhabitants of the western hemisphere as animals (and therefore incapable of owning land or engaging in trade) and those who, relying upon the scientific distinctions of Aristotle, maintained that the inhabitants did have souls, were men, and therefore had some rights, albeit undefined, to the lands they occupied.

The argument was decided in one of those uniquely unsatisfactory compromises for which European Christians have been justly noted. It was decided that, while Indians were indeed men whose right to lands was to be respected by European nations, God had intended man to engage in commerce and trade and that just wars could be waged against any tribe and nation of the New World that interfered with the trading activities of the Europeans. Since the Europeans were sailing west only for trading purposes, any resistance by the western peoples was an interference with God's proposed commerce. Conquest of the New World was thus justified by religious and ethical standards understood by the Europeans. Settlement and colonization quickly came to occupy an important role in the activities of the European nations in the New World. Later some nations would use the lands they had discovered as penal colonies and places for political exile.

The doctrine that evolved to justify displacement of the native populations was called the doctrine of discovery. In practical terms it meant that the European nation that claimed to have discovered the lands occupied by a non-Christian people had exclusive rights to take their lands away from them.

The legal minds of Europe hesitated to probe too deeply into the implications of the doctrine. One theologian suggested that according to the doctrine, an Indian prince could sail along the coast of Europe and claim all the lands of the Europeans without even getting his feet wet. No one wanted to contemplate the possibility that they might all become subjects of an obscure maharajah, so the doctrine was not explained to the peoples of the western hemisphere except in piously religious terms of bringing the Gospel to the heathen.

There was a major flaw in the doctrine of discovery: it did not cover the problem of perpetual land tenure. No provision was ever made for the natives of the "newly discovered" lands to obtain a final decision on their titles. Suppose they immediately became Christians—did this mean that their lands were not to be invaded by Christian nations and that they were to have privileges of national existence comparable to those of the many small states that existed in Europe at that time? This question was never decided. Once the riches of the New World began to pour into the coffers of Europe, any consideration of native land tenure was conveniently put to rest in favor of absolute rule of landholding by the conquering power. The natives of the western hemisphere would at no time have an opportunity to hold their lands in good title.

During the struggle for control of the eastern coast of the North American continent the race for land was hotly contested. Claims to title of lands passed from nation to nation as various wars forced European countries to cede their North American claims to one another in partial settlement of European conflicts.

The American Revolution provided the new United States with a justification for its claim to the right to settle the remainder of the interior of the continent, Canada excluded. American political theorists contended that the United States had stepped into the shoes of England with respect to the doctrine of discovery.

With the United States claiming the right to extinguish all Indian titles to lands on the continent within its domestic borders, the Indian tribes were deprived of any right of appeal. It became merely a matter of when, not if, the United States would take the lands. The unarticulated assumption upon which American Indian policy was based, therefore, was that land title could only be acquired from the federal government. Indian titles were considered nonexistent.

That is not to say that there was total agreement to disfranchise Indian tribes. Because of the uncertainty about Indian title in the minds of the states and federal departments of government, the executive branch in days of confederation assumed the significant responsibility of ensuring that all Indian lands would be subject to its control. While the purpose of land cession by the tribes was to benefit individual white settlers and immigrants, no individual was allowed to deal directly for purchase of Indian lands without a federal official being present to endorse the transaction.

The Northwest Ordinance of 1787 was passed by Congress in an effort to make settlement of the Great Lakes region more orderly and to raise revenues for the federal treasury through sales of Indian lands. It defined in the most precise terms the basis upon which Indians would hold their lands and what policy would be taken toward them:

The utmost good faith shall always be observed towards the Indians; their lands and property shall never be taken from them without their consent; and, in their property, rights, and liberty, they shall never be invaded or disturbed, unless in just and lawful wars authorized by Congress; but laws founded in justice and humanity shall from time to time be made for preventing wrongs being done to them, and for preserving peace and friendship with them.

Perhaps no better statement of lofty ideals and humanitarian motives could have been devised. But the philosophy of the Northwest Ordinance was promptly forgotten, and when it was invoked, it was used to justify the exercise of naked congressional power against the tribes, a violation of both the spirit and letter of the law.

The earliest policy on Indian lands envisioned the gradual removal of the eastern tribes to the stark plains of the West, where it was thought that no white man could exist. The policy was a step above genocide. The savagery of the Indian, his obvious inability to use the land according to Christian principles of commerce, and his persistence in his pagan religions were used to justify his banishment to the great American desert, as the Great Plains were then called. Indian land policy was thus shifted from one of original ownership to allocation by relative levels of civilization, a wholly cultural conception lacking any legal basis whatsoever.

Where did Congress get the power to distribute Indian lands to non-Indians? With the adoption of the Constitution, the colonies became a federal government in which individual states ceded certain powers to that government and retained other powers that they thought should be denied it. Functions were allocated to the various branches of government and the executive and legislative branches received the powers and responsibilities to deal with Indian tribes.

The president, with the advice and consent of the Senate, could make treaties with the Indians that had the same legal status as those made with foreign nations. But treaties never gave the tribes a totally sovereign and independent status in the eyes of the United States because the doctrine of discovery lurked in the background. The early treaties were a frantic effort by the United States to gain Indian allies at the expense of England and other European nations who had not forgotten that a rich continent was still available for the taking. It would seem that these treaties would have given the tribes a semi-independent status, since they still had, at that time, the option of aligning themselves with nations other than the United States.

While the executive branch of the government could establish the first legal relationship between Indian tribes and the United States and was responsible for maintaining any relationships the United States might enjoy with these tribes, the Constitution split the subject of Indian relationships between Congress and the executive. The interstate commerce clause authorized Congress to make laws with respect to trading with Indian tribes and with foreign nations. The first laws passed by Congress concerning the Indians were primarily of this nature. They defined the manner in which trade could be carried on with the Indian tribes.

The expansion of the role of Congress in other matters inevitably carried over to the field of Indian affairs. With constant pressure from western settlers and a growing block of manifest-destiny expansionists in Congress to articulate this pressure into legislative proposals, Congress began to alter its duties from mere trade regulation to total control over every aspect of Indian programs and policies. This trend has been particularly noticeable over the past half-century.

The traditional interpretation given to the interstate commerce clause by the federal courts has been to regard trade as a political, rather than an economic, reality. Thus, sticky questions of property rights and instances of enforcement of Indian treaty rights have been dodged by the federal courts as being too politically controversial. The courts have generally ruled that Indian questions are, in an ultimate sense, political and, as such, must be handled by Congress through legislation rather than under the usual Constitutional guarantees of due process and equal protection given to other American citizens. The courts have accepted the presumption that Congress always acts with wisdom and in good faith when dealing with Indians. It is a fanciful notion rather than a fact of life.

As the role of the federal government in Indian affairs has grown, various agencies have come into being that deal with nearly the same questions in regard to Indian lands as to the agencies dealing primarily with Indian tribal rights. When the Bureau of Indian Affairs was transferred to the Department of the Interior in 1849, it was placed in competition with a number of the department's other agencies, all addressing themselves to the task of supervising national physical resources. For the most part these agencies have been devoted to the confiscation of Indian lands rather than to developing them to safeguard them for their Indian owners. The twentieth century has shown a rapid growth of policies devoted to the exploitation of Indian lands by government agencies, with the Interior Department supervising the rape of Indian legal rights in a most interesting manner.

Within the Interior Department, the Division of Public Lands, which oversees all public lands except Indian reservations and agricultural forest lands, has developed such exotic branches as the Reclamation Service and the Wildlife Service, which from their very inception have coveted Indian lands. These agencies, supported on the outside by powerful groups of citizens and commercial interests, have generally determined what position would be officially taken by the parent Interior Department as protector of Indian reservation lands and waters.

It would be fair to say that if a private trustee were discovered acting in the same manner as the Interior Department does toward the Indians, he would immediately be indicted for gross violation of his trust. In all but a few cases, bureaucrats in the department have deliberately thwarted attempts by the Indian tribes to keep their lands under tribal ownership.

The situation is far beyond the point of simple scandal. It is so blatant that even the president has been forced to concede the total abdication by federal officials of their responsibilities for the protection of Indian rights. In a special message on Indians sent to Congress in July 1970, President Nixon outlined new legislation of major proportions. He called for the creation of an Indian Trust Counsel Authority, a special agency independent of both the Justice and Interior departments, to defend Indian rights. In the words of the president,

The first Americans—the Indians—are the most deprived and most isolated minority group in our nation. On virtually every scale of measurement—employment, income, education, health—the condition of the Indian people ranks at the bottom.

This condition is the heritage of centuries of injustice. From the time of their first contact with the European settlers, the American Indians have been oppressed and brutalized, deprived of their ancestral lands and denied the opportunity to control their own destiny.

Even the federal programs which are intended to meet their needs have frequently proven to be ineffective and demeaning.

Both as a matter of justice and as a matter of enlightened social policy, we must begin to act on the basis of what the Indians themselves have long been telling us.

The Indians have been saying this sort of thing for a long time. What was unprecedented in the situation was that a president of the United States felt so strongly about the Indian situation that he would actually mention wrongs done and injuries suffered because of federal dereliction of duties.

A case in point: an effort to take away the water rights of a number of tribes on the Colorado River in Arizona and the Rio Grande in New Mexico was made in the courts in 1971 in the *Eagle River* decision. Indian tribes had been aware that they might lose their water rights, rights that were essential to their existence in the southwestern deserts, where their reservations were located.

A number of tribes made official appeals to the Justice and Interior departments. In a letter to Minerva Jenkins, the tribal chairwoman of the Fort Mojave Tribal Council, at Needles, California, Erwin N. Griswold, solicitor general of the United States, promised that the Justice Department would fully defend the rights of the tribe to water on the Colorado River.

"Please be assured," he wrote in early November 1970, "that the government intends to make the Supreme Court fully aware of its obligations as trustee of Indian water rights in this matter [the *Eagle River* case], and of any bearing that the decision may have on those rights." When, however, the Justice Department filed its brief in the case in which it was to assert the Indian water rights before the Supreme Court, it said in an obscure footnote, "To the best of our knowledge, none of the reserved water rights claimed by the United States in Water Division No. 5 relate to Indian lands."

The result of the *Eagle River* decision was to place all Indian water rights at the mercy of the court systems of the various states, courts that are notoriously anti-Indian. The tribes issued loud protests and finally a subcommittee of the Senate, headed by Senator Edward Kennedy, looked into the deprivation of water rights, concentrating on conflicts of interest within the Interior Department. Questioned by the committee, Harrison

Loesch, assistant secretary of the interior for land management, who oversees the administration of Indian programs, lamely related that he did not "know" that Indians placed a high priority on water.

Loesch was less than frank with the committee. Indian tribes had waged an unceasing war against Loesch over water rights for nearly a year when he appeared before the committee. But it was generally conceded by everyone concerned that Loesch, a patronage appointment of Senator Gordon Allott, reactionary senator from Colorado, had been placed in his position to carry on precisely this kind of war of attrition against Indians.

The traditional major argument used by anti-Indian officials at both state and federal levels centers on the legal status of Indian tribes themselves. They seem to feel that the longer a tribe exists, the fewer legal rights it actually has. Thus, mere passage of time is used to justify abrogation of right and refusal of officials to recognize legal principles of property rights where they might apply to Indian people and tribes. This argument was early laid to rest by the Supreme Court of the United States in the *Kansas Indians* case (1866).

The state of Kansas, attempting to tax the Shawnees, argued that the members of the tribe had settled down and were farmers and therefore no longer Indians deserving of, or entitled to, federal protection. The Supreme Court ruled, "If the tribal organization of the Shawnees is preserved intact and recognized by the Political Departments of the Government as existing, then they are 'a people distinct from others,' capable of making treaties, separated from the jurisdiction of Kansas, and to be governed exclusively by the government of the Union. If they have outlived many things, they have not outlived the protection afforded by the Constitution, treaties and laws of Congress." In spite of this rather clear definition of federal responsibility for American Indians, current attitudes of Congress and the administrative branches of government make it clear that these protections will not be afforded Indians except on those occasions when it is politically impossible to do otherwise.

The controversy over Indian water rights is merely one of a series of running controversies that have lasted over a century and whose origins go back to the days of discovery, when it was thought that the newly discovered natives had no rights whatsoever. Today we live in a supersonic world replete with political doctrines and social theory far more sophisticated than those accepted in 1492. The United States has made commitments in many fields and its accomplishments in space far surpass even its own expectations. Everything has been changed by the twentieth century except Indian policy.

Today, out of the vast continent once "owned" by American Indian people, slightly less than 100 million acres remain. Of this amount some 40 million acres only recently came into Indian hands through the Alaska land settlement, and groups of whites are now appealing that legislation in an attempt to reduce the Indian landholdings still further.

But the type of ownership that American Indians enjoy today is only theoretical. The federal government still holds Indian lands through the administrative structure of the assistant secretary of land management of the Department of Interior. It is still accepted in the halls of Congress that Indians do not really own their lands but live on them at the pleasure of Congress. This anti-Indian sentiment is well understood everywhere in Indian country and is the major inhibiting force in developing Indian reservations.

In this book we plan to review the specific lands now owned by Indian tribes, which make up the almost 100 million acres, relating, insofar as possible, how the tribes managed to retain their lands and how some lands have recently been restored to Indian people. In the course of American history, however, a great many specific wrongs have been committed against individual tribes, wrongs that can, and must, be corrected in the immediate future. We will thus discuss a number of cases in which tribes are petitioning Congress or the president for return of their lands.

One of the most recent confiscations of Indian lands came about less than two decades ago when Congress unilaterally severed its relationship with a number of Indian tribes. In the years since that legislation took effect, the results of the policy have created very great social and human problems for these tribes. If there is to be a resolution of Indian problems, the specific problems created by the action of Congress in passing termination legislation must be reversed and the tribes must be restored to federal trusteeship.

Finally, we will propose that the United States enter a new phase of its relationship with the American Indian by creating a new doctrine of Indian legal rights with respect to land titles and ownership. We propose a new category of legal status for Indian lands and a policy of Congress to stabilize the Indian land base at 100 million acres by restoring lands illegally taken from a variety of Indian tribes in the last century. We believe that this program should naturally be the first step in solving the problems of American Indians created by the accidents and inci dents of American history.

ONE HUNDRED
MILLION
ACRES

❧ 1 ❧

Everything You Always Wanted to Know About Indian Lands, But Didn't Know Who to Ask

INDIAN TITLE was originally one of aboriginal use and occupancy. This was confirmed in early laws in which Indian lands were given special status as "Indian country" and in which the jurisdiction over the lands was given primarily to the federal government. The allotments process was, however, to create a no-man's-land, because the heirship problems related to ownership of certain tracts and the series of laws in Oklahoma governing the Five Civilized Tribes created a set of false legal distinctions between trust lands and restricted lands and thereby complicated the entire field of Indian legal rights. It is the task of this chapter to interpret and decipher such sentences as those above, which are the result of a selective jargon that has come into use in talking about Indian lands. It is the jargon of busy, bustling bureaucrats intent on discovering ways to restrict Indian use of lands. Until there is a new definition of basic Indian land rights within which all the factors just mentioned can be reconciled and incorporated, there can be no comprehension, let alone solution, of the problem.

How complicated is the problem of defining basic land rights? The federally recognized Indian tribes in the United States presently have 39,663,412.09 acres of land, which are held in trust by the Department of the Interior. (A few tribes own lands in fee simple, without government trust responsibility being exercised over them.)

Generally, tribally owned land is held in one of two ways. The tribe can hold legal title (fee simple) to the land, but restrictions against alienation of that title can be placed on it by action of Congress. For example, the consent of the secretary of the interior is required before the land can be sold, encumbered, or exchanged. But the deed is in the tribe's name, and the tribe has true ownership of the property and extant mineral, water, and other property rights.

The alternative to fee simple is beneficial title, where the United States holds the legal title to the land but the tribe and its members can use and occupy the land and benefit from any income it may produce. But they do not, strictly speaking, own it since the deed describing the land reads "property of the United States."

In the first instance, fee simple, the tribe owns the beneficial interest and legal title but the title is said to be restricted because it can only be sold under certain conditions. In the second case the tribe has only an interest in the use of the land and the United States is said to hold the land in trust. The difference between trust and restricted lands being in practical terms non-existent, the land problem comes down to the secretary of the interior's interpretation of Indian use and occupancy—the alleged criteria for his decisions on Indian lands.

Although we have already discussed the doctrine of discovery sufficiently in one context, the whole concept of use and occupancy is so dependent upon this basic doctrine, we must re-examine discovery in these terms. According to the authors of *Federal Indian Law*, the Europeans had reasoned that discovery involved recognition of fundamental factors of existence of social groups. The conflicting claims of European powers to unpopulated areas in the New World were to be resolved, according to Vattel, in accordance with the precept of the natural law (or, as we would say today, the precept of international morality) that no nations can "exclusively appropriate to themselves more land than they have occasion for, or more than they are able to settle and cultivate." Vattel concludes, "We do not, therefore, deviate from the view of nature in confining the Indians within narrower limits" (*Law of Nations* [1733], bk. 1, chap. 18).

There are many problems with the foregoing statement, not the least of which is our own equation of international morality with natural law. However, we are concerned here with Vattel's rationalization of the imposition of foreign cultural values—not natural law—on the American Indian. Vattel's "natural law" was designed to uphold agriculture over other forms of economic ventures.

The Europeans could not conceive of alternative land use of the Indian tribes. Some land was valuable to the Indians for its religious significance, such as the Taos Blue Lake in New Mexico, and the Pipestone Quarry, where the Sioux, Chippewa, Sac and Fox, Iowa, and other tribes gathered stone for their pipes. Certain other places were set aside as neutral grounds for fishing, hunting, gathering salt, picking berries, and other specific activities; here no tribe dared assert exclusive land title. Some land was even held as informal buffer zones between two strong tribes, a no-man's-land where neither tribe cared to claim exclusive ownership.

Curiously, the natural law offered by Vattel overlooked the fact that the European powers had claimed title to lands they .themselves had never measured, did not settle, and at the time could not possibly have cultivated. It took the European invaders better than 400 years to populate, settle, and cultivate the area presently designated the United States of America, and even today there are remote parts of the western states in which few people live. Even at face value, Vattel's theory of natural law could not logically support more than a minimal portion of the European claims to the western hemisphere.

If the response to this argument is that the Europeans had at least a greater potential for populating and cultivating faster than the Indians, natural law as it pertains to land should dictate that whoever populates, settles, and cultivates the fastest gets the most. It would then follow that because the United States is the acknowledged superpower in technology it can, according to international morality, legally move into any under-developed area, even Soviet Siberia, and assume political control of the land. Or it might mean that China and India, because they have more people than other nations, have a legal right to whichever land area they would like to control. Clearly, the arguments used for four centuries by political scientists and philosophers make no more sense when applied to the question of the American Indian population than they do in international politics.

Vattel's assumption that agriculture was the dominant and probable predestined form of man's economic existence was later endorsed by the officials of the Bureau of Indian Affairs who wrote the *Federal Indian Law* (Felix Cohen *et al.*) explanation of Indian land rights, thus rushing in where even the Supreme Court of the United States feared to tread. The Supreme Court said in *Johnson* v. *McIntosh*, "We will not enter into the controversy, whether agriculturists, merchants, and manufacturers have a right, on abstract principles, to expel hunters from the territory they possess, or to contract their limits." In effect, this decision meant that Indians do have rights based upon the same conception of natural law that had been used to prove that they had no rights. From this irreconcilable set of propositions evolved the whole conception of trust status or trusteeship of Indian land.

At the time of the arrival of the Europeans, the Indians were perfectly capable of backing their claims to land by force. The Europeans may have had superior firepower, but they had a logistics problem that would have disheartened Hannibal. It would be another two centuries before whites would be able to develop sufficient economic strength to sustain a continued Indian war without severe economic consequences. While the United States may have been able to claim sovereignty over large stretches of land, it was unable to maintain continuous sovereignty over them.

The doctrine of discovery turned out to have three important effects on the development of American Indian policy. First, it vested the right to bestow legal title to specific lands in a sovereign power. To bolster its own claims the United States had to argue that it was holding Indian lands in "trust" against the day when the tribes would be strong enough to defend their legal title. Yet, its policies were designed to extinguish the political rights of tribal governments, thus forestalling the day when the lands would be held legally by the tribes.

By asserting in theory, and denying in practice, the concept of Indian tribal sovereignty the United States forced the tribes to maintain an ambivalent relationship with the federal government. Even so, some tribal governments have been able to take effective political action, depending upon the extent to which their respective land titles allow them to exercise self-government over certain land areas. But, as the ultimate title remains with the United States, ultimate political control over themselves also rests with the United States. It is this final, ironic twist to the land problem that a new congressional policy could solve.

In the early years of this country the primary political consequence was that sovereignty had to be asserted against foreign nations and their Indian allies. That is, an attempt by a foreign power to intrude upon or claim lands on the continent would constitute an act of war. While sovereignty could be invoked against the foreign nation, its assertion against the Indian tribes was useless since that tribe did not share either the benefits of discovery or the status of a European power. While a tribe was included with their foreign allies for purposes of war, the successful conclusion of the war saw the larger power forced to sign treaties with the Indian tribes of the region in order to maintain its exclusive control over the lands it had won. Other consequences of the peace were not nearly as important as was the maintenance of alliances with Indians occupying the newly acquired lands. Nations victorious in war thus incurred legal liabilities with their additional lands. And treaty rights defined contractual responsibilities while preserving the undefined state of Indian use and occupancy titles under discovery.

The designation of "aboriginal use and occupancy" prevented the United States from embarking on a program of total conquest so long as there were European nations stalking the shores with the ever-present possibility of alliance with Indian tribes. Had the United States backed away from the doctrine of discovery it would have reopened the whole question of title by conquest, a question that had been foreclosed by the cession of discovery rights to England during the wars prior to the Revolution. America claimed to have stepped into England's shoes with respect to discovery and it had to maintain that pretense before the world in its first decades of national existence. By the time of the Monroe Doctrine, effective legal precedents had been established that entangled the federal government in the affairs of American Indians. One is tempted to conjecture that discovery was an effective doctrine in preventing any solution to the Indian question since it concerned lands and domestic political programs and policies related to people. The federal government asserted primacy in Indian affairs to protect its land title and unwittingly complicated matters by providing social services as a replacement for lands.

Indian sovereignty could have been upheld legally had the doctrine of discovery not been used to displace the various tribes. It would have required a recognition of tribal governments by the nations of the world. In practical terms the result of maintaining both the rights of tribal governments and the doctrine of discovery, which forbade any recognition of Indian ownership of land, was that tribal sovereignty remained a viable legal doctrine long after tribes had been dispossessed of their lands. Justice Johnson, concurring in the famous *Cherokee Nation* v. *Georgia*, developed what might be called a doctrine of incipient nationhood when he compared the Indian tribes to the Hebrews of old wandering in the desert, anticipating the exercise of sovereignty over a piece of land although not yet invested with it.

Without a viable land title vested in their governments the respective tribes became in many instances long lists of names of people enrolled in a tribe on the basis of ancestral participation. Thus, a person might leave a tribe, but his great grandchildren, because they had some measure of Indian blood, would be regarded by the United States as Indian and therefore subject to the prohibitions against drinking liquor, signing contracts, or maintaining a separate residence with full control over private property. Perhaps what the United States wished to assert was a change of culture so thorough that the peculiar problems of the administration of Indian lands would cease to exist. But in weakening tribal sovereignty the federal government destroyed the ability of the tribes to solve their own problems.

The final effect of the doctrine of discovery was, as we have seen, that it depended upon the assertion of title against other titles recognized by European powers at a time when they themselves had a series of alliances with Indian tribes, who supposedly could not have treaties with respect to lands because of the same doctrine. This quasi-independent status of Indian allies of European powers enabled the tribes to maintain a treaty-making power and status long after there was any danger of them effectively forcing the termination of settlement of any particular European power.

Between the end of the French and Indian War in 1763 and the 1815 Treaty of Ghent, which ended the War of 1812, Indian tribes, relying on their occupancy and use of lands and their military prowess, in effect parlayed their claims to land into claims for services from the new American government. This transformation is seen today in the many federal agencies that purport to serve Indian reservations. The historical roots of their responsibility for Indian programs are in the earliest treaty days, when the federal government, as part of treaty bargaining, made commitments to provide services needed by Indians, including all those things that the land itself had provided so freely prior to its cession.

It was in the process of making some 400 treaties and agreements that a new concept of title began to emerge with respect to Indian tribes. Some of the early treaties mentioned that the lands reserved to the tribes would be "held as Indian lands are held." No one knew the legal consequences of this language, since it seemed apparent that everyone at the treaty ceremonies understood what was meant. But since treaty records are rarely introduced into court or mentioned in the halls of Congress, the phrase has rarely been defined in comprehensive legal terms. It was simply a case in which the two words "Indian" and "title" began to be seen together more and more often until they became a sort of legal concept.

"Aboriginal use and occupancy," under the doctrine of discovery, meant that the occupants could be displaced at the pleasure of the European nations. It also meant that the United States could take the aboriginally-held Indian land and not be liable to compensate the Indian tribe under the Fifth Amendment to the Constitution.

"Indian title," however, has evolved to mean that the United States has recognized the Indians' right to use and occupy the land. Under this title, the United States is liable to pay the tribe when it decides to extinguish the Indian use and occupancy.

The doctrine of discovery implies no recognition of the national aspect of an Indian community; the concept of Indian title derives from treaties that recognized the Indians' political status.

The first such treaty was with the Delawares on September 17, 1778. In that treaty, signed in the darkest days of the Revolution, the United States went to great lengths to disclaim any designs on the tribe's lands. Article 6 of that treaty states,

Whereas, the enemies of the United States have endeavored, by every artifice in their power, to possess the Indians in general with an opinion, that it is the design of the states aforesaid to extirpate the Indians, and take possession of their country; to obviate such false suggestion, the United States do engage to guaranty to the aforesaid nation of Delawares, and their heirs, all their territorial rights, in the fullest and most ample manner, as it hath been bounded by former treaties, as long as the said Delaware nation shall abide by, and hold fast the chain of friendship now entered into.

The title of the Delawares to their lands and their property interest were recognized; the treaty viewed them as more than mere occupants on the land and established their communal and compensable rights.

It was in the treaty of October 22, 1784, with the then-hostile Six Nations of the Iroquois League that language was used that not only recognized the Indians' right to their lands but also helped to lay the foundation for eventual federal trusteeship. The United States received the tribes into "their protection" and recognized that the "Oneida and Tuscarora Nations shall be secured in the possession of the lands on which they were settled."

The evolution of the concept of Indian title took a big step in a treaty signed some four years later on January 9, 1789, with the Wyandots, Delawares, Chippewas, and Ottawas. This treaty recognized the tribes' right to use and occupancy in language that provided for the United States to relinquish and quitclaim certain territory to the Indian nations. Article 3 of this treaty added the language that today identifies trust land with Indian title. The tribes could not

sell or dispose of the same, or any part thereof, to any sovereign power, except the United States; nor to the subjects or citizens of any other sovereign power; nor to the subjects of citizens of the United States.

The First Congress, by the Act of July 22, 1790, confirmed this transformation of Indian land title when it declared

that no sale of lands made by any Indians, or any nation or tribe of Indians within the United States, shall be valid to any person or persons, or to any State, whether having the right of pre-emption to such lands or not, unless the same shall be made and duly executed at some public treaty, held under the authority of the United States.

In outlining so broadly the federal interest in land sales by Indian tribes, Congress was asserting the exclusive federal right to grant the fee simple title to Indian land after it had been ceded or sold under the supervision of the federal government. With few exceptions, the treaties with the tribes that followed this statute contained like provisions.

Later statutes, passed after the dissolution of the governments of the Five Civilized Tribes of Oklahoma and before the admission of the state into the union, contained similar restrictions on sale of Indian lands. This, then, is the origin of the concepts of trust and restricted Indian land tenure.

The major portion of lands now in Indian hands is held in Indian title in communal or tribal status. That is to say, lands are held in undivided tracts owned by the tribal members together and not in divided tracts with interests owned by individual Indians. Why are lands held in tribal status in this system of landholding on a tribal basis? The answer probably lies in the seemingly innocuous addendum to every grant in fee simple or guarantee of use and occupancy that is written into many treaty articles. For example, a "tract of country west of the Mississippi River [was granted] in fee simple to [the Choctaw] and their descendants, to inure to them while they shall exist as a nation and live on it" in the famous Treaty of Dancing Rabbit Creek, which resulted in the removal of the Choctaw tribe from Mississippi in 1834. Or again, "The United States will grant a patent, in fee simple, to the Creek nation of Indians and the right thus guaranteed by the United States shall be continued to said tribe of Indians, so long as they shall exist as a nation, and continue to occupy the country herein assigned." It has thus been long a part of Indian land policy that tribes would hold their lands in communal status.

But the tribal method of holding lands is, in a sense, a different interpretation of communal status from any other in the world. The closest approximation to it is the way property is held corporately. However, since the title to tribally owned Indian land is vested in the tribe as an entity, not in its members as tenants in common, it also differs from corporate ownership as most Americans would conceive it. The difference is stated by the Supreme Court of the United States in the following definition:

The distinctive character of communal property is that every member of the community is an owner of it as such. He does not take an heir, or purchaser, or grantee; if he dies his right of property does not descend; if he removes from the community it expires; if he wishes to dispose of it he has nothing which he can convey; and yet he has a right of property in the land as perfect as that of any other person; and his children after him will enjoy all that he enjoyed, not as heirs but as communal owners.

Federal Indian Law gives an excellent illustration of the difference between tribal ownership and tenancy in common, a distinction that must be understood before we analyze the landholdings of individual Indians:

The distinction between tribal ownership and tenancy in common may be clearly seen if we consider the fractional interest of an Indian in an allotment in heirship status where there are so many heirs that every member of the tribe has a fractional interest, and then consider the interest the same Indian would have in the same land if the land belonged to the tribe.

In the first case, the individual Indian is a tenant in common. He may, under certain circumstances, obtain a partition of the estate. His consent is, generally, necessary to authorize the leasing of the land. His interest in the land is transferable, devisable, and inheritable.

In the second case, his interest is legally more direct, *although economically it may be more valuable.* He cannot, generally, secure partition of the tribal communally held estate. He can act only as a voter in the leasing of tribal land [usually through an elected representative]. His interest in the communal property is personal and cannot be transferred or inherited, but his descendants, if they are members of the tribe, will participate in the tribal property in their own right. (Italics ours.)

What benefits accrue to the individual member of the tribe under the communal-ownership arrangement? Tribally owned land can be leased by tribal members at preference rates or as part of tribal rehabilitation programs on the basis of need where no other mechanism would be available to assist a disadvantaged member of a comparable community.

Income from tribal lands is usually used to develop programs for tribal members. Scholarship programs, police protection, operation of tribal courts, building of community halls, ceremonials and celebrations, administration of tribal programs, and small loan funds for tribal members all come out of tribal revenues from tribally-held lands. The closest analogy we can find is that of a small, compact rural community in which all the revenues from the immediate region would be used to provide a variety of services for every resident without regard to his individual income or economic status but simply because of his long-time residency and participation in the community.

In addition to the economic benefits of tribally-held lands the religious and social significance of tribal lands has an importance not usually found in comparable non-Indian communities. A great many tribes hold the lands upon which they have lived for thousands of years. The Hopi and Rio Grande Pueblos, for example, can trace their continuous occupancy of their lands back far into the mists of history. The Indian people feel that this continuous occupation of lands has given the lands a special significance that cannot be understood by others. The Yakima, for example, have a saying that you would have to dig down almost a foot to reach soil; that the top of the ground you walk on is the dust of generations of Yakimas that has made the lands of the reservation theirs regardless of what others might say.

The difficulty that lack of tribal land creates in an Indian community can be illustrated in the problems of the Lumbee Indians of Robeson County, North Carolina. The Lumbees lived in an isolated region of North Carolina and never posed a threat to white settlement. Without a history of conflict, no treaties were ever signed with the tribe and no reservation was set aside for them. They had some extensive landholdings prior to the Civil War; but the land records in the county courthouse were burned during the war, and they lost all of their holdings through white chicanery shortly after Reconstruction.

Although today a majority in Robeson County, the Lumbees are not in control of the lands of the county, and subsequently, the political structure has been manipulated to deprive them of control of their own schools. This situation has been particularly galling to the Lumbees in recent years because they had always been denied the right to attend schools with either blacks and whites and had operated their own rural schools. But, with the advent of school consolidation programs in rural areas, the Lumbees have been deprived of the one facet of life that enabled them to coalesce their community—the schools.

In 1972 the final effort to destroy the Lumbees was made by the state of North Carolina. Pembroke State College, located in Robeson County, had started in the last decades of the nineteenth century as a small log cabin where the Lumbees held classes for their children. In the 1890's a series of fund-raising drives enabled them to build a suitable schoolhouse, now fondly called Old Main.

As the years went by, the state of North Carolina began to think of the school as its institution rather than the Lumbees'. Where once only Indians enrolled, the college now has only 150 Indian students out of a total student body of 2,000. In 1971 the state decided to close Old Main, creating a direct confrontation with the Lumbee community, which regarded the building as the only visible evidence of their once extensive tribal lands and government. Extensive rallies were held to "save Old Main" and the state surrendered.

When an Indian community will tenaciously hold to a building as the last remnant of their tribal property, it should be apparent that land holds the highest value in their community. At the present time almost all Indian responses to proposals by both political parties to changes in the federal relationship with Indian tribes is based on preserving the communal land base. The most important part of any new policy dealing with Indian people—indeed, the fundamental value to be considered when dealing in areas touching Indian communities in any way—is establishing, as a policy of the United States government, a disclaimer that the United States will take any more Indian lands, regardless of its alleged need for federal purposes.

With the nearly 40 million acres now held in Indian hands, any future Indian policy must be built around the concept of adding to the existing tribal lands, returning them to one consolidated tract for each tribe for easier planning and management, and guaranteeing that tribal lands will remain as a home-land for Indian people and will not be subject to fluctuating ideas and policies of senators and congressmen. It is upon this existing base of landholdings that we propose a national Indian policy to be built.

❧ 2 ❧

A Little Love Nest,
Somewhere in the West

ORIGINALLY there were no lands owned by individual Indians. All land was held in tribal status, and its tribal governing body, the council, or headmen would allot pieces of land for each family to use. This form of land tenure was directly opposed to the manner in which the new colonists intended to hold their lands, although the Boston Common was similar to the Indian type of landholding.

The difference between Pilgrim ideas on land and those of the Indians near them was based, of course, on the nature of both groups. The Indian tribes had long before settled the land question by developing tribal society and governmental forms that called for a closely organized clan or family structure. The Pilgrims had a family structure but no political organization outside of informal agreements such as the Mayflower Compact. Thus, it was incumbent upon the colonists to organize both community and individual property rights simultaneously. Being individuals before God, according to their religion, they had no choice but to be individuals before their government.

As the whites grew stronger politically and began to insist upon Indians behaving like them, they started to advance the idea that the major ingredient in their success was the individual landholding concept. So strongly did they believe in private property that they elevated it to a status just short of magic. Missionaries, in addition to teaching the word of their god, ardently worked to convince their Indian neighbors that they

should demand their own tracts of land outside of tribal ownership, where they could prosper according to God's divine plan to
allot the whole earth to individual garden spots.

The early treaties were often complemented by long additional articles in which the various Christianized Indians or half-
blooded traders and guides would receive allotments of land in
the areas that the tribe had just ceded to the United States
government. The belief of the treaty-makers was that by offering these individuals the chance to own lands outside of the
tribal land areas, they could effect a transition to civilization for
those who had converted to the new religion or who had sufficient white blood to understand the magic of farming. Thus,
land allotment became, in the treaties of the first two decades of
the last century, a process by which citizenship was granted. The
change from tribal citizenship to citizenship of the United States
was described in treaty terms as "leaving tribal relations."

A typical example of leaving tribal relations occurred in the
South, where the removal treaties of Andrew Jackson forced the
Five Civilized Tribes to cede large portions of Georgia, Alabama, and Mississippi and to migrate to Oklahoma. The treaties
of the Cherokee, Chickasaw, Creek, and Choctaw provided that
any Indian not wishing to move to Oklahoma could sever himself from tribal relations and take an allotment of land and
remain in the South, submitting himself to the laws of the state
in which he resided.

A number of books have been written concerning the wisdom
of this policy. Under the Chickasaw and Choctaw treaties young
girls could receive allotments if they desired to remain. Unscrupulous white men married them at a tender age, obtained
their lands under a variety of guises, and promptly got rid of
them when the land title had been transferred in the county
land office.

A number of Indians of the Five Civilized Tribes desired to
remain in the South and took allotments, becoming citizens of
the respective states, and looked forward to participating in the
developing southern society. They were greatly disappointed. In
a series of land transactions, the Indians who remained were
stripped of their lands and sent packing. Many later straggled
sadly to Oklahoma to join their kinsmen, having learned that
county courts are most effective instruments of tribal extinction.

The removal treaties of the Ohio Valley and Great Lakes regions did not, as a rule, attempt to induce massive defections from the tribal ranks. More often they were used as a means of settling the debts of tribal governments by allowing traders to obtain large tracts of land in payment of exorbitant debts that had been run up by the chiefs. Allotments to chiefs to make treaty cessions more attractive to them was a standard practice in dealing with the Great Lakes tribes, whereas the southern tribes appeared to resist the whole idea of what was in effect a bribe for their leaders. It would be fair to say that almost all of the lands east of the Mississippi allotted on an individual basis in the early treaties have long since gone out of Indian hands.

In 1854 a decision was made to begin a general policy of breaking down tribal societies through the deliberate use of individual allotments of tribal land. The Omaha Treaty of 1854 contained a famous provision for allotment of tribal lands that was repeated in numerous treaties signed with smaller tribes, which did not have the power to reject the article. Article 6 of the treaty, signed by the Otoes and Missouris on March 15, 1854, exemplifies the type of allotments that federal policy forced on Indians at that time:

The President may, from time to time, at his discretion, cause the whole of the land herein reserved to be surveyed off into lots, and assign to such Indian or Indians of said confederate tribes, as are willing to avail [themselves] of the privilege, and who will locate on the same tract of land as a permanent home.

And the President may, at any time in his discretion, after such person or family has made a location on the land assigned for a permanent home, issue a patent to such person or family for such assigned land, *conditioned that the tract shall not be aliened or leased for a longer term than two years*; and shall be exempt from levy, sale, or forfeiture.

And if any such person or family shall at any time neglect or refuse to occupy and till a portion of the land assigned, and on which they have located, or shall rove from place to place, the President may, if the patent shall have been issued, revoke the same, or if not issued, cancel the assignment, and may also withhold from such person or family, their proportion of the annuities [which were to be paid to the members for the land they had already ceded] or other moneys due them, until they shall have returned to such permanent home, and resumed the pursuits of industry; and in default of their return, the tract may be declared abandoned, and thereafter assigned to some other person or family of such confederated tribes, or disposed of as is provided for the disposal of the excess of said land. (Emphasis added.)

The true purpose of the section on allotment is of course revealed in the words "rove from place to place." The traditional economic pursuits of the Plains and river tribes of the Midwest was a combination of small farming and hunting. With buffalo dominating the landscape to a far greater extent than cattle do today, it appeared ridiculous to the Indians to settle in one place and raise vegetables.

The federal policy in settling the rich river valleys and prairies of Iowa, Missouri, Arkansas, and eastern Nebraska and Kansas required that small homesteads be established and agricultural towns be developed. The government planners felt that if the tribes were restricted to certain land areas of limited scope in an orderly fashion, they could eventually merge the Indian farming communities into the developing rural society of the Middle West. Thus, the lands that the tribes had held in communal status were reduced to only the amount of land that a tribe could hold in a contiguous block of individual allotments; the remainder of the tribal lands were declared to be "surplus" to tribal needs. They were then sold to the immigrant settlers brought west by the railroads or opened to homestead settlement.

The policies of the 1850's were halfway between the old idea of severing Indians from their tribal relations by offering them citizenship and individual landholding, and the later idea of the destruction of tribal culture by abolishing tribal governing bodies. Over the years most of the lands were eventually sold out of Indian hands, thus precluding the preservation of any large tribal landholdings. Yet the tribal governments themselves were not abolished, and the members of the tribes retained their original sovereign political status. The situation was ambiguous to say the least.

As these tribes adapted to rural American society of the last century, the various states began to assert what has been a familiar argument of states wishing to grab Indian lands. They attempted to tax the Indian lands while they were still held by the federal government for the individual Indians. The claim was that the tribal members had so completely been accepted as members of the local communities that any distinctions that appeared to remain were superficial. On the basis of apparent cultural conformity, therefore, states attempted to levy taxes that in effect were discriminatory and to take Indian lands by default.

The question with respect to the Kansas Indian tribes, particularly the Shawnee, was taken to the Supreme Court by Bluejacket, a Shawnee chief. The court rigorously defended the political status of the tribe and enunciated what was to become a very famous doctrine in the field of Indian law. The court stated that unless and until Congress determined that the political existence of the Shawnees had been totally dissolved, the tribe was entitled to an enforcement of all protections of the Constitution and treaties signed under the Constitution.

The members of such tribes as the Omaha, Otoe and Missouri, Ponca, Oneida of Wisconsin, Stockbridge-Munsee, Shawnee, Quapaw, and Seneca-Cayuga allotted in the 1850's were thus placed in a most difficult position. They were allowed to retain their political identity while being denied the most important part of that identity—tribal lands. The Indians' present social and economic conditions can be traced directly to this allotment policy, which sapped their tribal governments of any significant tribal income during the decades when even small amounts of tribal income or a tribal land base would have qualified for extensive government programs.

This policy was applied, as we have seen, primarily to the small tribes that were not military threats to white settlement. By 1885 over 11,000 patents and 1,290 allotments had been issued. There are no hard data on how successful this process was except for the existence today of towns predominantly white with Indian names and cemeteries located in Nebraska, Missouri, Kansas, and Wisconsin. If one searches carefully in the neighborhood one can find several Indian families still clustered around the remnants of a reservation with a few acres of land still remaining in Indian hands.

In the following decade the government was confronted with the task of stopping the larger tribes from "roving from place to place." It was one thing to bludgeon a small group of Poncas gathered peacefully along the Missouri River near Yankton, South Dakota, and another thing to march into Montana and tell Crazy Horse, Sitting Bull, and Red Cloud to become farmers. Most of the national cemeteries in the western United States are the sites where this activity was suggested to the tribes of that region.

Allotment of tribal lands was approached very gently when dealing with the strong tribes of the southern and northern plains. In the series of treaties of 1868 with the Sioux, Cheyenne, Crow, Navajo, Blackfeet, and others, a formula was gingerly suggested by the government treaty-makers that if any Indian "desired" to take an allotment, the agent in charge of the particular agency that surveyed the land within the tribal estate would mark out the allotment for the person and carefully record it for him in the tribal "land book" to be carefully kept at the agency headquarters. There was not much enthusiasm among the agents to advocate this provision within hearing of any of the chiefs of the tribes.

The tribal land book concept did not, as we have seen, get a rousing welcome from any of the Plains tribes. But the idea of settling the Great Plains did not lessen either, and pressure continued to build up for the allotment of the massive landholdings of the tribes of the Dakotas, Montana, and western Oklahoma. A combination of missionaries who devoutly believed in the sanctity of private property over the sanctity of keeping treaty promises and an increasingly influential cattle interest that understood the sanctity of money began to tell Congress what it should do to help Indians.

On February 8, 1887, after nearly five years of conflict, Congress enacted the famous General Allotment Act, also known as the Dawes Act after Henry Dawes, senator from Massachusetts, whose expertise on the plight of Indians could not be denied. Dawes was convinced that within a very short period of time the magical qualities of individual property would transform the stolid warriors into happy churchgoing farmers.

It must have been Dawes's primitive belief in magic that led him to advocate allotment of the Plains Indians' landholdings. A minority of his Indian committee recommended against the plan, declaring that those tribes that maintained their lands in tribal tracts were notably lacking in poverty, whereas those tribes already allotted under the preceding treaties of the 1850's were poverty-stricken and demoralized. The minority view, unfortunately, did not carry the day, and the legislation passed to the cheers of the churches and cattlemen. The main provisions of the General Allotment Act were as follows: (1) a grant of 160 acres to each family head and of 80 acres to each other single person under eighteen; (2) a patent in fee (simple) to be issued to every allottee but to be held in trust by the government for twenty-five years, during which time the land could not be alienated or encumbered; (3) a period of four years to be allowed the Indians in which they should make their selections after allotment should be applied to any tribe (failure of the Indians to do so would result in selections for them at the order of the secretary of the interior); and (4) citizenship to be conferred upon allottees and upon any other Indians who had abandoned their tribes and adopted the habits of civilized life. These provisions were applied to each reservation of major size in the West as the occasion arose. In 1871 Congress disclaimed the practice of signing treaties with the various Indian tribes, maintaining that any legislation pertaining to Indians had to be approved by both houses of Congress. Thus, no treaties could be signed with the respective tribes for land cession and yet Congress could not, as we have seen in our whole discussion of Indian title, merely displace tribes whose title had been recognized.

The administrative departments in the executive branch of government devised a technique by which they were able to make it appear that justice was still being practiced in the handling of Indian problems. The "agreement" with tribes was specifically created to make the American public think that the United States was still dealing fairly with the tribes.

The format of the agreement hardly varied from tribe to tribe. Most of the treaties signed with large and militarily powerful tribes early in the nineteenth century proclaimed that the United States would never take any Indian land without either a two-thirds or three-fourths agreement by the adult males of the tribes. The commissioners sent out to swindle the tribes always took along some well-known military hero, preferably one who had fought very recently against the tribe, and implied with his presence that if the tribe did not come to terms and agree to further land cessions and allotment, the army would very shortly march into the reservation and kill everyone concerned.

Even after the tribes had been given an "offer they couldn't refuse," few tribes agreed to surrender their lands to the United States. At the Great Sioux Agreement of 1889, prior to the admission of South Dakota to the Union and the dissolution of the immense Sioux reserve, fewer than 10 percent of the eligible males signed the agreement. The commissioners returned to Washington and reported that the Sioux had agreed to cede their lands and accept allotment, which was, of course, patently false. The program went through, regardless of the illegality. It has recently been upheld in the United States Court of Claims as a valid transaction.

When tribal land was allotted in severalty to the tribal members under the provisions of the General Allotment Act, Indian title was extinguished for large tracts of land. This procedure was followed despite the fact that the Indian tribes had not ceased to exist "as a nation." However, the individual Indian was only given the beneficial title to the allotment when it was made. Legal title was kept by the United States until the end of twenty-five years, at which time it was thought the individuals would be sufficiently de-Indianized to conduct their own affairs.

Some reservations were not large enough for all tribal members to receive allotments. Their tribal estates had already shrunk to a minimum area, while their populations had grown. After all the lands of the original tribal holdings had been allotted, the remainder of the Indians as yet unallotted were told to go out some place on the public domain and find land for themselves. Thus, several tribes were scattered and often decimated simply because the government would not provide lands in the immediate locale.

The General Allotment Act did not include the Five Civilized Tribes which were removed to Oklahoma, the Cherokees, Creeks, Choctaws, Chickasaws, and Seminoles. Their treaties generally forbade either allotment or the inclusion of their lands within the boundaries of any state without the permission of their general councils or tribal governments. And they were skillful politicians who had resisted the efforts of the United States to destroy their governments for over half a century.

A series of law suits almost eliminating the powers of tribal governments ensued—each, strangely enough, expanding the powers of the federal government over the five tribes on such narrow grounds that federal Indian rights became a farce. But this was the Supreme Court that also decided *Plessy* v. *Ferguson*, which justified the separate-but-equal civil rights theory. It is not, therefore, surprising that it was able to come to the conclusion sought by the land-hungry settlers of the old West.

A number of commissions were sent to Oklahoma to negotiate land cessions. The Atoka Agreement stripped the Choctaws and Chickasaws of their lands, the Jerome Agreement finished the Kiowas, and various other agreements spelled out the systematic reduction of Oklahoma Indian tribes to a conglomerate of legally incompetent individuals with small land allotments under minimum legal protections. The tribal governments of the Five Civilized Tribes were reduced to mere shadows and perpetuated only for the sake of disposing of any final tracts of tribal lands that could not be distributed to individual members.

Perhaps no people resisted allotment as fiercely as did the Indians of eastern Oklahoma. The traditional full-bloods refused to register for their allotments. Some fled into the hills rather than touch the pen that would indicate their approval of the massive land fraud. Finally, the Bureau of Indian Affairs rounded up almost every Indian of the five tribes that they could locate and forced them to accept the allotments. The real distinctions between Indian and white could be clearly seen in this instance. While the full-bloods were hiding to prevent the allotment of their lands, the towns of Oklahoma were filled with whites who claimed a smidgen of Indian blood in order to get some of the tribal lands.

The final indignity suffered by the Oklahoma Indians was the admittance of Oklahoma into the Union. As part of the organic act, Indians were placed under the state courts of the new state for probate purposes. Needless to say, corruption flourished when oil was discovered on their lands shortly after they had been placed at the mercy of the Sooners and Boomers who had taken their lands. Full-blooded Indians began to die mysteriously and with their dying breath showed their appreciation by leaving their estates, not to their families, but to the friendly white lawyers who gathered to usher them into the Happy Hunting Grounds.

The situation in Oklahoma became so scandalous that legislation had to be introduced reimposing restrictions on the Osage Indians and expanding the role of the secretary of the interior to protect the Indians from total destruction. So many deaths of

Osage had been recorded that people feared for the total extinction of the tribe without a strong federal authority overseeing the Oklahoma situation. If oil and water do not mix, oil and helpless Indians are hardly more compatible when placed in an Oklahoma court.

In 1877, Secretary of the Interior Carl Schurz recommended allotment because "the enjoyment and pride of the individual ownership of property [is] one of the most effective of civilizing agencies." He visualized a transition period of short duration, in which the tribal members learned how to farm and conduct business at the local bank. He and many others concluded that the members of various tribes would be so content with their new life that the Indian problem would be solved.

By the first years of the twentieth century the facts had begun to emerge. Allotment was not as successful a program as predicted. Indians were losing their allotments in a variety of ways, few of them legal. Swindles were so commonplace that the widespread optimism based on the belief in the magic of individual property rights had to be tempered with the reality of the immediate situation on each large reservation.

The Appropriation Act of May 27, 1906, permitted the president to extend the period of restrictions on the sale of Indian lands beyond twenty-five years. At first people thought that this magnificent gesture would enable the Indians to maintain some sense of balance in losing their allotments. But the Appropriation Act of 1907 gave the secretary of the interior permission to remove the restrictions prior to the expiration of twenty-five years. Thus, he was given dictatorial powers over Indian property. At the agency level, where the authority Congress grants to the executive branch always exists in the person of the agent, the Bureau of Indian Affairs could indefinitely extend the restrictions or lift them according to whims of those in charge of the agency.

When the allotment period ended in 1934, a total of 246,569 allotments had been made. They comprised 40,848,172 acres of land on some 100 different reservations. The actual land loss to the various tribes was much greater, however, than the mere loss of individual allotments. Many tribes had owned millions of acres of prime grazing land and farmlands. When this land was divided into individual allotments, the lands in excess of the actual amount needed to satisfy immediately tribal members' requirements was declared "surplus" to the tribes' needs and sold by the United States for a pittance. The proceeds were placed in the federal treasury, where churches went immediately to get the funds for mission schools. In total some 90 million acres were taken from Indians as easily as checking out a book in the library.

One would have thought that, having wiped out any semblance of communal existence, the United States would have rested from its labors. Such was not the case. If individual allotments complicated matters, they were only the prelude for a really exciting scrambling of land matters. Through a series of incredibly ignorant policy decisions the federal government proceeded to further subdivide the individual allotments by insisting that upon the death of an original allottee his lands be divided among his heirs according to Anglo-Saxon ideas of descent rather than in accordance with traditional Indian customs.

Courts had consistently placed the domestic matters of the tribes in the hands of tribal governing bodies, such as they were at the time. Thus, Indian marriages according to tribal customs were recognized by state and federal courts as valid marriages. Adoption of a child in the traditional Indian manner was held to be a correct exercise of inherent tribal rights of government. The tribes were given some leeway in determining how decisions were to be made on a communal basis. The Iroquois, in particular, maintained their traditional Peacemakers Court throughout the entire allotment period.

But the descent of real property was held to be subject to state laws of inheritance, so that when an allottee died his lands were divided among his living heirs. The lands themselves were not divided; the agency records were merely changed to reflect the existence of the new Indian owners. A casual glance at the process will indicate how quickly the situation was complicated beyond the processes of rational thought.

An Indian has an allotment of 160 acres. He has a wife and five children. His oldest son is married and has three children. Suddenly the Indian dies. His wife inherits a third interest in the lands, each child receives one-fifth of two-thirds of the lands. The existing interests read as follows:

Wife	5/15ths of 160 acres
Child *A*	2/15ths
Child *B*	2/15ths
Child *C*	2/15ths
Child *D*	2/15ths
Child *E*	2/15ths

The day of the funeral the wife and the oldest son are coming back from the cemetery and the horses bolt, overturning the buggy and severely injuring both. The wife dies that night, and three days later, the son. On hearing of the wife's death, the bureaucrat eagerly grabs his pen and makes the following entries in his records:

Mr. Indian Allotment No. 1887

Child *A*	3/15ths
Child *B*	3/15ths
Child *C*	3/15ths
Child *D*	3/15ths
Child *E*	3/15ths

Then he learns that son *A* has just died. He takes out the book and makes the following notations:

Child *B*	3/15ths or	9/45ths
Child *C*	3/15ths	9/45ths
Child *D*	3/15ths	9/45ths
Child *E*	3/15ths	9/45ths
Grandchild *F*	2/45ths	2/45ths
Grandchild *G*	2/45ths	2/45ths
Grandchild *H*	2/45ths	2/45ths
Wife *I*	1/15th	3/45ths

And what if the children of *B*, seven in number, who inherit from *B*; wife and step-children of *C*, eleven in number; *D*, a bachelor; and *E*, a sower of wild oats with three children by each of three wives, all die in a flood?

Allotments had scarcely been handed out when this devastating process of repeated subdivision of interests in individual allotments began. It is a favorite subject of Bureau of Indian Affairs personnel, and many have made a career of simply continually recording and re-recording the various interests as Indians marry, divorce, have children, and die, leaving a complicated series of relations not only bereaved but bewildered at the apparent loss of lands they thought their late relative owned.

It has been the practice of the Bureau of Indian Affairs to lease out the lands where so many interests exist that it is impossible for anyone to get consent to lease the lands. An extreme example of the problem, now popularly designated the heirship problem, is the Nancy Cloud Allotment on the Standing Rock Sioux Reservation in North Dakota. The figures given are as of 1959, almost a decade and a half ago. The present status of the land and number of heirs is unknown.

An Extreme Heirship Case

Description: S½ sec. 33, T. 19N., R. 29 E., Black Hills Meridian, South Dakota, containing 320 acres.
Allotment no. 299, Standing Rock.
Original allottee: Nancy Cloud, or Mahpiya.
Number of subsequent probates since the death of original allottee: 99.
Summary of present (1959) heirs and their share is as follows:

NAME OF HEIR	SHARE
Gertrude Looking Horse	8,268,220,800/115,755,091,200
Thomas Looking Horse	8,268,220,800/ ″
Emeran Red Tomahawk	387,572,850/ ″
Barney Red Tomahawk	387,572,850/ ″
Harry Boneclub	954,147,600/ ″
Maude Boneclub	954,147,600/ ″
Moses Striped Face	12,612,600/ ″
Edward Striped Face	12,612,600/ ″
Innocent Striped Face	12,612,600/ ″
Mabel Carrier	2,449,483,200/ ″
Mathew Soft	248,812,200/ ″
Lulu Soft	248,812,200/ ″
Angela Soft	248,812,200/ ″
Louise Did Not Butcher	295,293,600/ ″
Mrs. Luke Goodfur	5,512,147,200/ ″
Eunice Red Bird	1,990,497,600/ ″
Hazel Red Bird	1,990,497,600/ ″
Joseph Dog	301,445,550/ ″
Annie Dog	301,445,550/ ″
Bede Dog	301,445,550/ ″
Moses Dog	301,445,550/ ″
Johnson Brown Eagle	100,481,850/ ″
Levi Brown Eagle	57,418,200/ ″
Victor Brown Eagle	57,418,200/ ″

NAME OF HEIR	SHARE
Kate Buckley	86,127,300/115,755,091,200
Phillip Dog	86,127,300/ "
Luke Eagleman	2,480,466/ "
Oliver Eagleman	2,480,466/ "
Glenda Eagleman	1,654,644/ "
Stephen Hawk	43,063/ "
Margaret High Cat	3,124/ "
Helen White Bird	3,124/ "
Rose High Cat	3,124/ "
Alice Harris Lovejoy	101,481,850/ "
Lydia Harris Lucero	101,481,850/ "
Mary Harris Gilbert	101,481,850/ "
Enid Taken Alive	295,293,600/ "
Ruth Walking Shield	1,033,527,600/ "
George W. Walking Shield	1,033,527,600/ "
Laura White Bearking	306,230,400/ "
Rose Ellen Firecloud Pheasant	516,763,800/ "
Milo Ironroad	689,018,400/115,755,091,200
Gertrude Duncan	9,569,700/ "
David Duncan	9,569,700/ "
Daniel Duncan	9,569,700/ "
Edward J. Duncan	9,569,700/ "
Jefferson Duncan	9,569,700/ "
Bertha Duncan	9,569,700/ "
Imelda Duncan	9,569,700/ "
George E. Duncan	9,569,700/ "
Robert Duncan	9,569,700/ "
Edward One Horn	344,509,200/ "
Martin George Bliner	2,067,055,200/ "
Annie Hawk	306,230,400/ "
Cora Faye Pheasant	129,190,950/ "
Thomas M. Pheasant	129,190,950/ "
Samuel Fly	295,293,600/ "
Caroline Brown Wolfe Eagle	612,460,800/ "
Felix Eagle	918,691,200/ "
Anita Yellow Earrings	75,675,600/ "
Andrew Yellow Earrings	75,675,600/ "
Eunice Ellen Red Bird	1,378,036,800/ "
Hazel Red Bird	1,378,036,800/ "
Mrs. Luke Goodfur	2,756,073,600/ "
Nellie Cottonwood	1,033,527,600/ "
Muriel Warner Proulx	1,033,527,600/ "
Donald G. Warner	1,033,527,600/ "
Carries The Bow	168,739,200/ "
Thomas Creek	37,837,800/ "
Kule Creek	37,837,800/ "
James Creek	37,837,800/ "

NAME OF HEIR	SHARE
Daniel Creek	151,351,200/115,755,091,200
Daniel Brings Plenty	98,431,200/ "
Magdaline Buck Elk Thunder	54,684,000/ "
Phillip Blue Coat	5,512,147,200/ "
David White Wolf	738,234,000/ "
Anna Makes Room	12,811,680/ "
Elizabeth Elk Head	5,124,672/ "
Hazel Elk Head	5,124,672/ "
Lawrence Elk Head	5,124,672/ "
Phillip Elk Head, Jr.	5,124,672/ "
Belle E. Elk Head	5,124,672/ "
Joseph High Elk	14,372,550/ "
Alice J. High Elk	5,749,020/ "
William Swimmer	5,749,020/ "
Alma Swimmer	5,749,020/ "
Vivian Carter	5,749,020/ "
Ford Swimmer, Jr.	2,874,510/ "
Patricia Swimmer	2,874,510/ "
Lorraine Hayes	6,249,600/ "
Clarence Hayes	6,249,600/ "
Linda Blue Coat	3,124,800/115,755,091,200
Audrey Blue Coat	3,124,800/ "
Josephine Laundry	114,836,400/ "
Daniel Counting	62,496,000/ "
Sarah Counting-Little Dog	17,856,000/ "
Simon Counting	17,856,000/ "
Robert Counting	17,856,000/ "
Amy Garter	17,856,000/ "
Olive Little Wounded	17,856,000/ "
Rosalie Dog Eagle	17,856,000/ "
Cleveland Two Crows	8,928,000/ "
Cora Two Crows	8,928,000/ "
Joseph Laundreaux	43,063,650/ "
Sophia Laundreaux	43,063,650/ "
Sidney Benoist	43,063,650/ "
Rose Running Battle	17,717,616,000/ "
Marian High Elk	50,778,000/ "
Silas High Elk	50,778,000/ "
Royal Phil High Elk	50,778,000/ "
Samuel Blue Coat	25,389,000/ "
Marilyn Deborah Blue Coat	25,389,000/ "
Alice Hollow Horn	261,437,000/ "
Sadie Hollow Horn	261,457,000/ "
Lydia Hollow Horn	261,457,000/ "
Annie Garter	1,653,644,160/ "
Eli Bad Warrior	203,112,000/ "
Lucy Looking Horse	203,112,000/ "

NAME OF HEIR	SHARE
Nancy Buck Elk Thunder	5,468,400/115,755,091,200
John Buck Elk Thunder	9,569,700/ "
Caroline Buck Elk Thunder	9,569,700/ "
Bonny Lou Buck Elk Thunder	9,569,700/ "
Arnoldean Buck Elk Thunder	9,569,700/ "
Nancy Elk Head	38,435,040/ "
Joshua Elk Head	38,435,040/ "
Annie Yellow Hawk	38,435,040/ "
Nancy Elk Head	16,873,920/ "
Hannah Red Horse	16,873,920/ "
Emma Drops At A Distance	1,837,382,400/ "
Henry Drops At A Distance	918,691,200/ "
Earlwin Drops At A Distance	918,691,200/ "
Annie Drops At A Distance	918,691,200/ "
Evelyn Drops At A Distance	918,691,200/ "
Moses Bad Male	187,488,000/ "
Hanry Janise	46,872,000/ "
Jesse Janise	46,872,000/ "
Dorothy Janise	46,872,000/ "
Francis Janise	46,872,000/ "
Angeline Poor Dog	9,374,400/ "
Evelyn Brings Plenty	21,873,600/ "
Laurine Brings Plenty	21,873,600/ "
Leroy Brings Plenty	21,873,600/115,755,091,200
Charlotte Two Bulls	172,254,600/ "
David White Wolf	246,078,000/ "
Jacob Hollow Horn	61,519,500/ "
Susie Hollow Horn-Knife	61,519,500/ "
Elizabeth Inamongst	30,759,750/ "
Edward Inamongst	30,759,750/ "
Emmet Hollow Horn	15,379,875/ "
Martin Rufus Charger	10,936,800/ "
Sharlene Charger	7,291,200/ "
Adel Joyce Charger	7,291,200/ "
Annie Industrious	98,431,200/ "
Anna Eagle Chasing-Red Bird	98,431,200/ "
Stella Slides Off-High Elk	6,249,600/ "
Eunice Slides Off-Walks Quietly	6,249,600/ "
Owen Slides Off	6,249,600/ "
Esther Woodring	84,369,600/ "
Edith Woodring	84,369,600/ "
Claude Running Bear	328,104,000/ "
Joseph Running Bear	328,104,000/ "
Grover Cleveland	295,293,600/ "
David Tiyona	2,067,055,200/ "
Elizabeth Greenhill Smith, Cass Lake Chippewa	2,067,055,200/ "

NAME OF HEIR	SHARE	
Hazel Douglas Red Tomahawk		
(Canadian)	387,572,850/115,755,091,200	
Jessie Sword	98,431,200/	"
Sallie Randall	1,968,624,000/	"
George Red Bear	137,803,680/	"
Joseph Red Bear	137,803,680/	"
Edward Standing Soldier	68,901,840/	"
Ben Red Bear	137,803,680/	"
Robert No Neck	137,803,680/	"
Jennie Crow Dog-Little Bear	344,509,200/	"
Frank Belt	8,858,808,000/	"
Nellie Standing Bear	328,104,000/	"
Charles Spotted Eagle	1,968,624,000/	"
Oscar Spotted Eagle	1,968,624,000/	"
Katie Looking Cloud	6,249,600/	"
John Looking Cloud	4,166,400/	"
Martha Looking Cloud	4,166,400/	"
Clyde Looking Cloud	4,166,400/	"

Total number of heirs to this allotment as of April 22, 1959, is 183; of this total, seven are undetermined estates, they have not been probated; sixty-seven are Standing Rock enrollees (three undetermined estates); ninety-one are Cheyenne River enrollees (three undetermined estates); four are Rosebud enrollees; one is a Fort Peck enrollee; one is a Crow Creek enrollee; one is a Cass Lake Chippewa; one is a Canadian; and seventeen are Pine Ridge enrollees (one undetermined estate).

In recent years a number of legislative proposals have been advanced to stop the continual division of Indian land interests into smaller and smaller fractions. The problem has been that proposed solutions have been worse than the original state of affairs. By and large they have consisted in efforts to force the quick sale of individual allotments, thus completing the historic mission of separating the Indian from his land.

A step toward solving this heirship problem was made in 1934, when the Indian Reorganization Act (I.R.A.) was passed. This law prohibited further allotment of tribal lands for those tribes that accepted its provisions and organized constitutions under it. A revolving-loan fund was created to be made available to I.R.A. tribes for land-consolidation programs. A few tribes have made substantial progress under the provisions of this act. However, Congress has been notoriously stubborn in providing funds for the revolving-loan program. At present prices a loan fund of some $100 million would be needed to allow tribes to consolidate their lands by repurchase programs from individual Indian heirs desiring to sell their interests and put the land back into tribal ownership.

The situation is constantly changing. The last comprehensive account of individual Indian landholdings showed that 10,697,-612.58 acres of land are in individual Indian hands, with almost 6 million in the complicated heirship status. Much land simply cannot be used because any leasing of the lands requires full consent of all heirs. Many heirs simply cannot be found. Their interests are so small that any lease money from the past would be smaller than the 25 cent service charge the bureau levies for making out Indian lease checks. Thus, the heirs never receive any money from their share of the land and do not even know if they actually own any of it.

There is an immediate need for additional funds in the revolving-loan fund so that tribes can borrow sufficient capital to purchase the allotments in selected areas of the reservations and create manageable tracts of income-producing lands. The administrative costs to the federal government at present for allowing this deplorable situation to continue go into the millions of dollars every year. It would be not only feasible but entirely rational in every sense to solve this problem.

When added to the basic 40 million acres of presently-held tribal lands, the more than 10 million acres of individual Indian lands provide an additional land base upon which a new federal relationship with Indians can be built. But continued loss of individual allotments only increases the administrative tasks of both the federal government and the tribes.

❦ 3 ❦

A Snowball in Hell

Asubstantially large portion of the currently existing Indian land base came into Indian hands only just recently. The Alaska Native Land Settlement Bill, which President Nixon signed into law in late 1971, is a compromise agreement between the natives of Alaska and Congress acting as representative of the federal government. The settlement bill concluded one of the strangest histories of aboriginal people ever told. For nearly a century the natives had existed without identity in a legal sense and with claims extending back into the complexities of international wranglings of the pre-Revolutionary days. The whole story is worth telling.

The Eskimos, Indians, and Aleuts of Alaska numbered approximately 74,000 at the time of the first official Russian voyage to the Alaskan mainland in 1740. The native inhabitants, though diverse in language and culture, were landlords over a land area totaling some 375 million acres. For millennia Eskimo, Indian, and Aleut people had occupied particular regions of Alaska under the varied conditions of that land. Their adaptations to the diversity of Alaskan lands ranged from the whale- and caribou-hunting Eskimos on the Arctic Slope in the Far North, to the fishing societies of the coastal village peoples such as Tlingits and Haidas in southeastern Alaska, and to the stern fog-bound island chain of the Aleutians, which reach to the doorstep of Japan thousands of miles to the west.

Until the late nineteenth century, Alaskan natives were scattered throughout Alaska in villages and family groups, thriving on the bounty of nature. Trade centers developed in which concentrated populations lived and traded with each other and with sailing ships that occasionally stopped for supplies and trade items such as skins, ivory, and furs. Trade routes covering the whole of Alaska were developed, bringing frequent contact between the different tribes in the region. European goods reached Alaska primarily through Siberia and the Bering Straits region.

The Russians colonized the southern portion of Alaska from 1741 until 1867 with a series of small coastal settlements designed to control trade rather than advance permanent settlement. During the Russian occupation the native population of Alaska plummeted from 74,000 to 35,000 because of outright and wanton slaughter as well as starvation and disease such as smallpox, diphtheria, and measles, to which the natives had no immunity.

The late nineteenth century also brought the influence of the Europeans and Americans through whaling expeditions, missionary activity, and teaching endeavors. The major influx of outsiders came, of course, with the frantic gold rushes in the last decade of the century when thousands of miners raced northward to the Klondike and other gold fields. The disappointed miners later trudged back to the countries they had come from, but a surprising number grew to like the territory and stayed to set up permanent homes.

Following the gold rushes came the canned-salmon industry, which took advantage of the native's traditional source of food and expanded it into a multimillion dollar industry, while depriving the natives of most of the fish through state regulations. Then came the military defense establishment of World War II and the cold war, creating an artificial economy into which few natives could enter. And finally came the oil companies, presaging total destruction of both the land and its people.

Today, the Eskimo, Indian, and Aleut peoples number about 60,000, with the Eskimo numbering slightly more than half. The native population is scattered throughout the state in some 200 villages and a few urban areas. These native communities range in size from 2,500 inhabitants down to as few as two or three families huddled in isolated inlets along the coast or clinging to a precarious existence in the northern icefields. But there is still one trait common to all the villages and people: they still look to the land for their primary means of survival. The whale, seal, fish (particularly salmon), moose, caribou, duck, beluga, reindeer, bear, ptarmigan, walrus, muskrat, and the many other animals of the northern wilderness allow the natives to survive today much as they did in olden times.

Alaskan-native land-occupancy patterns have been well-documented. In 1968 a federal field committee stated that "the aboriginal Alaska natives completely used the biological resources of the land, interior and contiguous waters in general balance with their sustained human carrying capacity and this use was only limited in scope and amount by technology." It also stated that aboriginal group or tribal territoriality with definable bounds did exist in Alaska, thus, in a sense, applying the doctrine of discovery to the Far North centuries after it had lost all meaning.

Thus, when the Russians turned toward Alaska to exploit its vast fur and mineral resources, they moved into territory that had to be taken by force, from nature and from its inhabitants. The Aleutian Islands were almost denuded of sea otter and fur seal. The Aleuts were forced into virtual slavery after their subjugation by the Russians, whose only edge in the conflict appeared to be a superior technology. The Aleut population skidded from about 20,000 in 1750 to less than 1,500 in 1910, indicating the near extermination of the people.

Fortunately for the Indians of the interior and the Eskimos farther north the Russians and early Americans limited their heavy trading activities to the Aleutians, the Gulf of Alaska region, Kodiak Island, and the warmer waters to the south. Intrusions into native life in the southeastern coastal area were fairly extensive. In these areas the natives were only rarely successful in protecting their villages and themselves from destruction. Generally, survival was accomplished by accommodating the foreigners, but occasionally the natives would fight back, repulsing the invaders.

The Russian colonizers never subjugated the entire native population in Alaska. Only those groups that lived near the fur hunting and trading areas came under Russian control. By 1867 the Russian government, plagued with administrative problems in Alaska and needing money, decided to sell Alaska to the United States. With a purchase price of $7.2 million the vast territory came under American control. Only 400 whites lived in the area at the time, while 150 times that number of natives had no knowledge that the territory was being transferred from one alleged owner to another half the distance of the globe from them.

The official transfer took place in southeast Alaska without any native participation. Most native communities were hundreds of miles from the Russian coastal settlements, and some truly did not even know that the Russians had ever claimed to own their lands. The only natives informed in any way about the transfer were those in Sitka and its immediate environs who heard the cannons and noticed a large crowd gathered for the ceremonies.

The native peoples of Alaska have always maintained that the Russians sold only what they had, a few forts and trading centers, but not the land over which the natives had almost complete dominion. How could they sell land over which they had no effective control? How could they sell land they had never seen and had no reason to suspect even existed?

The Treaty of Cession of 1867 did not grant citizenship to the natives of Alaska. The document was notoriously vague and simply stated,

The inhabitants of the ceded territory, they with the exception of the uncivilized native tribes, shall be admitted to the enjoyment of all rights, advantages, and immunities of citizens of the United States and shall be maintained and protected in the free enjoyment of their liberty, property and religion. The Uncivilized native tribes will be subject to such laws and regulations as the United States may from time to time adopt in regard to aboriginal tribes of that country.

Since the provision applied only to the 400 nonnatives, it seems rather ridiculous to bother to outline the disfranchisement of the natives.

With the stroke of a pen and some traditional phraseology the Alaska natives were thus thrown into the historical and legal quagmire of the continental American Indians' fate. Court decisions of another time, land, and political situation were made applicable to the natives of Alaska as if the totality of previous American history could be transplanted to the new environment intact. The solemnly intoned words of John Marshall became law for the Alaskan natives, clouding and confusing their own unique history and legal position.

Following the Treaty of Cession, the American military arrived to maintain an American presence in the new territorial capital and to protect the few whites that lived in Alaska.

By 1884 there had been a rapid increase in American economic activity in southeastern Alaska. Canning, timbering, and mining activated an increased trade with the continental United States and foreign markets. The whites in Alaska, of whom there was an increasing number, grew desirous of finding some means of securing title to the particular lands and resources they wanted to exploit. In 1884 Congress passed the Organic Act to provide some measure of relief for the settlers from what was a rather corrupt and inept military government of the territory. Coincidentally, the act provided for the specific protection of the lands of the Alaska natives by the United States:

Indians or other persons in said district shall not be disturbed in the possession of any lands actually in their use or occupation or now claimed by them, but the terms under which such persons may acquire title to such lands is reserved for future legislation by Congress.

This enunciation of national policy with respect to native rights followed the other great declarations of policy such as the Northwest Ordinance of 1787. It had about as much effect. The Homestead Act, the Mineral Leasing Act, federal withdrawals for game refuges, executive orders for national parks and national forests, establishment of military reservations, and then statehood all combined to deprive the natives of some 166 million acres in the years following this promise by the Congress.

By the early 1900's the full-scale invasion of Alaska by miners and prospectors created serious dislocations of the native peoples from one end of the territory to the other. It was argued that natives could not obtain title to land or file mining claims because they were not United States citizens. Consequently, whenever a miner wanted a piece of land that had natives on it, he simply filed on it and took the land, natives notwithstanding. Little heed was paid to claims to land by native people, even though the land under question may have been extensively used by them for uncounted generations.

Congress extended the provisions of the General Allotment Act of 1887 to Alaska in 1906. Although this act was designed, as was the General Allotment Act, to fragment and destroy communal life, when applied selectively to the conditions then exist-ing in Alaska, it could have been used to protect innumerable summer campsites and food-gathering places used by the smaller groups of natives from expropriation by others. However, most of the natives were not schooled in the white man's complicated legal system and did not know how to use the provisions of the act to benefit themselves. More importantly, the majority of the natives did not even hear of the act.

The act remained on the books until recent claims settlement, but the Bureau of Indian Affairs deliberately withheld any in-formation on it from the natives. Until very recent times there was only one realty specialist employed by the Bureau of Indian Affairs in Alaska, and his task was to cover the whole state, 375 million acres. Repeated requests by the natives for additional realty specialists to assist the native communities were unheeded. Consequently, in the first fifty-four years of the operation of the Alaska Allotment Act, only 80 allotments were issued, nearly all of them in southeastern Alaska. In 1968 only 15,216 acres of land were held by natives under the allotment act. Recently, through agencies other than the Bureau of Indian Affairs, about 600 filings for allotment have been made by the villagers who want to protect at least those areas that are used most intensively by their people from possible state selection (under the statehood act) or from other third-party encroachments.

Unfortunately for those who file for allotments in good faith expecting to receive certification of ownership of the allotments, there are a great many hurdles to top before they are given a hearing. Challenges can be made by outside parties while the certification process is still under way, and if the bureaucrats lag on processing the application or fail to do the necessary survey work, the whole application for allotment may come to naught.

In 1936 Congress extended the I.R.A. to Alaska; it authorized the secretary of the interior to designate as an Indian or Eskimo reservation any public lands occupied by them upon a vote of the adult native population of a village, a majority adopting a constitution and bylaws. This act could have provided a satisfac-tory means of settling the land titles around the villages and in certain traditional hunting and fishing areas. However, the bureau officials in Alaska were notoriously slow in informing the natives about their rights under this law and actively discouraged use of it by the people. Under this law only seven villages, with a native population of 1,111, held 1,540,270 acres of land in 1968. It appears to be a large amount of land for so small a population, but for a hunting economy it is hardly adequate.

In 1910, prior to the Indian Reorganization Act and its Alaskan counterpart, the president was given the authority to make executive-order withdrawals "for the Natives of the indigenous Alaskan race." By 1968 nine villages, with a native population of 1,713, held 1,259,679 acres by virtue of the exercise of the president's powers in setting aside executive-order reservations. Thus, prior to the fight for the Alaskan Native Land Settlement Bill, only 2,824 natives had any kind of title to their lands, holding reservation lands totaling 2,799,949 acres in trust with the government. This acreage does not include any other lands used for administrative purposes, school lands, or congressionally created reserves.

It should be noted that during the massive influx of white settlers during and after World War II there were numerous requests by the Eskimo, Indian, and Aleut peoples for a total land acreage suitable to their immediate needs. Ninety villages requested a determination of their area of use and occupancy for the purposes of acquiring definite boundaries to their reserves, but no action was taken on their petitions.

Alaskan politicians, businessmen, and prospectors generally opposed the creation of reserves, and native people were brainwashed into believing that they would be restricted to a certain land area if reservations were created, thereby further inhibiting their hunting and fishing economy. With the people fearful and fully believing the propaganda, the establishment of native land claims was unnecessarily confused and lengthened.

The tribes of the lower forty-eight states had traditionally gone to Congress for legislation permitting them to sue the United States for land claims and adjustments in treaty land cessions. In 1946, to forestall the incredible amount of legislation pending concerning admission of the tribes to the United States Court of Claims, Congress passed the Indian Claims Commission Act. The procedural rules of the Indian Claims Commission were drawn to conform to the conditions of the history of claims litigation as they had developed in continual conflict over the major treaties of the 1800's in the states. Senators and congressmen thought that they had solved the problem until they considered Alaska.

The act was virtually useless to the Alaskan natives. The Indian Claims Commission's causes of action were built upon the concept of settling the question of when the lands had been taken from the tribes. The 200 or more native villages had not suffered a "taking" in the strict legal sense of the word. The Treaty of Cession in 1867 did not extinguish Indian title nor did the Statehood Act in 1958. Neither law spoke directly to a cession by the natives or a taking from them by the United States of any lands. Some tribes in southeastern Alaska with a slightly different history with respect to the United States filed claims. Twelve native groups filed, but no claims were ever adjudicated by the commission.

It was understood by the native peoples that the Indian Claims Commission handled cases in which tribes were compensated for lands that had now, for all practical purposes, been settled and could not be returned. The natives did not want compensation, and since there was little settlement on the lands they claimed, to have attempted to litigate the land question in Alaska before the Indian Claims Commission would have been tantamount to requesting a forced sale of their lands at prices of 1867. They wanted the original confirmation of their title, which had been a right preserved for them through all legislation that affected Alaska. The only solution was to seek an agreement with Congress.

The door to a congressional solution of the land problem had been left open during the legislative acts dealing with the territory prior to statehood. After World War II a drive began to get statehood for Alaska. The native peoples were minor participants in the battle for statehood. There were few politically oriented native organizations existing at that time. They had never taken stands on issues that they considered peripheral to their interests. Many were fearful that statehood would come without a settlement of their claims. The native groups did not therefore become formally involved in the movement.

A great many natives saw the issue of statehood as one affecting them personally, however, and particularly those who lived in the cities of Alaska joined in the movement toward statehood. They represented a concern for the future of the social order rather than simply a more narrow and restricted native view.

Most native peoples were living off the land as best they could in the interior, far from the centers of communication and political turmoil. No radio, television, or press provided news of any kind to the majority of natives, and they did not realize the importance of many provisions of the statehood bill. The coastal press, however, did make it appear that native land interests were being "protected."

What the statehood act did, in effect, was to perpetuate the indecisiveness of Congress in failing to recognize the extent of native land to which the natives had clearly defined title. While making provisions for the new state to select 103 million acres of "federal" land, the fourth section of the act also stated that the new state of Alaska "forever disclaim"[ed] all right or title to any lands or property (including fishing rights), the right or title to which may be held by any Indians, Eskimos or Aleuts or is held by the United States in trust for said natives." Congress also made provisions that all questions concerning such land and property would be under the sole jurisdiction of the United States.

The new state, having a very small population, was expected to live off the fruits of the land. That is to say, having a small tax base, it was expected that the state of Alaska would select economically profitable lands as part of its 103 million acres from the federal government and then live off the income from the sale and leasing of this land. When the state began to make its selections, it picked the choice lands of the area, often intruding on settled native villages. The natives, especially in the interior, began to protest the high-handed actions of the state. The villagers in the interior and in the Tigchik Lakes area of western Alaska filed protests covering 5.8 million acres of land the state had selected in 1961. By 1968 forty protests covering 300 million of the 375 million acres had been recorded.

Then-Secretary of the Interior Stewart Udall was faced with a classic problem: to grant 103 million acres of native-claimed land to the state or to do his duty as the guardian of native property rights and disallow the state selections until Congress could act on native claims? He instituted in 1966 an administrative "land-freeze policy" that prevented transfers of title and oil and gas leasing on lands claimed by the natives until Congress could decide the issue of ownership. Between 1959 and 1966, however, over 5.5 million acres had been patented to individuals or the state.

The response of the state to Udall's freeze was naturally vehement, since the freeze on state selections was hitting the state in the pocketbook, where it hurt the most. The natives, on the other hand, were jubilant because state selections were impinging on their villages and continued selection of prime lands would have meant absolute loss of their lands and would have made the question of confirmation of title a moot point.

The state characterized the land freeze as illegal and filed a suit in 1967 in federal court to compel Secretary Udall to grant state selections whether or not they were protested by Indian groups. The state lost. In 1969 the United States Court of Appeals for the Ninth Circuit refused to hold that native-occupied land was eligible for selection by the state, thus strongly supporting the view that native title to Alaska was still unextinguished. This decision gave further impetus to the movement for congressional settlement and bolstered native bargaining points with congressional leaders. Settlement of the native land claims was crucial to any development of the state of Alaska and, in 1969, even affected the financial solvency of the state government.

The natives began to gird for the fight in Congress. Over the years the natives had been impotent to protect their land base because of the immensity of distance involved in attending meetings. More than 200 villages were scattered over an area one-fifth the size of mainland America. Transportation was in many cases simply a dog sled or a ride hitched with a bush pilot. No roads, trains, or buses existed for many of the villages.

In a political sense the natives were in even worse condition. No tribal groups had been officially recognized other than the Tlinget and Haida, who lived at the extreme southern tip of the state. Congress and the Department of the Interior dealt only with village-level entities and then on a superficial basis. A few native organizations had been formed with the objective of preserving their regional land base. The Tanana Chiefs Conference, the Northwest Alaska Native Association, and the Arctic Slope Native Association were among the strongest interior groups, while a few urban-based groups contributed some strength in the settled areas, where what communications media that existed were located. But the glaring need for the natives was total organization to maximize political strength and present a common front.

In October 1966 a statewide gathering of Eskimos, Indians, and Aleuts was called. After a rigorous debate and discussion of the crisis facing them, the natives created the Alaska Federation of Natives (AFN). The immediate stimulus to unity was the overwhelming recognition of the repeated losses of land through the state selection process and patents to private individuals. From 1966 on, the AFN, as it came to be called, pursued the single-minded goal of obtaining from Congress a legislative solution to the land rights question.

The initial act of the land claims committee set up at the founding convention was to draft a bill outlining the natives' proposed solution to the problem. The bill had two major purposes. It first sought confirmation of title to lands actually found to be used and occupied by natives, and then it advocated compensation for those lands that had already been taken in one way or another over the previous century.

While this was more a knee-jerk response than a reasoned legislative proposal, it was clear from the unanimity of the people that these two principles would have to be broken down into three points for negotiation: (1) a sufficient land base for the villages; (2) a generous financial compensation for the lands ceded to the government; and (3) native control of all lands and funds.

At the end of 1967 the state and the native peoples were at an impasse. Then-Governor Walter Hickel (later secretary of the interior) and the native leaders were reduced, in their frustration, to calling each other names. Both sides came to recognize that regardless of their immediate and heated arguments, the answer to the problem lay in the actions of Congress. It was agreed that nothing could be gained by further fratricide among Alaskans when other people would be making the final decision.

The AFN and Governor Hickel agreed to the creation of the Land Claims Task Force, which would be funded by the state. The purpose of this group was to propose a detailed land-claims package to submit to Congress and to the state. The task force was constituted of the entire board of directors of AFN and a number of others appointed by the governor.

It was fortunate that the state was providing the finances for the task force to carry on its business, because the natives had virtually no funds with which to conduct their struggle. So, in a sense the cooperation of the natives with the state meant that precious resources need not be expended fighting the state but could be preserved for the final push in Washington before congressional committees. The task force was chaired by Willie Hensley, an Eskimo who had won election to the Alaska House of Representatives by a rather impressive margin in the previous election. By early January 1968 a solution was hammered out acceptable to both the natives and the state officials.

The proposal had a number of features that made specific some of the earlier, more nebulous ideas of the native peoples. Forty million acres would be given in fee to the villages and the right to use surface lands for subsistence purposes for 100 years. The natives would be given a 10 percent royalty interest in the Outer Continental Shelf revenues and $20 million immediate advance royalties, and the state would give the natives a 5 percent royalty interest in all lands selected by the state after the freeze was lifted.

The task-force proposal, later reflected in S. 2906, a bill that was introduced in Congress, was the first major attempt to draw together a comprehensive native-land-claim settlement act for Alaska. In retrospect it was a mighty effort by native leadership firmly intent on molding the settlement pattern from the very beginning.

The important effect of the task force effort was the fact that the state, through Governor Hickel, came to accept the 40 million acre figure for native land ownership as a realistic figure and the idea of state contribution to the overall settlement through a royalty interest to the natives became an important negotiating tool. Further, and perhaps most important, total native participation in the settlement negotiations and the necessity of obtaining the consent of the people were built into the solution.

Following native agitation for protection of the land base in 1966 and the subsequent imposition of the land freeze, the Interior Department took it upon itself to dream up its own solution to the land claims problem. In June 1967 Secretary Udall offered a bill, S. 1964, which contained a proposed solution that reflected little knowledge of the village situation in Alaska and totally overlooked the political realities of the situation in the state. It offered a maximum of 50,000 acres of land in trust to each native village (overlooking the fact that some villages needed little land, others a great deal). It proposed that the state be authorized to bring suit on behalf of the natives in the United States Court of Claims for all other lands to which the natives claimed use and occupancy (forgetting that the two antagonists were the natives and the state). The bill arbitrarily designated March 30, 1867, as the date of "taking" of Alaska from the natives (this after everyone had accepted the fact that it had not yet been taken).

Only when the department's proposal is translated into terms comparable to the final settlement proposal of the task force does the treachery of the proposal become comprehensible. A limit of 50,000 acres per village was a land settlement of 10 million acres; the natives had already gotten the state to agree to 40 million acres. Claiming that the land was taken as of 1867 would be a compensable interest to the natives of land taken, 375 million acres, of $7.2 million, the price that Russia received from the United States for the original purchase.

Naturally, the AFN leadership, which was at that moment attempting to get the state to agree to the creation of the task force, was outraged at the stab in the back received from the Interior Department. The proposal was denounced as a fraud, and the natives refused to discuss anything but their original proposals with anyone.

In his March 6, 1968, message to Congress on "Goals and Programs for the American Indian," President Lyndon Johnson began to put pressure on everyone to find a solution to the land claims controversy. In the text of his message he stated that "it remains our unfinished task to state in law the terms and conditions of settlement, so that uncertainty can be ended for the Native people of Alaska." Johnson outlined three principles to consider in the passage of legislation: (1) Give the native peoples of Alaska title to the lands they occupy and need to sustain their villages. (2) Give them the rights to use additional lands and water for hunting, trapping, and fishing to maintain their traditional way of life, if they so choose. (3) Award them compensation commensurate with the value of any lands taken from them.

The president's message, more just and intelligent than the solutions advocated by the Interior Department, the alleged trustee of the natives, spurred a series of visits to Alaska by Secretary Udall and Undersecretary Robert Vaughn. The result was a new legislative proposal introduced as S. 3586 in April 1968, a month after the president's message. It contained the following new provisions: (1) The date of 1867 for figuring "taking" was dropped and a compensation figure of $180 million was proposed. (2) A specific compensation figure rather than a percentage of the receipts from the Outer Continental Shelf should be adopted. (3) The earlier court of claims provision should be dropped. On the whole the new proposals were primarily an indication that Udall and Vaughn had indeed been to Alaska and discovered that it was not 1867.

Native reaction to the new proposals was the same. They strongly objected to the drastic limitation on lands (the 10 million acre figure remained). The bill contained provisions for giving the secretary of interior rather extensive powers over the natives after settlement was reached. Many of the natives thought that the monetary compensation was still woefully inadequate. Yet there was an indication in the bill that the Interior Department was beginning to understand the complexity of the problem.

Early in 1969 President Nixon selected Walter Hickel as his secretary of the interior. Although there had been fruitful interaction between the natives and Hickel when he was governor of Alaska, the prospect of Hickel as head of the Interior Department chilled most natives of Alaska, as it did Indians in the lower forty-eight.

Within a year of his appointment Hickel had alienated every Indian on the continent. When asked about reservations in Portland, Oregon, Hickel said they were psychological crutches. When asked to save the water in Pyramid Lake, Hickel proposed it be drained to stabilize its shore line. And when responding to an inquiry on whether he would remove Udall's land freeze, he snapped, "What Udall can do by executive order, I can undo."

The AFN immediately sent four of its board members to the nation's capital to determine what Hickel would actually do with the freeze. The freeze was the only protection that the native peoples had against total rape by the state using the selection process. The AFN remembered how hard Hickel had fought against the freeze while governor of the state. They were, shall we say, worried?

The Alaskan press, thinking that Hickel would remove the freeze, viciously attacked the AFN when it refused to support Hickel's nomination as secretary until the Senate Interior and Insular Affairs Committee had wrung from him a promise not to withdraw the land freeze until a solution to the claims had been reached. When Hickel finally backed down on his plan to release the lands for state selection, the natives gave him their support and his nomination was confirmed.

In September 1969 the state of Alaska obtained $900 million in an oil and gas lease sale on 431,000 acres of land on the North Slope to which the Eskimos had tentatively approved title. The oil and gas potential of the land claimed by the North Slope Eskimos was enough to engage the attention of the world. The Trans-Alaska Pipeline System began to lay plans for the construction (through native-claimed lands) of an 800-mile, 48-inch pipeline from Prudhoe Bay to Valdez. The oil and gas industries and their backers in the financial world began a major effort to secure a permit from the Interior Department to build a pipeline.

By a series of strange coincidences events began to shift in favor of the natives. In July 1968, the Federal Field Committee for Economic Development and Planning had submitted a report to Senator Henry M. Jackson, Democrat of Washington, who headed the Interior Committee in the Senate. It painted a picture in very comprehensive terms of the massive extent of land use and occupancy of the native peoples and recommended a settlement of $1 billion and a small amount of village lands.

The report had a substantial impact when it was released, because it bolstered native claims terms and made them sound more reasonable. Its only acknowledged drawback was its concern for economic and social integration of the natives rather than any recognition of their deep interest in maintaining an adequate land base.

An interesting merger of diverse factors combined to place the natives at the focus of a decent settlement. The state of Alaska was nearly broke. Selections could not continue because of the land freeze protecting native lands. The oil and gas industry, under heavy attack by conservationists, were blocked in their efforts to obtain the permit to build the Trans-Alaska pipeline in part because of the freeze and in part because of threats of lawsuits by the natives if construction were attempted.

The conservationists, flexing their newly acquired political muscle on the environmental issue, pointed out that the proposed compensation for the natives was hardly adequate considering the discovery of oil on the North Slope. Jackson was hard put to oppose the natives. It was a standoff with every group glancing nervously at the others, wondering what the final coalition of forces would look like.

The AFN after resolving very serious internal divisions, agreed to a change of position that advocated (1) 60 million acres of land for the villages; (2) $500 million as partial payment for lands taken, to be paid out over nine years at an interest rate of 4 percent; (3) a 2 percent mineral royalty override payment for lands taken on all state and federal lands in perpetuity; (4) twelve regional corporations consisting of native villages. These native-owned corporations would manage all lands and funds channeled to them from the overall settlement.

Walter Hickel, a strong advocate of foreign-policy change within the cabinet, met an inglorious end in 1970 with, to use an Indian phrase he picked up while at the Interior Department, "an arrow in the heart." Following his departure the Nixon administration came forth with a new proposal that was reflected in a House bill, H.R. 432. This new position emerged after extensive lobbying efforts by AFN members. While it did not contain everything the natives wanted, it was a great improvement in the movement toward a decent bill and appeared to have sufficiently attractive features to pass Congress.

The new proposal, backed by the White House, had the following provisions:

(1) A federal payment of $25 million a year for twenty years for a total of $500 million

(2) A 2 percent royalty on mineral production on both state and federal mineral leases to a total of $500 million

(3) A confirmation of title to 40 million acres of land to the villages

(4) Creation of an Alaska Native Commission, to be appointed by the president and confirmed by the Senate, which would establish the

native enrollment and the administrative apparatus of the settlement

(5) Establishment of a statewide corporation appointed by the Alaska Native Commission with a board of seventeen members to administer the settlement proceeds.

The natives could not support the Nixon proposal as the lack of interest payments over the twenty-year period of payout actually meant a reduction to $492 million. Also, the land provisions did not allow the selection of land by villages, thereby reducing the beneficial aspects of holding the lands. One of the strongest objections raised was against the concentration of control in one statewide corporation. Many natives felt it would be too powerful and destroy their regional organizations, which had achieved increasing power during the struggle for settlement.

The more beneficial position indicated by the Nixon proposal in supporting the 40 million acre figure gave the natives a new bargaining tool in the House Interior Committee, however, and they badly needed it. Chairman Wayne Aspinall, long considered an Indian enemy in Congress, was the chief stumbling block to getting House approval of any settlement bill. He introduced his own version of the settlement.

Aspinall's bill, H.R. 3100, provided less than a half million acres of land in fee to the villages and subsistence permits for use of 40 million acres of land revocable at the pleasure of the secretary of the interior. Realizing that they were up against a closed mind, the natives concentrated their efforts on members of Aspinall's committee. Finally, on September 23, 1971, Aspinall relented and a coalition of Democrats and Republicans (the White House wanted this settlement badly) passed the most favorable of the proposals.

The bill provided for 40 million acres of land, $425 million in cash, a 2 percent royalty until a figure of $500 million had been paid out, and twelve regional corporations owned by natives and controlled by them. The only bad feature of the bill lay in the fact that only the first 18 million acres could be selected around the villages. The remaining 22 million acres could not be selected until after the state had chosen its 103 million acres. All the good lands would, of course, be taken by the state, making the choosing of the remaining 22 million acres a rather useless gesture. But the natives had come a long way since the first proposal by the Interior Department half a decade before.

The remaining task was to get the bill passed by the Senate. In 1970 the Senate had passed S. 1830, a rather extensive bill that had many of the features the natives wanted. But no action was taken in the House of Representatives because of Aspinall's opposition. In September 1971 the Senate Interior Committee reported out a bill that edged closer to the AFN demands but still felt short in many ways. The bill created seven regional corporations, allotted $1 billion, and set forth a rather complicated land provision. It took the 40 million acres and divided it into 20 million acres in fee, 10 million acres for investment, and 20 million for "subsistence" utilization, with presumably the 10 million acres not really belonging to the natives. It also allowed the option of taking the House division of 40 million acres.

The natives even then were not very enthusiastic about the settlement. Whatever legislation they approved meant a final disposition of any claims they might ever have against the federal government. They were extremely cautious about the various provisions that appeared to dangle like so many baubles before them. But everybody sensed that a final settlement was very close.

After some tough lobbying by the White House a final version acceptable to the Congress and the natives was drafted and passed both houses of Congress. On December 18, 1971, President Nixon called a convention of the AFN on the telephone and told them the terms of the settlement. He asked if they wanted him to sign it. The struggle was over. They told him to go ahead, realizing that he had personally intervened to get them a decent decision from the reluctant Congress.

The final version written into law was a compromise of the various proposals. It included surface and subsurface rights and title to 40 million acres of land to be divided between the 200 villages. Each village was allowed to become a corporation and twelve regional corporations were to be set up to carry out development plans on a regional basis. An amount of $462 million cash will be paid out over a period of eleven years and a 2 percent royalty on all revenue derived from the mineral leasing of state and federal lands up to a final figure of $500 million.

Thus, after a titanic struggle the Alaskan natives received a final settlement to their land claims against the United States. In terms of the potential wealth of Alaska it may prove to be very little, but when compared with the treatment received by the tribes of the lower forty-eight, it is the most generous gesture in history by the United States government.

The 40 million acres in Alaska is the largest single holding of lands by any group of American Indian people. It surpasses all the tribal lands in the continental United States by several thousand acres. Added to the over 39 million acres owned by tribal governments in the western United States it forms a major portion of the proposed 100 million-acre estate, which we believe should now be preserved for the aboriginal peoples of the United States.

Occupied Indian Lands

THE EXISTING national Indian land estate presently consists primarily of more than 39 million acres of tribally held lands, more than 10 million acres of individually held Indian lands known as allotments, and 40 million acres of recently acquired lands in Alaska under the new land settlement. The total acreage thus held by some 800,000 people is slightly over 90 million acres. It is less than 3 percent of the total land area once owned by American Indian people. As such it represents, in the negative sense, the almost successful displacement of American Indians from their homelands.

The past, however, is past. The task today is to gather what does remain of Indian landed estates and attempt to derive from the remnants a rational policy to ensure that no further depredations are committed by the United States government against Indian tribes and people. Our proposal is not merely to solidify the present land base but to advocate restoration of lands that rightfully belong to Indian tribes and have been taken from them in quasi-legal proceedings. We feel that this program would serve to erase the sense of betrayal that marks the feelings of Indian people toward the agencies of the federal government and the non-Indians of this nation.

In addition to tribal and individual Indian lands there is an exotic category created by administrative fiat known as occupied Indian lands. The presumption is that tribal and individual lands do not have much relevance for the government because they are crammed to overflowing with Indians. Therefore, some type of land name is required to be used by the government to indicate that some form of civilization has come into Indian country over the past century. These lands are occupied lands. Lands, that is, occupied by the Bureau of Indian Affairs and regarded as so totally the bureau's as to be nearly devisable to succeeding generations of bureaucrats.

The Bureau of Indian Affairs presently has under its jurisdiction 5,067,828.2 acres of land. Of this 4,064,568.11 acres are located in Alaska. Of this amount some 1,540,286.75 acres were set aside by the Alaska Welfare Act of 1936 as reservations for six native groups. The Alaska Welfare Act was the far northern version of the I.R.A. of 1934. While the lower forty-eight states' tribes received a clarification of their titles under new constitutions issued under the I.R.A., no such event occurred with the natives of the north.

The Alaska title problem, as we have seen, plagued bureaucrats and congressmen for over a century. The United States was reluctant to allow the natives of Alaska to sign treaties because of the vague suspicion that treaties in the lower forty-eight states had converted aboriginal title to that legal problem known as Indian title—a title hardly negotiable but highly compensable if the federal government acted too high-handedly with respect to the occupants of the land.

While the act of 1936 paralleled the I.R.A. in almost every respect, the bureaucrats in Alaska feared for their power over the natives if Indian title were allowed to prosper in that state. It was hard enough to keep track of the Indians, Eskimos, and Aleuts during the long winters, and no one knew what they might come up with if left alone too long. Because some anonymous file-fiddler decided that the natives of Alaska were getting "something for nothing," the lands were given the classification of "no compensable interest lands." A strange category, unique in legal annals.

"Compensable interest" apparently means that if the United States decides to take the lands, it must compensate the people for the loss. The problems in classifying the lands of Alaska in this manner are apparent. The land has value to the natives because of its ability to sustain the wildlife upon which the natives depend. Since the federal courts have no way of measuring what hunting lands mean to a people today, it appears that the linguistic gymnastics are for naught. If, on the other hand, the lands were to be evaluated for their worth to nonnatives and the question of oil producing values were raised, then the problem would become very interesting when natives are told to move.

But the more fundamental legal question raised by the Alaska Welfare Act is how a tribe organized under a federal statute that recognizes its title to its lands can have no compensable holdings or interests in the land. The statute appears to convert the lands into lands held by Indian title, which, as we have seen, severely limits the right of the United States to move the people hither and yon at its whim. Clarification of the status of legal title to the lands apparently owned by the six native Alaskan tribes is not only imperative but progressive. The concept of Indian land title cannot be continually split into more and more complicated versions of the title recognized by Columbus. At some point it must be given a meaning that will persist over a period of time.

Another 1.25 million acres of land were set aside as a reindeer reserve by the federal government. The reindeer reserve has formed an integral part of Eskimo existence for some time. Reindeer have become as important to the natives of the frozen north as the buffalo were to the Plains Indians and the salmon to the Indians of the northwest coast. In spite of the alleged progress in the nation's coldest state, the economic existence of the people of interior and northern Alaska is still partially dependent upon hunting and fishing. Reindeer form a crucial difference between life and death during the long winter months when game is scarce. With the development of oil fields in the frozen wastes there is no guarantee that the natives will be allowed to maintain their reindeer herds until an adequate and sustaining substitute for reindeer is found.

We would thus advocate turning over the reindeer reserves to the natives to be held in trust for them by the United States. In this way the herds would be preserved as a national asset and yet the people who are most in need of their continued existence would be allowed to participate in perpetuating them. The lands would thus form a last land base for the aboriginal peoples in the original ecological setting. Other lands involved in the Alaskan land settlement are designed to serve as the base of what is expected to be a large industrialization of the state. As such, they are not as extensive as they might be and totally useless for supporting large herds of animals.

Another 1,275,000 acres of land are in the process of being sorted out by the government and the natives as part of the gigantic land settlement. Some of the lands used and occupied by villages for generations will not be given to the villages but will be used to support activities of the Department of the Interior in its various functions. Anyone who believes that the Interior Department will not continue to assert total ownership of as great a land area as it thinks it can get away with is deceiving himself. The whole attitude of the bureaucrats seems to be that the federal government has given the lands to them personally. Woe to he who advocates changing that conception and reminding the career civil servants that they do not own the lands. The danger in this distribution of lands now in controversy between the Interior Department and the natives is that when the dust clears, it will be apparent that the Interior Department has once again created a new category of lands for its own use in direct derogation of either public or native interest.

In order to prevent the Interior Department from fooling both the state of Alaska and the Alaskan natives and carving out a whole new empire for itself in the north, we advocate a restoration of the lands in contention to the natives on a village basis. These lands should be granted to the native villages in spite of the recent land settlement, because they have formed a distinct category of lands in controversy for some time. We are fairly certain that when people think of the Alaskan settlement, they do not realize that the Interior Department has a vested interest in keeping everybody confused until it is assured of its continued domination of the interior of the state.

In the lower forty-eight the Bureau of Indian Affairs has almost taken over a million acres intended for the use of Indians and converted it to a private bureaucratic estate. 1,003,300.09 acres are held by the bureau in the western states under the excuse that these lands are "needed" for their administration of Indian affairs. Some 344,811 acres form a distinct category called "submarginal lands." We shall devote a later chapter to a discussion of them because of the importance these lands have in general Indian land problems.

The remaining lands, approximately 577,651 acres, are lands that the United States acquired from third parties, in special forced cessions from the respective tribes, in simple confiscation from reservations, or in transference of lands from one category of public lands to another. The lands are used by the Bureau of Indian Affairs or the United States Public Health Service in a variety of ways. By and large the functions performed by these agencies for Indians are now being performed in many cases by the tribes themselves under programs funded by other government agencies. The continued use of a landed estate of this magnitude by two government agencies must therefore be questioned at this point in history. It is very interesting, however, to learn the manner in which these lands were originally acquired from the tribes.

During treaty-signing days a treaty would often provide for the operation of schools for the children of the tribe. Some article would contain provisions that required the federal government to provide schools and teachers for certain tribes according to a set formula. The treaties of 1868, for example, provided a school and teacher for every thirty children who could be induced to attend school. No provision was made for land purchase for the school sites, however, and when the schools were set up, many were simply built upon lands taken from the tribes concerned.

The excuse was always that the United States was providing an education for the children of the tribe and that the tribe had to contribute whatever the government required to carry out its task. Thus, little tracts of land were taken for school purposes. With settlements on many reservations organized around the traditional stations for distribution of treaty annuities, school districts reflected the practices of isolated rural America to an amazing degree. Little schoolhouses on lands taken from the tribes were scattered throughout the interiors of many of the large reservations.

In recent years, as roads have become available and transportation facilities have been modernized, school districts have been consolidated. The many small tracts have somehow continued in government hands. In some instances the land theft is clearly apparent. Records indicate that the lands were taken "for school purposes" to be returned to the tribes whenever the lands were not used for school purposes.

Other treaties made provisions for sawmills, for blacksmith shops, for cattle grazing, for road yards, and for a number of other service-oriented functions that the government promised to provide the respective tribes. Again the pattern followed was that lands were taken outright or taken with a reversionary interest, with the promise that when the lands were no longer used for the purposes for which they were taken, they would be returned to tribal hands.

For example, a treaty with the Kansas Indians in 1815 mentioned that the United States would provide a blacksmith for the tribes. It was logical, in those days, that the smithy be established at agency headquarters so that the majority of the tribal members could take advantage of the services. Over the years the blacksmith was provided sporadically, so that people began to forget even that the blacksmith was a treaty service. As the service was phased out, new uses came into being for the lands and the old smithy would be converted into a storehouse, shed, shop, or office according to the needs of the agency. Some tracts of land came down through the years serving a variety of purposes without ever having their titles clarified or updated.

The opposite was also true. Lands that had already gone out of Indian hands were purchased from their white owners and made into government school or administrative lands. The funds came sometimes from the tribe inhabiting the reservation, sometimes from congressional appropriations, and sometimes from gifts from sympathetic whites. For every piece of land acquired in this manner a different story could be told. The lands would become part of the agency compound or classified as lands under the supervision of the different branches of the government. For all practical purposes the lands gradually became lands that were occupied by the Bureau of Indian Affairs or the Public Health Service and thus served only to establish a different land title within the reservation itself.

During the Depression lands in the West dropped to their lowest value in years. Some fell almost below the price of their original cession by the tribe, which is to say in the neighborhood of 45 cents an acre. To help bail out the white landowners, the government purchased lands within the reservations that had gone out of Indian hands and were now sitting virtually worthless in the hands of the white owners.

Taking all three categories of lands and merging them into one in the general concept of occupied administrative lands, we emerge with nearly a half million acres of land that is used for the administration of Indian affairs. A problem arises as soon as the lands are no longer needed for administration of programs by the bureau. Whose lands are they? What is to be done with them?

Generally, the lands are declared surplus. The question rises, then, surplus to whom? To the bureau, which is pulling back its own functions while the tribes are beginning to provide these same services for themselves? Are they surplus to the tribes who are being slowly pushed off their lands by federal termination policy? Or are they surplus to the bureau but vitally needed by the Fish and Wildlife Service, which wants to put in a duck marsh for white sportsmen coming from the cities on weekends?

The whole concept of surplus lands implies that in order to administer the reservations the bureau had to colonize certain parts of the reservations by establishing a landed beachhead. As its power declines, then, the federal government has to make a choice between invading reservation lands anew or turning the lands over to the tribes involved. No realistic effort has ever been made to determine exactly how each piece of land came into government hands. Rather, the whole idea is to throw them on the General Services Administration market and see which government agency can think up a use for them.

The secretary of the interior has authority under the I.R.A. simply to sign a statement of transfer giving the lands to the tribe within whose reservation they are located. However, the Interior Department officials have taken the position that they do not have to use the law because it is "old"—that is to say, was not passed in the last Congress.

The fear of transferring lands to Indian tribes is built upon the desire of high Interior Department officials to remain on the good side of congressmen. They live in mortal fear that they will be questioned during the annual hearings on appropriations and that Congress will discover that they have helped Indians get more land. Everyone assumes that Congress will froth at the mouth if they discover that 2 acres of surplus school lands were given out to some tribe without consultation. Thus, the provisions of the I.R.A. stand as mute witnesses to the absence of backbone in the Interior Department.

The return of the tiniest tracts of lands are thus subject to the great process of legislation during every Congress. A bill is submitted by a sympathetic senator or congressman to return 2.56 acres of school lands to a tribe that already has the magnificent sum of 300 acres of tribal lands. Surely, the heart and mind of America pour out during this rational process. Sometimes it costs more to print up the legislation than to purchase the lands outright. Reports are asked of the Department of Interior, the Office of Management and Bureau of the Budget, and other agencies, such as the Department of Health, Education, and Welfare and the Department of Justice, which might conceivably be concerned to learn that the government proposes to hand over this vast estate to the tribe. The Interior Department generally returns a negative report on the bill, stating that it is its policy to take lands away from Indians and not to help them preserve their lands. The reports generally indicate that a small identity crisis has arisen in the Bureau of Indian Affairs at the idea of giving Indians a square deal.

The Office of Management and Budget, which approved such trivial things as the Lockheed loan and financing of the SST, virtually hemorrhages at the idea that this small tribe will get an inflationary grant of property. It promptly files a report saying that if the tribe receives the land, the president's wage-price guidelines—indeed, the whole war against inflation—will be jeopardized.

After several congresses in which tribal members are promised a great many things, among them the return of the lands, a crucial event occurs: a sympathetic senator or congressman from another state embarrasses the tribe's congressmen, and the bill begins to move. Finally, forces totally unexpected merge to provide sufficient pressure to get the local congressman busy, and the bill is finally put into law. The administration promptly claims credit for the legislation and a great many politicians are made honorary tribal members. On the whole, it is an uneven and demeaning process. The whole struggle is so costly that the tribe has been set back many years in both funds and time that could have been devoted to other more constructive programs. But Indian people feel that reclaiming even a little land is the highest task they can undertake.

The administrative forces of the Bureau of Indian Affairs could save everyone a lot of confusion, emotional exhaustion, and expenditure if they would simply use the procedures of the I.R.A. and return the lands to the tribes without precipitating a major crisis every time a piece of land within a reservation becomes surplus.

On the advent of the antipoverty program a lot of tribes thought that restoration of lands would be the first step in fighting the economic conditions on the reservations. Many programs called for a matching in kind or cash by the tribal governing bodies. Some of these smaller pieces of land, being ideally located in prime locations for development near tribal headquarters or small villages on the reservations, would be perfect sites for tribal programs. It seemed natural that the government would return lands so that new industries and programs could be based upon them.

Instead, the attitude of the Interior Department only hardened. Officials there tried to pretend that small tribes could make a good showing in the poverty war without any community buildings, industrial sites, or offices. Reports on land restoration became more and more designed to prevent the tribes from receiving the lands at any price. Thus, the issue raised at the 1972 Democratic National Convention in the fight over the Indian plank revolved around surplus federal lands. One delegate strongly opposed the plank, stating that it meant the rip-off of many valuable parcels of land to Indian tribes.

We have listed lands (p. 60) that are currently surplus on or near reservations that might be returned to tribes under a new federal policy on stabilizing the Indian land base.

At the Democratic Convention of 1972 a delegate from Louisiana opposed a minority plank of the American Indians asking for restoration of lands declared surplus to the federal government to Indian tribes. His argument was that the lands would constitute millions of acres that could possibly be worth billions of dollars. One of his examples concerned prime industrial land within an eastern urban area. The table above hardly constitutes a massive land base, does it? The grand total of lands presently available for restoration is all of 369.255 acres. Hardly something to fight over, is it?

In most cases the struggle is not really necessary. The secretary of the interior has the power under the I.R.A. to return lands to any tribe that is organized under the provisions of that law

TRIBE	ACREAGE	PAST USE AND PRESENT NEED
Covelo Indian Community Round Valley, California	20	Former Indian school and now being used by tribe anyway
Grand Portage, Nett Lake, and White Earth Bands of Chippewa, rural Minnesota	90	Small tracts of former fire stations, roads, sheds, could be used by tribes to consolidate with existing tribal lands. The pieces are very small.
Lac du Flambeau Lac du Flambeau, Wisconsin	40	Former school lands needed for tribal development
Blackfeet Tribe Browning, Montana	3	Former school lands, needed to use as industrial park
Cheyenne River Sioux Eagle Butte, South Dakota	100	Former school tracts, needed for homesites for homeless Indians
Reno-Sparks Indian Colony Reno, Nevada	28.38	Former school lands, needed for homesites for homeless Indians
Creek Tribe Muskogee, Oklahoma	5	Former school lands, needed for community building
Flathead Tribe Arlee, Montana	82.875	Former school lands, needed for homesites for homeless Indians

Most Indian tribes accepted the law and have constitutions approved in accordance with its provisions. In fact, in the first few years after the passage of the I.R.A., lands were not only restored to tribes but surplus lands were made into Indian reservations, particularly in California, and people were encouraged to settle on them. In some instances the bureau simply went out and purchased lands on the open market and gave them to newly created Indian tribes.

The reasons why many tribes want surplus lands appear simple enough but in fact are more complex and significant than simply adding another few acres to a tribal holding. Many Indians living upon reservations or in former reservation areas are homeless. In Oklahoma, for example, Indians live on the old prestatehood allotments of the Five Civilized Tribes. Many of these allotments are but 40 acres. They are not taxable, however, as long as they are in the hands of the original allottees or restricted from taxation by other federal provisions.

With the high cost of profitable farming it is no longer feasible to farm a tract of 40 acres unless one has an outside income and grows food for the family on the land. But the situation is more complicated than simply finding a supplemental income to combine with agricultural enterprise. As Indian families have lost their lands in Oklahoma or as new families without allotments have grown up, they have moved on the 40-acre tracts owned by other Indians at the invitation of the owners. Indians cannot say no to their relatives or people in need.

The result, particularly in eastern Oklahoma among the Creeks and Cherokees, has been that the small tracts of Indian land have become small reservations in themselves. Government policy with respect to all services, particularly educational and health services, often depends upon residence on trust land. In essence, the people are forced to cling to the last trace of federally related lands in order to maintain any eligibility for services other Indians within reservations receive as a matter of course. So, providing lands to tribal governments may enable them to provide homesites for homeless Indians, to start housing projects or to ease the crowded conditions in some areas. Thus, even a small tract of land is vital to a great many people.

Some lands are wanted for industrial sites. These sites are hardly valuable in and of themselves at the present time. Rather tribes are setting aside funds to scour the nation seeking to attract industries of various kinds to their reservations. The National Congress of American Indians has sponsored conferences in recent years at which tribes display exhibits of the resources of their reservations with the hope that they can provide an attractive site for some corporation to consider in its expansion plans.

Often an industry will require a certain type of land for its proposed activity on a reservation. It may need great amounts of water, speedy access to transportation facilities, access to power lines, sand and gravel in tremendous quantities, rugged and untouched lands for testing of heavy equipment, or isolated lands for experiments. Thus, land takes on an industrial use or perhaps even recreational use only when a tribal government has the initiative to develop it in conjunction with other tribal programs and the economic needs of the immediate area. No lands presently needed by tribes that are surplus are valuable at the moment. They may become valuable if the tribe can develop them.

Another important need to be considered when discussing surplus lands is the need for tribes to consolidate their lands into feasible units for farming or grazing. Often the remnant school lands are in the middle of a proposed tribal consolidation area. Ranching and farming are dependent upon the use of large tracts of land and modern techniques of utilization. Tribal governments often mark out areas of tribal and individual lands that could be consolidated into one unit for either farming or ranching, sometimes for recreational development. The success of such projects depends upon being able to work with a solid block of land. Surplus lands that are not in tribal hands frustrate this type of development and reduce the income potential of all lands envisioned to be used in the lease.

The final, and perhaps most sensible, reason for restoring surplus lands to tribes is simply the cost in administration if the lands are left in their present status. Someone has to look after them. They have to be fenced and surveyed. If an income is expected from them, someone has to look for potential lessors who would be interested in small and often weirdly shaped tracts.

In tribes with woodlands and lakes such as those in Minnesota, the tracts are simply small and annoying. They stick out as areas which tribes are forbidden to use and yet they could only be used for such selective activities that even to mention them is to bring down ridicule upon the person suggesting it

On the other hand, a new category of lands is more and more coming to be surplus that may prove to be extremely valuable for some tribes. On some reservations one of the branches of the armed services may set up a radar station, a coastal outpost for ship patrolling, or a testing ground for equipment. Former ammunition dumps, training camps, or airbases adjacent to reservations are also becoming surplus. In many cases these lands have extensive buildings and facilities on them. They may be considered obsolete to the army or air force, but even in a deteriorated condition they are far better than the buildings used as tribal headquarters. Tribes are very desirous of obtaining these sites as places on which they can operate training centers for their antipoverty programs and programs for job training funded by the Labor Department.

Many tribes would take a big jump ahead if they could have the use of these surplus military installations. Most are quite near, or even on, the reservations concerned. Giving them to tribal governments could in most cases be accomplished simply if the Bureau of Indian Affairs would file a request for them.

In rare instances the government has given a tribe a chance to proceed under full steam with solutions based upon adequate land-restoration programs. The Eastern Cherokee Band of North Carolina got a bill passed in the Ninety-first Congress that made it possible for the secretary of the interior simply to give them lands they need when and if the lands become surplus. Law 91–501, 84 Stat 1097, gives this one tribe the benefits all tribes were meant to enjoy under the I.R.A. but which the Interior Department refuses to provide.

The solution to this problem would appear relatively simple. Since Interior Department officials regard the mere passage of time as tantamount to the repeal of legislation, each session Congress should pass a resolution reminding them that the legislation is still valid until officially repealed. In that way every tribe would have a current authorization from Congress to support its struggle with the bureaucrats.

However, we would rather see something along the lines of the following resolution made the official policy of the government regarding any lands that may become surplus on or near reservations in the future:

That the secretary of the interior is authorized, upon request of the tribal governing body of any federally recognized tribe, band, or identifiable group, together with the improvements thereon, that now Register, that the United States holds in trust for the requesting Indian group, subject to valid existing rights, all of the right, title, and interest of the United States in any of the federally owned lands within or contiguous to other lands held by the Indian tribe, band, or identifiable group, together with the improvements thereon, that now or in the future may become, excess to the needs of the government as determined by the secretary of the interior or secretary of any government department which presently has title to such lands.

With respect to the "occupied Indian lands" presently in the hands of the government, we would recommend immediate transfer of the title or clarification of the Indian interest to the tribes concerned. This action would include, as we have discussed, transfer of title to 4,723,017.2 acres of land to Indian tribal governments. For those lands that are presently being used for government activity and therefore not yet surplus, we would simply advocate continued federal use at no cost to the government. But when the land is eventually declared surplus, it should immediately go into tribal ownership. Added to the present Indian estate, the following figures (numbers of acres) result:

Tribal lands	39,663,412.09
Individual Indian allotments	10,697,621.58
Alaska native lands	40,000,000
Occupied Indian lands	4,723,017.2
	95,084,050.87

It would provide a permanent Indian land base approaching 100 million acres.

✤ 5 ✤

Submarginal Lands Are
Alive and . . . Well?

Iᴛ ᴡᴀs," as Dickens said in another context, "the best of times and the worst of times." The United States, in the throes of a vast economic depression, had elected a president who had promised a New Deal. Of the incoming administration, Will Rogers said, "It's the only time when the fellow with money is worrying more than the one without it." For America's native population, to whom all previous administrations had dealt approximately the same cards, the time offered new promise. After all, things could hardly get much worse.

The little land base that had remained in Indian hands after the one-sided horse trades of the treaty period ending in 1871 had been systematically eroded after the enactment of the General Allotment Act of 1887. In his inimitable hairy-chested rhetoric, President Theodore Roosevelt had described the General Allotment Act as "a mighty pulverizing engine to break up the tribal mass."

Even at the time of the adoption by Congress of this legislation, the cynical purpose behind it was understood. A minority report, filed at the time of the congressional debate on the General Allotment Act, made this perfectly plain:

The real aim of this bill is to get at the Indian lands and open them up to settlement. The provisions for the apparent benefit of the Indian are but the pretext to get at the lands and occupy them. If this were done in the name of greed, it would be bad enough; but to do it in the name of humanity, and under the cloak of an ardent desire to promote the Indian's welfare by making him like ourselves, whether he will or not, is infinitely worse.

During the forty-five years that followed, the land in Indian ownership diminished from 140 million acres to a little more than 50 million acres of the least desirable land. Not only was the Indian land base eroded, but so was the land itself. The Bureau of Indian Affairs classified the lands that remained in Indian hands as "14 million acres critically eroded, 17 million acres severely eroded, and 25 million acres slightly eroded."

As President Franklin Roosevelt took office in 1933 with a mandate to overcome the economic crisis, the nation had a quarter of its work force unemployed and 40 million people living in poverty. "Farmers, struggling to keep on their feet amid plummeting crop prices, were knocked down for good by a series of natural disasters—floods, droughts, plagues, and dust storms" were the words used to describe this era. And, of course, the poorest of the nation's poor were American Indians.

Indians, perhaps surprisingly, were not overlooked in the rush by the New Dealers to do something about the nation's economic ills. President Roosevelt selected Harold Ickes, a conservationist and reformer, to be secretary of the interior, and Ickes picked John Collier to be commissioner of Indian affairs. Even then, Collier was described as a "life-long defender of the American Indian against official rapacities." His twelve-year tenure marked the longest period of service of any Indian commissioner and undoubtedly the most progressive. Collier set about shaping a "New Deal for American Indians" under three policy guidelines: (1) economic rehabilitation of the Indians, principally on the land; (2) organization of the Indian tribes for self-government; and (3) civil and cultural freedom and opportunity for the Indians,

The keystone of the Collier era was the passage of the Indian Reorganization Act of 1934, which officially ended the allotment period. Under the authority of this far-reaching statute, tribal governments that accepted its provisions were reorganized and an effort was made to repurchase land within preexisting reservation boundaries and thereby to restore to each tribe an adequate land base.

The I.R.A. authorized an expenditure of not more than $2 million in any one year for the purpose of consolidating land until 1936, and then only $1 million a year, which was simply not enough to meet the obvious need. Even at depression prices, many tribes needed that much money themselves if an adequate job was to be done. Projecting a national need of $2 million a year was grossly inadequate.

It was in this context that the problem arose of what to do with those "submarginal" lands that the United States government was purchasing from bankrupt farmers. The solution seemed readily apparent, and the New Dealers moved fast. On March 4, 1933, President Roosevelt was inaugurated; on May 14, 1933, the Federal Emergency Relief Administration (FERA) was established by Congress to cooperate with states in relieving hardships caused by unemployment and drought. On July 17, Harry Hopkins, then administrator of the FERA, authorized state emergency relief administrations to spend some of the funds appropriated under the federal program for the relief of both "ward and non-ward Indians."

At the same time, a national land program was undertaken. Its overall objective was the "purchase and retirement from farming of unprofitable, thin-soiled and exhausted land, and the removal of the occupants to other more promising areas where they could be rehabilitated and thus taken off the relief rolls."

In keeping with the mood of the times, Congress had been most generous in the authority it conveyed to the president to use the monies appropriated under the Emergency Relief Appropriation Act of 1935 for the development of a national program of land conservation and land utilization. The legislation provided that "the sums so allotted may be used, in the discretion and under the direction of the President, for the acquisition of sub-marginal lands and their use for such public purposes as the President shall prescribe."

Much thinking was done on behalf of the president to determine the public purposes for which the submarginal lands might be used. After all, it takes a degree of creativity to find a significant use for "unprofitable, thin-soiled and exhausted lands." But such creativity was not beyond the brain trusters. Most of the land was placed in protected federal areas, where, allowed to refurbish itself, it became a substantial part of what is now the national forest system. A sizable portion of the remainder was earmarked for those people who had become experts in survival on thin soil—the American Indians. Once again, giving eroded land to the Indians became a recognized federal policy.

Discussions over a three-month period took place at the highest levels in formulating the land program. President Roosevelt, Secretary Ickes, Secretary of Agriculture Henry A. Wallace, Hopkins, and others personally participated. Finally, the program was announced. Specifically included in the land use proposals were demonstration agricultural projects, recreational projects, wildlife projects, and "projects in which land to be purchased is to be used primarily for the benefit of the Indians, under the jurisdiction of the Bureau of Indian Affairs, Department of the Interior." The objective of these Indian projects was "readjustment and rehabilitation of Indian population by acquisition of lands to enable them to make appropriate and constructively planned use of combined land areas in units suited to their needs."

On July 14, 1934, John S. Lansill, director of the Land Program, wrote to Commissioner Collier that a grant of $25 million had been made to the FERA by the Public Works Administration for the purchase of submarginal farmlands and that $2.5 million of that grant had been reserved for Indian land projects. He requested that Collier submit "at the earliest moment" projects totaling the amount authorized and also proposed another $1.5 million in future submarginal-land acquisition projects. Landsill stressed the urgency of action: "It is extremely important that the land purchase program begin at once. Any help that you can give to speed up operations will be appreciated. The Land Program is anxious to cooperate with you fully."

By October 22, 1934, the amount available for acquisition of land for Indian land projects had been doubled and five types of demonstration Indian land areas were being described. These included the elimination of "checker-boarded" reservation areas by returning to Indian control lands that had been alienated; purchase of lands within watershed or water-control areas where necessary to protect the water supply of a reservation; purchase of additional lands to supplement inadequate reservations, whether the land was necessary for homesites, subsistence farming, grazing, or timber supply; purchase of lands for homeless Indian bands or communities forming relief problems; and purchase of lands needed for proper control of grazing areas.

On January 1, 1935, Collier and Lansill issued a joint memorandum that restated the proposals for Indian rehabilitation through land acquisition under the land program and that fixed final funding for Indian projects at $5 million. The two men made a joint policy statement: "It is desirable to acquire lands for Indian use which will improve their economy and welfare, and lessen relief costs, provided it is possible to provide for the present users." The proviso proved to be no problem. Most of the "present users" were on their way to California anyway.

Not to be overlooked in this program is the assumption that Indian life could be improved by giving to tribes land on which white farmers could not make a living. The assumption is correct, of course. This fact alone is a good indication of the economic deprivation of the Indian people.

The FERA began acquiring submarginal lands for Indians in 1934. In 1935, the Resettlement Administration was created and took over this responsibility. In October, 1936, a "memorandum of understanding" between the Resettlement Administration and the Bureau of Indian Affairs spelled out the agreement between the two agencies. The opening clauses make very clear the conditions under which the land was acquired:

Whereas, the Resettlement Administration is now engaged in a land acquisition program in connection with certain projects for the exclusive benefit of Indians; and
Whereas, the lands being acquired under this program are situated almost entirely within existing Indian reservations to which they are intended for addition for the purpose of providing subsistence farm sites and consolidated grazing areas for the exclusive use of Indians.

The memorandum went on to list ten submarginal-land purchase projects totaling 265,944 acres that the Resettlement Administration was in the process of acquiring. The purpose of the memorandum was to spell out ground rules allowing the Bureau of Indian Affairs to exercise temporary supervision over the lands during the prolonged period anticipated as necessary to complete acquisition of land title by the federal government. The memorandum concluded,

Upon the consummation of its land acquisition program in connection with the projects listed, the Resettlement Administration will concur in appropriate recommendations made by the Department of the Interior to Congress for incorporation of these project lands into the Indian reservations respectively indicated.

For the tribes involved, this was indeed a consummation devoutly to be wished.

The Resettlement Administration became a part of the Department of Agriculture on January 1, 1937. On August 11, Secretary Wallace wrote to Secretary Ickes, asking that eleven additional submarginal-land acquisition projects be included under the terms of the previous memorandum of understanding, making a total of twenty-one projects in all, encompassing approximately 402,533 acres of land.

Among the new projects there were five that, for the first time, were neither wholly nor partially within the boundaries of existing Indian reservations. These were projects designed to provide land for Indian tribes that had no lands: two projects for the Cherokees of Oklahoma and one each for the Seminoles of Florida, the Burns Paiute colony of Oregon, and the Stockbridge-Munsee community of Wisconsin.

Thirteen of the remaining sixteen projects were attempts to return to Indian dominion lands entirely within the boundaries of existing reservations. The other three projects were partly within and partly without the reservations for which they were intended. They were all located in a contiguous band of states stretching across the western half of the northern United States from Michigan to Idaho.

On April 15, 1938, President Roosevelt signed an executive order transferring jurisdiction over the lands within the twenty-one projects to the secretary of the interior, subject to the retention by the secretary of agriculture of such jurisdiction as was necessary to complete acquisition of the lands.

In May of the same year, Assistant Commissioner of the Bureau of Indian Affairs J. M. Stewart, wrote to all affected tribal agency superintendents explaining the land program and the effect of the executive order:

The title to these lands is taken in the name of the United States, and they will not become the property of the Indian tribe for whose use they were purchased, until Congressional action is obtained specifically transferring such title. However, the lands should, from the standpoint of administration, be treated as though they were tribal lands and any use thereof should be taken with the tribal council.

Additionally, the superintendents were told that although

these lands were purchased for Indian use if it is found impracticable at the moment for the Indians to use a portion thereof you are authorized to issue use permits to non-Indians in accordance with regulations now in force governing Indian tribal lands. The revenue obtained from that source should be taken up and carried as "Special Deposits" until such time as more definite instructions are given you.

It had taken more than four years to reach this point, in spite of the rush with which the land program had started. Moreover, the New Deal for American Indians was beginning to have problems with Congress. Between 1937 and 1944 there was constant friction between Commissioner Collier and the Senate and House Indian Affairs committees.

The agency superintendents had quickly spread the expectation that congressional action would soon turn over parcels of land to the tribes for whom they had been purchased. Tribes were encouraged to use the land as though it were already their own. At L'Anse Reservation, in Michigan, where the housing situation was desperate, thirteen homes were built on the submarginal land parcel with federal rehabilitation funds. The homes were occupied by tribal members who maintained them on the assurance of Bureau of Indian Affairs officials that the Indians would soon own them. After several years, however, uncertainty began to grow as the Indians became aware that the federal government could dispossess them at a moment's notice since title to the land remained with the federal government. Under these conditions, the Indians were reluctant to expend their scarce resources on any maintenance, and the housing fell into disrepair. Much of it was abandoned, although the need for housing on the reservation remained.

A similar situation existed at the Stockbridge-Munsee Reservation, near Bowler, Wisconsin. The tribal history is similar to that of many of the small eastern tribes. The Mohican Indians originated in Massachusetts but were pushed westward during the early colonial period into New York State. There they joined the Stockbridge, Brotherton, and other small tribes and became known as the Stockbridge band of Mohican Indians.

This confederation first signed a treaty with the United States in 1794. Less than thirty years later, in 1822, the government broke the treaty, pushing the tribe farther west into Wisconsin, where they were again told they could live in peace on the shores of Lake Winnebago. It was at this time that additional bands of Delaware Indians known as Munsee joined them. They became now known as the Stockbridge-Munsee. Again, peace was short-lived, and in 1856 the Stockbridge-Munsee were forced to cede their lands at Lake Winnebago to the government in exchange for a tract of land encompassing the present reservation, which was purchased by the government from the Menominee tribe for them. The original reservation included 23,040 acres. In the 1870's, valuable pine lands on the reservation were sold by Congress without notice to the tribe. Lumbermen removed the timber, leaving the tribe with no means of subsistence beyond the sale of produce from meager gardens. By the end of the allotment period, little more than 100 acres of the reservation remained under Indian ownership.

Landless and in desperate economic straits, the Stockbridge-Munsee community received early attention from Commissioner Collier. The Resettlement Administration approved Collier's request to buy 13,077 acres of submarginal land for the tribe and recommended to Collier the purchase of an additional 3,000 acres with I.R.A. funds. The supplemental purchase, it was felt, would block out the entire area for the tribe and, coupled with the submarginal lands, provide a reasonable land base. The co-operation between the two agencies was complete. Collier authorized the purchase of 1,250 acres with I.R.A. funds, all that were then available. The Resettlement Administration transacted the purchase, and a reservation was proclaimed on March 19, 1937, for the use and benefit of the Stockbridge-Munsee band of Mohican Indians of Wisconsin. Subsequently appropriated I.R.A. funds were used to purchase an additional 1,000 acres of land for the tribe.

No one considered the purchased acreage adequate for the needs of the tribe, except in conjunction with the 13,077 acres of submarginal land, which the tribe was promised would soon be theirs. More than thirty years later, that promise has still not been kept by the government.

Relying on the assurance of officials of the Bureau of Indian Affairs and acting under their supervision and assisted by federal rehabilitation funds, the Indians built forty residences on the Stockbridge-Munsee submarginal land parcel. There are now

152 people living in these houses, considerably more than live on the tribally owned, I.R.A.-purchased land. Yet the title to the submarginal land remains with the United States, and for reasons similar to those given at L'Anse, about half of these houses are now in poor condition.

The failure of Congress to enact the necessary legislation giving title of the submarginal land to the tribe has, in the words of tribal elder Elmer Davids, "wrought havoc with our plans and thoroughly depressed our spirit." Speaking in 1961, Davids told of the aspirations of his people, to which has been added ten more years of frustration:

Our present reservation is a cut-over tract. At the time of purchase it was about to be abandoned by the lumbermen as worthless. However, it is quite well-suited to our Indian needs. There is some arable land, a forest that will again in time come into production, and several streams of good fishing water. We have made good progress here. Our basic need is a land base, made secure for all time. In and on this hangs our future. Members of our tribe, scattered far and wide, are constantly applying for land and asking membership in the community. They wish to establish a home among their people. If we were to be assured that this little oasis of land would be ours indefinitely, the effect upon our spirit would be out of all proportion to the real or sale value of the land. It is a home for the aged, refuge for the unemployed, handicapped or ill. It would restore our faith that people of these United States would have it that way if they really understood Indian nature. The white public should be educated to look upon a reservation in the true meaning of the word: something the Indian tribes have reserved for themselves out of the vast territory of this country which was once their domain and for which, in some cases, they so valiantly resisted the invaders.

At the end of 1941, the nation had gone to war. President Roosevelt was preoccupied with the conduct of the fighting, and matters of domestic concern were placed on the back burners. Among them was the legislation transferring submarginal lands to Indian tribes. The bills to complete this aspect of the land program had begun appearing in the Congress in 1938 on behalf of certain tribes. But progress through the sluggish Indian Affairs subcommittees had not been rapid enough to result in enactment of legislation, although some of the bills had passed the House of Representatives but never the Senate. During the war years, the Bureau of Indian Affairs was moved from Washington to Chicago and funds were drastically curtailed. Collier was in no position to push for action on the bills.

The friction between the bureau commissioner and Congress reached a climax in 1944. In the midst of the war with Hitler's Germany, a select committee of the House of Representatives, with incredible insensitivity, offered its recommendations for what it called "the final solution of the Indian problem." The recommendations were for a return to the policy of Indian cultural genocide by coercive assimilation. The report suggested a reversal of most of Collier's programs—a return to the old, discredited ways. Collier resigned the following year. President Roosevelt, starting his fourth term, died in office. The New Deal for American Indians was over.

The 1944 report ushered in the beginning of the "termination period," during which Congress sought to eliminate as many tribes as possible by withdrawing federal recognition, protection, and services. It was not the climate in which legislation to add lands to Indian reservations could be expected to pass.

Until 1944, the submarginal-land projects purchased for the Indian tribes had been assigned to the tribes for their use without charge. Six of the projects, including those at the Stockbridge-Munsee and L'Anse reservations, consisted of cutover timberlands. Additionally, two parcels at the White Earth Reservation in Minnesota and one each at the Lac Court Oreilles and Bad River reservations in Wisconsin were in this category. At the Devils Lake Sioux Reservation in North Dakota, the submarginal land parcel was used for the Fort Totten Indian School farm. The remainder of the submarginal land parcels were predominantly grazing lands that had been assigned to the respective tribes.

Aware of congressional attitudes in 1944, Bureau of Indian Affairs officials stopped assuming that legislation transferring title of the submarginal lands to the tribes was imminent, although the Interior Department continued to support such legislation. One by one, the assignments of submarginal grazing land the land at any time. Initially, the revocable permits were for sized the power of the government to withdraw the right to use to tribes were canceled, and the tribes were authorized to use the land under the authority of "revocable permits," which empha-

ten-year periods. Later, the permits were issued for much shorter periods, in some instances for as short as a year or two.

Meanwhile, Congress was cutting back on bureau appropriations. In 1947, drastic budget cuts forced reduction of bureau personnel at the agency level. The tribes were compelled to employ personnel to administer realty functions normally handled by the bureau. Tribal income from their profit on submarginal-land permits enabled them to pay the salaries of the employees.

Although the only authority under which it was authorized to administer the lands was for "the exclusive benefit of Indians," the bureau started charging the tribes for the issuance of the permits. At first, the charge was only a token amount.

By 1949, the congressional desire to terminate federal Indian reservations had gained considerable strength. Still, the congressional attitude toward Indians reflected considerable ambivalence. This had always been present, but it was never more clearly shown than during the termination years. The submarginal-land program proceeded and got more favorable attention from Congress during the termination period than at any other time since the program had been undertaken.

Not all of the submarginal lands acquired for Indians were covered by the 1938 executive order mentioned earlier. Under a separate series of executive orders signed by President Roosevelt, 457,530 acres of submarginal land had been transferred to the Bureau of Indian Affairs for the benefit of the Jemez, Zuni, San Ildefonso, Zia, Santa Ana, Acoma, Laguna, and Isleta Puebloes. In all, some 828,000 acres of submarginal lands were transferred to the bureau for the benefit of Indians.

Under the direction of the powerful senator from New Mexico, Clinton Anderson (who four years before had been secretary of agriculture and who before his retirement in 1972 had been the ranking member of the Senate Interior and Insular Affairs Committee), title to the New Mexico land was delivered to the respective tribes on August 13, 1949. Anderson had been a field administrator of the FERA from 1935 to 1936 and knew well the purposes for which the Indian submarginal lands had been purchased. The same legislation conveyed title to an additional 154,502 acres of land withdrawn from the public domain to the Canoncito Navajo tribe, also of New Mexico. The funds on deposit in the "special deposits" accounts, which had accrued from the issuance of livestock-crossing permits and grazing permits, were awarded to the tribes. When the Indian Claims Commission had been created three years earlier, it had not been given jurisdiction to consider whether the value of the land transferred should be set off against any tribal claims.

On May 8, 1950, Dillon Myer became commissioner of Indian affairs, giving the proponents of the termination policy control of the whole bureau. The Indian Claims Commission was created in 1946 to settle Indian land claims arising out of the land thefts during the treaty period; the commission can only award money compensation. Most services and lands received by the Indians from the federal government since the taking of the land are subtracted from the amount of the award. The goals of the policy of the new commissioner were to "get rid of Indians and Indian trust land once and for all by 'terminating' federal recognition and services and relocating Indians into cities off the reservations." Myer had no previous experience in Indian affairs to qualify him for the appointment, but he was an expert in relocation. During World War II he had administered the program that "relocated" thousands of Americans of Japanese descent from their homes on the west coast to concentration camps in the Southwest. Myer was commissioner until 1953, when the termination policy received the official sanction of Congress with the passage of HCR 108.

Still, the submarginal-land program was not dead. The same House of Representatives that had originated and passed HCR 108 passed and sent to the Senate three bills that together would have delivered to several Indian tribes trust title to their submarginal lands. The Interior Department, by whom Commissioner Myer was employed, continued to support adoption of this legislation, as it had consistently since the program had been conceived under President Roosevelt and Secretary Ickes. Now, however, the support was coming under President Eisenhower from Secretary of the Interior Douglas McKay. It was as though the delivery of their submarginal lands to the Indian tribes was so clearly the only appropriate disposition of the lands purchased for them that even an apparent conflict with the prevailing general policy would not be allowed to stand in the way.

Actually, of course, the conflict was more apparent than real.

Although the termination policy called for the eventual elimination of all tribes, the plan was to begin with the most economically self-sufficient. The submarginal lands, on the other hand, had been purchased for the tribes that were most needy. Delivery of the lands to these tribes to get them on their economic feet was necessary, therefore, whether or not termination was the eventual goal.

Secretary McKay's support of passage of the Indian submarginal-land legislation may have been completely consistent with the past policy of the Interior Department, but it enraged Senator Hugh Butler, Republican of Nebraska, who was then enjoying the beginning of his short, year-and-half reign as chairman of the Senate Interior and Insular Affairs Committee. Butler died in office in July 1954. The bills also died in his committee.

On April 23, 1953, Butler wrote to McKay asking to have the departmental reports "restudied." He made explicit his opposition to the bills and his reasons for it:

If these bills are enacted it will open the way for other such bills and eventually will permit the transfer of all of these sub-marginal lands and the money now on deposit in the special accounts. In addition, it would create new Indian reservations or add additional areas to existing reservations. It would tend to perpetuate the Indian Bureau and its supervision over the Indians indefinitely. Such a policy will not aid in freeing the Indian from governmental control.

Butler's simplistic concept of the land program ignored its history as well as its authorization by Congress in 1935 and its ratification again by Congress through transfer of the New Mexico lands in 1949. He reasoned that the money came from the United States Treasury; therefore, the land belonged to the United States. Because the land belonged to the United States, the income derived from its use belonged to the United States; and the United States did not include the Indians.

All was well, according to Butler, as long as the money was collected and placed in special deposits. "This money," he said, "belongs to the taxpayers of the United States and should now be covered into the Treasury. It was the taxpayers' money which was used to acquire the land." Never mind that the land was mostly within the boundaries of Indian reservations. Never mind the terms of the federal emergency relief legislation, which had authorized the land program and appropriated the funds for it. Never mind the economic condition of the tribes. Land was not good for tribes: it tended to perpetuate them.

The Bureau of Indian Affairs had responded to what it believed was the congressional mood by creating the revocable permits. The tribes did not like the permit system, which emphasized the temporary nature of their right to use the land and under which they were charged for the first time for the use of the land. Only non-Indians had been charged before the revocable permit system was instituted. Other than the inaction by Congress of the turnover legislation, there had been no previous indication that the government might renege on its promise to deliver the land. The revocable permit was the first tangible indication.

But Butler saw in the revocable permit something more sinister. "Someone within the Indian Bureau worked out a scheme whereby the various Indian tribal councils were permitted to lease these lands from the government for two cents per acre and in turn to re-lease the same lands to the actual users at rates of from ten cents to several dollars per acre, thereby making a tremendous profit. This scheme in effect cheated and defrauded the United States Government out of large sums of money." Only four years earlier the Congress had taken that money in their special accounts and had given it to the various Puebloes of New Mexico; President Eisenhower had signed the bill. Apparently, *everyone* was involved in the conspiracy to defraud the United States!

Senator Butler's letter might not have made much sense, but it could not be taken lightly in the Interior Department. After all, Butler was chairman of the Senate Interior Committee. The ripples from the letter were traceable all the way down the bureau's chain of command, from the secretary of the interior to the commissioner on Indian affairs, to the area directors, to the agency superintendents, and back again. A memorandum from the commissioner to the area directors summarized Senator Butler's three-page letter in one paragraph about the submarginal-land bills: "Senator Butler has taken objection to such legislation. He, apparently, is of the opinion that there is not ample justification shown whereby the various tribes should have ownership of the land and the accumulated proceeds therefore now held in special deposit accounts." The commissioner asked the area directors to obtain answers to a series of specific questions. It was obvious that the purpose of obtaining such answers was to provide the necessary justification.

The Billings, Montana, area director responded in great detail. He reached two general conclusions:

> It is evident from our files and information obtained from personnel associated with this acquisition program that these lands were being acquired at that time for Indian use and the matter of transferring to the Interior Department for Indian use or to the Indian tribes themselves was a mere formality. It is obvious that the differences in income received by the United States Treasury for surface use of such lands which are now in Indian use in respect to such lands used by non-Indians is inconsequential. However, in the matter of leases for oil and gas, a far more adequate return from the submarginal lands within the Indian Reservation boundaries would have been realized had those lands been officially transferred to tribal ownership as was contemplated at the time of purchase. It seems to me that the time has come to settle this issue and have the Congress enact the necessary legislation to vest title in the United States in trust for the respective tribes.

Nineteen years later, the issue is still unsettled.

In the meantime, the Bureau of Indian Affairs responded to the pressure created by Butler's letter. In a carefully worded memorandum to area directors and accounting offices dated November 23, 1955, Assistant Commissioner Barton Greenwood explained that the special deposit accounts should be deposited in the United States Treasury to the credit of the appropriate miscellaneous receipts account and subsequent receipts should be treated in similar fashion. "No purpose would be served," Greenwood wrote, "by continuing to hold this money in special deposits in support of such legislation since it may be provided in this legislation if so desired that such funds on deposit in the Treasury could be credited to the account of the tribe." If there was no purpose in reserving the funds in special deposit accounts, where they earned no interest for either the tribe or the government, why had it taken the bureau from 1938 to 1955 to discover that the accounts had no purpose?

There was, of course, a purpose in keeping the money set aside. Once in the treasury, the money was not likely to come back out, no matter what the books said. Putting the money in the treasury meant it no longer had to be dealt with. Presently proposed turnover legislation introduced at the request of the Nixon administration in 1971 does not even mention the sub-marginal-land receipts in the treasury, although the amount there has increased tremendously since 1955, substantially exceeding the original purchase price of the land. Instead, at the insistence of the president's Office of Management and Budget, it authorizes the Indian Claims Commission to consider setting off the value of the land against pending tribal claims. Thus, instead of getting the land plus the income, as Roosevelt and Collier intended, the Indians may get the land with an opportunity to pay for it twice. If, that is, they can persuade the Congress to deliver the land at all.

The bureau also responded to Senator Butler's other complaints. As the ten-year revocable permits on submarginal grazing lands expired, two administrative changes were made: the time periods for the permits were considerably shortened and the formula for computing rents was changed to make it "more realistic." The result was a roughly tenfold increase in the rent payable by each tribe to the United States for the revocable permit to use the grazing lands. The terms of the new permits were presented to the tribes on a "take it or leave it" basis. The Cheyenne River Sioux tribe respectfully declined.

The new rates were based on an estimated 50 percent of what the tribe could expect to obtain by subletting the lands to the actual users. Again, the bureau position made no sense except as a facile political compromise with the Senate Interior Committee. There was a serious question as to whether a government agency charged by a presidential mandate with administering lands for the exclusive benefit of Indians could legitimately charge the beneficiaries anything at all. But, if Senator Butler's contention that allowing the tribes to make a "tremendous profit" on the use of lands purchased with taxpayer's money constituted a fraud on the taxpayers made any sense, reducing the profit margin to 50 percent did not cure the fraud. Rather, it added bribery to the list of crimes. At the Rosebud Sioux Reservation, the annual cost of the tribal grazing permit jumped from $358.68 to $6,889.64 as a result of the change in policy.

Given their impact on bureau policies, one would have thought that the late Senator Butler's contentions about Indian submarginal lands had the support of his surviving colleagues. Instead, three years after the letter was written, on July 20, 1956, Congress as a whole repudiated this assumption by turning over the 27,000-acre submarginal land parcel in Florida (to which Butler specifically referred in his letter) to the landless Seminole tribe for whom it had been bought, creating a new reservation. In addition, on August 2, of the same year, Congress conveyed beneficial title to 78,372 more acres of submarginal land to the Jemez and Zia Puebloes in New Mexico.

Meanwhile, Congress was implementing its termination policy. In 1954, legislation was passed ending the legal existence of six different tribes. In 1956, the Congress terminated federal supervision over three Oklahoma tribes on successive days. The impact on the individual tribes was, of course, devastating. The impact on American Indians generally was to unify them in protest and resistance to the policy. Reacting to the protest, on September 18, 1958, Secretary of the Interior Fred Seaton announced in a speech at Flagstaff, Arizona, that no tribe would be terminated without its consent. Although the policy remained on the books, the termination of tribes stopped. The delivery of submarginal lands to tribes during the termination period appeared as an inconsistency, but it really was not. Rather it was a process of fattening for the slaughter. Having lost political support for the termination policy, the terminationists in Congress successfully blocked enactment of further submarginal-land legislation within the congressional interior committees. There have been no tribal terminations since 1958, but neither has there been any favorable action on submarginal-land legislation.

The various parcels of land had once been called submarginal because they were unable to profitably support the farming or timber operations on them. As the years passed, the submarginal land, like most other land in the country, appreciated in value. In 1955, the presence of oil and natural gas below the surface of this land was suspected at the Fort Hall Reservation in Idaho; at the Pine Ridge, Rosebud, and Cheyenne River reservations in South Dakota; and at Fort Belknap, Blackfeet, and Fort Peck in Montana.

Under the administration of the Bureau of Land Management within the Interior Department, mineral leases were issued and considerable revenue derived from the issuance and placed in the United States Treasury. At Fort Peck alone, the federal income solely from mineral leases and royalties during the period from 1955 through 1970 was $2,194,611. Coupled with the rents the government had collected for surface rights (another $182,-740.92), the amount collected from the Fort Peck submarginal land parcel through 1970 was $2,377,351.92. The Fort Peck total is, of course, exceptionally high. It was the one place where oil was actually found.

Since the submarginal lands at Fort Peck had cost the government only $412,302, the government has realized a profit of $1,965,049.92 from its purchase. Not bad going on the use of Federal Emergency Relief funds, which were appropriated "for the exclusive benefit of Indians." Meanwhile, the Fort Peck Indians, like the other tribes, have not received the lands.

On the twelve submarginal land parcels consisting of grazing land, the government has collected more than $1.5 million dollars over its initial cost. The exact figures are as follows:

	Parcel Cost	U.S. Receipts	Difference
Pine Ridge S. Dak.	$207,792.00	$115,144.50	($92,647.50)
Rosebud, S. Dak.	155,004.00	97,864.70	(57,139.30)
Lower Brule, S. Dak.	56,990.00	25,358.20	(31,631.80)
Crow Creek, S. Dak.	81,591.00	30,348.20	(51,242.80)
Cheyenne River, S. Dak.	18,202.00	4,548.00	(13,654.00)
Standing Rock N. Dak.	24,911.00	17,741.72	(7,169.28)
Devils Lake, N. Dak.	11,869.00	2,318.40	(9,550.60)
Fort Peck, Mont.	412,302.00	2,377,351.92	(1,965,049.92)
Fort Belknap, Mont.	89,936.00	75,831.62	(14,104.38)
Blackfoot, Mont.	31,076.00	45,079.90	(14,003.90)
Fort Hall, Idaho	133,213.00	12,205.86	(121,007.14)
Burns Paiute, Oreg.	14,620.00	2,938.36	(11,681.64)
Totals	$1,237,506.00	$2,806,731.38	($1,569,225.38)

The other submarginal land parcels were timberland. When purchased, the land consisted of cutover timber. Bureau of Indian Affairs officials allowed housing construction on these parcels at L'Anse and Stockbridge-Munsee as described above and at the Lac Court Oreilles Reservation in Wisconsin, where about ten homes were built. Three of these were "paid off" by the people living in them who now own the homes—but not the land under them. At Stockbridge, a small portion was cleared and cultivated for tribal farming needs. The rest of the timberland parcels with minor exceptions were held by bureau officials to give second-growth timber a chance to grow.

The bureau permitted salvage cutting pursuant to cutting permits, for which a fee was paid, of dead and dying timber only. In 1962, by directive from Washington, the policy was changed to permit commercial timber-cutting. From that point on, the federal income from these parcels soared. Originally held in special accounts, this money too was deposited in the federal treasury. In most cases, the bonding requirements and competitive bidding procedures used by the bureau excluded the small Indian operators from participating in the commercial harvesting of the timber. On every one of these reservations, the United States Treasury has received more than was paid for the land. The exact figures are as follows:

	Parcel Cost	U.S. Receipts	U.S. Profit
L'Anse, Mich.	$16,121.00	$21,510.00	$5,389.00
Stockbridge-Munsee, Wis.	69,546.00	92,283.12	22,737.12
Bad River, Wis.	32,093.00	47,631.60	15,538.60
Lac Court Oreilles, Wis.	25,598.00	52,490.00	26,892.00
White Earth, Minn.	175,664.00	175,896.00	232.00

The very policy change that had occurred in 1955, made because the bureau commissioner had said that special deposit accounts no longer served any purpose, was itself a deterrent to favorable congressional action on the turnover legislation. The longer Congress waited, the more money could be milked from the land for the federal treasury. Perhaps it was a coincidence that the issuance of mineral leases commenced the same year that the special deposits were eliminated and that commercial cutting of timber began a few years later. Perhaps not.

The interest of the tribes in obtaining title to their submarginal lands has been unflagging. As a result, numerous bills have been introduced in each session of Congress that would, if passed, deliver title to the respective tribes. In 1962, proponents tried an omnibus approach. At the request of Senator Anderson, then chairman of the Senate Interior Committee, the comptroller general of the United States prepared a lengthy report designed to find reasons for not passing the legislation. The listed criteria used in the report were whether the various tribes had demonstrated a need for, and would constructively use, the submarginal land, whether the conveyance of submarginal land would influence eventual termination of federal supervision over the tribes, whether the present financial resources of each tribe warrant the proposed donation of the land, and whether the current and potential income from submarginal land is of significant proportions. When these criteria could not be used to recommend against the legislation, the report invented new criteria. Delivery of land to the landless Burns Paiute colony was improper, the report said, because it "may establish a precedent that would encourage similar groups to seek like benefits."

There were, of course, no other landless Indian groups for whom submarginal lands had been set aside that were not already seeking "like benefits." The Stockbridge-Munsee community, landless except for the I.R.A. lands purchased for it in the 1930's, and the Cherokee tribe of Oklahoma, which had two parcels of land set aside for it in the original executive order of 1938, were already actively seeking this legislation.

That the report would use the "precedent" argument at all was evidence of how hard its authors were trying to find reasons against delivering the land. Although written only six years after the Seminole legislation had passed and although it repeatedly concerns itself with the question of legislative precedent and has a separate section on the historical background of submarginal lands, the report totally fails to mention the existing legislative precedents. This oversight must reflect on either the competency or objectivity of the report.

The "legislative precedent" issue is a red herring anyway. Since 1956, Congress has been ignoring the Seminole precedent set by the legislation for the various New Mexico Puebloes. Clearly, Congress can, and often does, ignore its own precedents. It makes little sense to deny the transfer of land to the deserving Burns Paiute colony solely on the grounds that someone else may come along seeking similar treatment. Each case can stand or fall on its own merits if Congress chooses to hear it.

Somewhat ironically, in the instances in which the comptroller general's report approved of delivery of submarginal lands to the Stockbridge-Munsee, White Earth, and Fort Totten (Devils Lake) tribes, the congressional interior committees simply ignored these recommendations. From 1962 until 1970 there were no further legislative hearings on any of the bills to deliver submarginal lands to the tribes, although bills in support of this action were repeatedly introduced. At one time, there were as many as thirty such bills pending in the Ninety-first Congress.

Meanwhile, the untenable position the Bureau of Indian Affairs had taken with respect to grazing fees as a result of the pressure from Senator Butler was under counterattack. After the series of increases in grazing fees that had commenced in 1955, the bureau rented to Indian tribes grazing land acquired, and supposedly being administered, for the exclusive benefit of those same Indian tribes at rates even higher than authorized by law for rental of lands in the public domain. Attorney Marvin Sonosky, representing five of the tribes using submarginal grazing lands, pointed out this absurdity to the Interior Department.

On March 28, 1963, the Department of the Interior approved a change in fees charged on submarginal land for grazing purposes only to bring such rates in line with those charged for use of public domain lands under the Taylor Grazing Act. This resulted in a substantial reduction in the rental rate. Even though the Interior Department conceded that its previous charges had been excessive, no refund or credit of the funds deposited in the United States Treasury was made to the tribes.

Under continuing pressure from Attorney Sonosky, the Interior Department continued to reexamine the legal basis of its administrative policy. Such a reexamination, conducted with any degree of reasonableness, could only produce one result: on October 22, 1964, Acting Secretary of the Interior Frank P. Briggs issued a memorandum entitled "Discontinuance of Fees Charged to Tribes for Use of Submarginal Lands." The memorandum began, "Bearing in mind the purpose for which submarginal lands were originally acquired, our continuing reevaluation of policy considerations leads to the conclusion that the Bureau of Indian Affairs is not justified in making a charge for the permits to these lands."

The purposes for which the lands had been acquired were not at all in doubt: The records disclose a complete understanding between the federal agencies involved in the acquisition and administration of the submarginal lands that such lands had been selected for acquisition in connection with demonstration

Indian projects, that they were needed by the Indians in connection with utilization of Indian-owned lands, and that proper recommendations would be made at the appropriate time for the enactment of legislation to add permanently those lands to Indian reservations. This had been the conclusion of everyone who had completely reviewed the submarginal-land program with the exception of Senator Butler. Briggs reviewed the history and concluded: "Although there have been some deviations from the policy established in early years, and from time to time the purpose of the purchase has been overlooked, nonetheless, the true intent of the purchase was for the exclusive benefit of Indians. With this purpose in mind, the conclusion has been reached that no further charge will be made after this date."

Thus, twenty-six years after the Bureau of Indian Affairs had begun to administer the lands and twenty years after it had begun to charge tribes for permits to use it, the Interior Department was returning to the policy with which it had started. To do otherwise would have required the department to again "overlook" the purposes for which the land had been acquired and delivered to its charge—that is, to violate the express terms of the executive order that authorized it to administer the land. For twenty years, departmental policy had admittedly violated that mandate, but again no attempt was made to recompense the tribes. Secretary Briggs had an answer for that one, too: "This entire question of charging fees is strictly a matter of policy and not a question of law." There is no explanation of this strained conclusion. But it is the only one that the department could reach without becoming liable to the Indians. Perhaps, that is explanation enough.

The government had no intention, of course, of cutting off all the income the submarginal land was producing. Exceptions to the "no charge" rule were quickly carved out: (1) The rule applied only to surface use, not to the removal of minerals. The income from mineral leases still went into the United States Treasury. (2) Although surface crops could be grown and harvested, timber was not such a crop. Timber was like minerals. The income from timber-cutting permits still went into the treasury. (3) Sonosky only represented tribes in the Dakotas. At Stockbridge-Munsee, the meager tribal income had never enabled the tribe to obtain legal representation. The income from surface rents on their submarginal lands should not have gone to the treasury. But, since nobody had explained this to the tribe, the government continued to collect it. Surface rents for a ranger station and used-car lot on Stockbridge submarginal lands netted the government another $1,122.02 during the years 1964 to 1970. And, at Fort Hall, the tribe continued to be charged for the use of farmland.

In 1970, the National Council on Indian Opportunity (NCIO), an arm of the vice-president's office, began to look into the question of submarginal lands. As a result, a researcher visited each of the seventeen northern reservations for which submarginal lands were being held.

At Fort Hall, Idaho, Tribal Chairman Kesley Edmo presented a diagram that represented a portion of the Shoshone-Bannock submarginal land parcel with a fence line around it. There were two deviations from the boundary line that left portions of the submarginal land outside the bureau-built fence. One was a section of farmland 137.1 acres in size. The other only cut off 2.8 acres but was obviously deliberately created by putting a wedge-shaped area in the otherwise straight fence line. A small circle on the diagram, inside the wedge area, indicated the place where a natural spring emerged from the ground. The bureau officials had built the fence so that the spring was outside of it, allowing the non-Indian farmer (who also got the benefit from the 137.1 acres) to come onto the submarginal lands, place a pump sunk in concrete on the spring, and pump the scarce water off of the submarginal lands onto his own. His lands were irrigated from the spring and were productive. The submarginal lands inside the fence, the surface use of which had been rented to the tribe, were dry and dusty.

Confronted with an outraged "investigator from Washington," the agency superintendent and real property officer admitted that the situation "looked kind of funny." Assured that the situation looked more scandalous than humorous, the officials hastily assured the investigator, "We will move the fence to the property line any time the tribe requests." The tribal council, before which the entire conversation had taken place, quickly passed a unanimous resolution instructing the officials to move the fence to the line immediately. Asked when they intended to take such action, the real property officer asked, "Will this afternoon be soon enough?" He was assured that it was. That was in August 1970. The investigator left on the afternoon plane. The fence has not been moved.

On August 15–16, 1970, a joint meeting was held in Minneapolis, Minnesota, to which each of the concerned tribes sent two delegates. The tribal delegates concluded the meeting with the adoption of resolutions unanimously supporting a joint effort to obtain title to their respective submarginal land parcels.

As the Ninety-second Congress opened in 1971, changes on the staff of the Senate Interior and Insular Affairs Committee were indicative of changing attitudes on the part of some of its ranking members, particularly Chairman Henry M. Jackson, who had been labeled a hard-nosed terminationist. On March 26, 1971, for the first time since 1956, hearings were held before the full Senate Interior Committee on two bills sponsored by the Nixon administration to turn over title to their submarginal lands to the Stockbridge-Munsee and White Earth reservations. The bills, which were a direct result of the NCIO investigation, included for the first time language insisted upon by the Office of Management and Budget (over the weak protest of the Interior Department) authorizing the Indian Claims Commission to consider setting off the value of the land against pending tribal claims. The bills failed to mention all the money deposited in the United States Treasury from the use of the land since 1938, although in both instances the amount received exceeded the original cost of the land to the United States.

With some reservations about the language of the bills, all of the witnesses at the hearing supported delivery of the lands to the tribes. But the committee never reported out the legislation.

In the meantime, NCIO published its report on submarginal lands, concluding:

The land was purchased with special funds to be consolidated with other tribal landholdings and held in trust for the tribes. The accrued revenues were intended to go with the land. As the amount of accrued revenue has increased through the years, the desire on the part of the government to retain it has increased. But, legally and morally speaking, it is difficult to justify rentention by the government of any more than that amount which redeems the original purchase price of the land.

Thus, the fulfillment of this promise made long ago requires passage of legislation delivering trust title to the submarginal lands to the respective tribes for whom they were purchased, for use in accord with land use plans that have been legislatively approved, and delivery of that amount of accrued revenue which is appropriate. The sooner that these ends are achieved, the sooner that these tribes can move toward providing a better economic life for their people.

America's Indians have often seen much of what the foregoing history reveals: the high-minded promises that were never kept; the programs started for the benefit of Indians that ended providing benefits for the government or for rapacious officials and their friends while Indians waited; the apologies, but not compensation, for previous acts of the government that were admittedly unconscionable, illegal, or both; and last, the feeling that lands to be given to Indians must first be milked for every bit of value that could be drawn off. What makes this case different is that here the promise has not yet been broken: it has simply never been kept. The opportunity to keep it is still available. How much better than more apologies and expressions of guilt the fulfillment of this promise would be.

We recommend congressional action on all of the submarginal-land restoration bills. Prompt enactment of this legislation would mean a restoration of 344,811 acres to the Indian land base. Combined with the previous totals of land held in the other categories, the basic Indian land estate (in acres) would be as follows:

Tribal lands	39,663,412.09
Individual Indian allotments	10,697,621.58
Alaskan native lands	40,000,000
Occupied Indian lands	4,723,017.2
Submarginal lands	344,811
	95,428,862.87

❦ 6 ❦

The Tricky Transit
at Flathead Lake

Part of the continuing problem of Indian lands involves the
clarification of boundary lines set aside by treaty cessions or executive orders. Tribes cannot make intelligent plans for the
development of their reservations unless and until they have their
boundaries firmly established. Much of the confusion has come
about because of errors in either surveying or describing boundaries nearly a century ago. The tragic part of boundary errors is
that the government has consistently claimed that errors, even
on the part of its own employees, redound to its credit and are
not evidence that the tribe has a valid land claim against it.

No new policy for Indian lands can be promulgated without
having at its root the proposition that where tribes have been
unfairly deprived of their lands, these lands should, insofar as
possible, be restored to them. In the following chapters we will
discuss a number of instances in which tribes have been deprived
of lands because of a refusal by the United States government
and its constituent agencies to admit their errors and return the
lands they have wrongly taken.

The land restoration of the Flathead Lake area to that tribe is
a case in point. From the earliest times, the Salish, Kootenay,
and Upper Pend d'Oreilles tribes of Indians lived in the area
roughly bounded by the high plateau of western Montana and
northern Idaho. They were visited by Lewis and Clark in their
1805–1806 exploratory trip to describe the Northwest Territory
and to find a path to the Pacific Ocean. The Flatheads welcomed

them, and after the harrowing experiences of Blackfeet country, the two explorers were happy indeed to meet the tribes.

While almost all of the coastal Salish peoples practiced the flattening of the heads of young children by binding boards to their foreheads in early childhood, only these bands of Indians were officially called Flatheads by the Americans who began coming to their country. Missionaries and mountain men in search of furs began to come into the Flathead country shortly after the journey of Lewis and Clark had opened up the vista of new frontiers and wealth to the world outside. Throughout the first several decades of their contact with the whites the Flatheads maintained a rather remarkable pattern of friendliness toward the invaders.

But the pattern of settlement began to demand that the Northwest fall to the settler's plow, and by the 1850's the government had begun a long series of treaties with the tribes of the Columbia plateau area for the cession of lands and the establishment of reservations. James Buchanan was president in 1855 when Governor Isaac Stevens was dispatched to the Northwest for the purpose of gaining as much Indian land as possible through a series of treaties with the tribes of the area.

After finishing the negotiations of treaties with the tribes of the Puget Sound area and along the Columbia River, Stevens and his party set out for the eastern Washington area to sign treaties with the Nez Perce, Yakima, and Flatheads. On July 16, 1855, a treaty was concluded with the Salish, Kootenay, and Upper Pend d'Oreilles tribes of Indians at Hell Gate, a rugged defile where the Bitter Root River runs through the mountains somewhat east of present-day Missoula, Montana.

It took Stevens many days to conclude his treaty with the Flatheads, because they did not believe the many promises that he had made them and because he seemed particularly vague as to the exact location of their reservation. Many of the Flatheads wanted to remain in the Bitter Root valley and Stevens wanted them to move to the Flathead valley. To allay their fears Stevens promised the tribes that the president would send out a party to determine which valley would be best for the people. If the president determined that the Bitter Root valley was better, it would be marked off as the reservation. If the Flathead valley was thought to be best, the people would be expected to move there within a year after the ratification of the treaty. Thus, at the conclusion of the treaty no one really seemed to know exactly what had been ceded and what had been set aside as a reservation. Stevens acted as if the Flatheads had agreed to move to the Flathead valley and many of the Flatheads continued to live in the Bitter Root valley, anticipating the arrival of the president's men who would make the final determination.

The government officials apparently had no hesitancy about which reservation had been set aside, because they continually acted as if the Flatheads remaining in Bitter Root valley were outlaws living off the reservation. For years after the signing of the Treaty of Hell Gate there was continuing agitation for a determination of a reservation, and the Flatheads constantly demanded the survey of their lands in order that they might allocate lands according to traditional tribal living practices. But the government continued to act puzzled either when the subject of reservations was mentioned or when the Flatheads asked for a survey according to the treaty provisions.

The war for the West continued in the interim, and the Flatheads, zealous about keeping their part of the treaty, never involved themselves in the struggle of the other tribes to remain free. Thus, they remained peacefully living on their reservation in the lower Flathead valley while the Sioux, Northern Arapaho, and Northern Cheyenne gave General Custer his hair-raising reception in Montana and slept blissfully while their cousins, the Nez Perce, rode silently by in the night in their desperate effort to reach Canada and freedom.

With the destruction of the buffalo and the starvation of the strong warrior tribes of the northern plains, the government was in an ideal position to force its will on the tribes that still lived in the northern tier of states, stretching from Minnesota to Washington on the Pacific coast. Thus, in 1882, Congress, aware that the question of a permanent reservation for the Flatheads had never been determined, passed the Act of June 5 and provided for the removal of the Flatheads living in the Bitter Root valley to the reservation in the lower Flathead reservation. It was never a question of the president sending out someone to determine where the reservation should be located. Someone in the nation's capital simply took out a map and began drawing lines, and later the soldiers came and escorted the remaining Flatheads to the reservation.

Less than five years after the removal a crisis occurred on the reservation. Congress had passed the General Allotment Act believing that by vesting each individual Indian with the profound and magical gift of private land ownership he would forsake tribal customs and be transformed into a god-fearing farmer like his white neighbor down the road. The problem at Flathead was that no boundaries had ever been set for the reservation. It was virtually impossible, then, to divide something of an unknown quantity equally.

In 1887, therefore, the government surveyors arrived at the Flathead reservation to begin surveying the reservation. Surveying had been promised in the treaty of 1855, and had it been done then, perhaps the result would have been different. But in 1882, more than a quarter of a century later, there were no whites around who knew about the original promises, and no one who worked on the survey would take the Flatheads' word, simply because they were Indians.

The treaty had been rather specific about the boundaries of the lower Flathead reservation. The second article of the treaty read:

Commencing at the source of the main branch of the Jocko River; thence along the divide separating the waters flowing into the Bitter Root River from those flowing into the Jocko to a point on Clarke's Fork between the Camash and Horse prairies; thence northerly to, and along the divide bounding on the west the Flathead River, to a point due west from the point half way in latitude between the northern and southern extremities of the Flathead Lake; thence on a due east course to the divide whence the Crow, the Prune, and the So-ni-el-em and the Jocko Rivers take their rise, and thence southerly along said divide to the place of beginning.

It is not recorded whether the surveyors actually read the article of the treaty before they embarked on their great venture, but the similarity between their final description of the reservation and the treaty article left something to be desired.

The problem was not that difficult. The southern, eastern, and western boundaries of the reservation were the crests of mountain ranges or the dividing lines of watersheds. Thus, it was not difficult, once having climbed the mountain, to determine what was the crest. The northern boundary, however, presented a difficulty of great magnitude. It was supposed to represent a line parallel to the midline of Flathead Lake. With a shifting shoreline and the continual rise and fall of lake shoreline, determining the midline was almost totally subject to the time of the year at which the survey was taken. When the dust cleared, the surveyors had underestimated the midline by a considerable distance, excluding at least 4,000 acres that clearly should have been included in the reservation and an undetermined number of acres that possibly could have been included. The line, it appeared, sagged.

One can forgive surveyors for what appeared to be a mistake of not too great significance but not for their determination of the southwestern corner of the reservation. This corner, as you will recall, was to be determined by the confluence of the Bitter Root and Jocko rivers, a fairly easily identifiable landmark. It seemed, however, that a group of hardy pioneers had already gathered at this particular point. The boundary thus skipped a few steps magically avoiding the settlers (thus making their titles good) and came to rest in the west, having excluded some 12,000 acres of prime Indian river-bottom land.

Now it did not take a very smart Indian in those days to understand that rivers do not set their course in conformity with recent settlement patterns in the neighborhood. The tribe complained vigorously, with few tangible results. The survey was finally completed in 1892, with a straight face on the surveying party, and was entered in the government records as having conformed to the provisions of the treaty.

Had the tribe been left in peace at this point, the issues would be fairly clear and the bureaucrats would have no basis for continuing to keep the Flathead lands. But the nation was in the midst of closing the frontier and opening up the remaining Indian reservations for white settlement, and so, confirmation of a boundary at Flathead made the tribe eligible for allotment under the 1887 act. Settlers began to cast envious eyes at the reservation, which occupied a valley they considered too valuable for a tribe of happy savages. Pressure began to mount in the West for allotment of the Flathead lands and sale of the surplus to white settlers.

Even this would have been only a slight impediment to the title, but a force intervened that gave the government agencies the chance to complicate land titles to an amazing degree. In 1891, the year before the completion of the survey of the reservation, Congress had repealed the Timber Culture Act to appease the rising conservation movement and to foreclose further settlement of forests by fraudulent claims under this old statute. Two sections in the repeal had particular importance for the Flatheads. The tenth section stated

> that nothing in this act shall change, repeal, or modify any agreements or treaties made with any Indian tribes for the disposal of their lands, or of land ceded to the United States to be disposed of for the benefit of such tribes, and the proceeds thereof to be placed in the Treasury of the United States; and the disposition of such lands shall continue in accordance with the provisions of such treaties or agreements, except as provided in section 5 of this act.

It would seem, therefore, that the original reservation boundaries, as outlined in the treaties, were preserved by this act and that title derived from the treaties was good against anything but a subsequent land cession by the tribes under federal law. This theory might have subsequently held up had not the act contained another section dealing with the new policy of setting aside public lands. Section 24 provided

> that the President of the United States may, from time to time, set apart and reserve, in any State or Territory having public land bearing forests, in any part of the public lands wholly or in part covered with timber or undergrowth, whether of commercial value or not, as public reservations, and the President shall, by public proclamation, declare the establishment of such reservations and the limits thereof.

The effect of this section on public lands of the United States was to trigger a race between two sets of bureaucrats, in the Interior and Agriculture departments, as to the amount of land each might control. In the middle of this titanic struggle of executive departments were the unfortunate Flatheads, with an erroneous boundary not of their making.

Two separate forces had been unleashed by federal law and were headed for a confrontation on the lonely and hitherto isolated reservation of the friendly Flatheads. On June 10, 1896, Congress passed a law specifically directing that a commission be formed to discuss further land cessions from Indian tribes. The

Flathead Indians fell under this statute, and a commission proceeded to Montana intent upon stripping them of their lands and reducing them to another western farming community through allotment.

In the following year President Cleveland issued a proclamation under the authority of the Act of 1891, which had given him powers to set aside forest lands. Citing section 24 of the act, the presidential proclamation stated that "the public lands in the State of Montana, within the limits hereinafter described, are in part covered with timber, and it appears that the public good would be promoted by setting apart and reserving such lands as a public reservation" and proceeded to list the lands that would be withdrawn—including the Flathead lands excluded from the reservation in the erroneous survey of 1887–1892.

It was apparent that the Flatheads were about to lose their lands either to the settlers if the allotment commission declared the southwestern corner of the reservation surplus or to the government in the new forest reservation even if the land were restored. Their argument was that all claims were preserved because of the treaty, which gave them priority in title over the lands. Events were moving so fast and in such a complicated manner, however, that the argument was never heard by the busy bureaucrats.

On April 23, 1904, Congress passed a statute confirming the allotment of the reservation and opening the Flathead reservation lands to white settlement and entry. The act virtually destroyed the Flatheads. Early adherents to the Catholic religion, they had planned their reservation life according to the new ways learned from the missionaries. Many were cattlemen with large herds of cattle and horses, and some were raising sheep, while still others continued to live off the herds of buffalo that had found refuge on the reservation from the relentless white hunters.

When allotments were given out the pattern was less than haphazard. Families could not receive their lands as contiguous parcels, and so, many had to sell off their livestock and reduce their herds to a size consistent with their small tracts of land. Ranching provided less than a subsistence income; farming was virtually nonexistent because of a lack of irrigation facilities.

The people were forced to near-starvation conditions. Congress had destroyed a successful ranching community in favor of its new policy to turn Indians into farmers.

As whites began to move into the ceded Flathead lands, they discovered what the Indians had learned all too well: the country was not suited for farming. It was ranching land with tremendous forest areas more suitable for recreation and the life of the hunt than for farming, particularly grain farming. Tumult began among the new white entrants for an irrigation project to make the lands arable. In 1908, at the request of whites who wanted to settle the Flathead lands but who could not for lack of water, Congress authorized an irrigation project—to be paid for out of funds received by the tribe for sale of the lands the whites were about to enter. If ever a heartless Congress wrote a rotten land deal, this was it.

The conservation movement, on the other hand, did not exactly provide the Flatheads with any relief. Shortly after the president had set aside the forest lands in Montana, along with over 10,000 acres of disputed Flathead lands, Congress provided in a general appropriations act in 1897 that

the President is hereby authorized at any time to modify any Executive Order that has been or may hereafter be made establishing any forest reserve, and by such modification may reduce the area or change the boundary lines of such reserve, or may vacate altogether any order creating such reserve.

President Cleveland left well enough alone. But the stage was set for some real sleight-of-hand activity by the bureaucrats pending the arrival of a president they could hoodwink.

In November 1906, President Theodore Roosevelt under the impression that he was preserving the West of his youth, issued an executive proclamation to expand the boundaries of the Lolo National Forest. The Agriculture Department had won the fight against the Interior Department.

The proclamation cited the act of June 4, 1897, under which the president was given virtually a blank check for adjusting boundaries of public forest lands. The Lolo National Forest was "enlarged to include the said additional lands, and . . . the boundaries of the reserve are now as shown on the diagram forming a part thereof." The proclamation was not to "take effect upon any lands withdrawn or reserved, at this date, from settlement, entry or other appropriation, for any purpose other than forest uses, or which may be covered by any prior valid claim, so long as the withdrawal, reservation, or claim exists."

The important point to keep in mind is that in all of this legislation there was always a disclaimer clause stating that wherever titles or claims to titles existed, they were not to be disturbed. At no point did any of the legislation purport to change any recognition of land ownership that existed prior to the statute involved. Therefore, it would appear that the Flatheads' claim to the 12,000 acres on the southwestern corner of the reservation was as good as gold. Or rather as good as an Indian title ever had been.

Some of the Flatheads continued to maintain that the boundaries of the reservation were not as they should be, but they were beginning to be ignored even by tribal members. After all, the treaty had been signed in 1855, and it was now the early years of the twentieth century; few old timers were yet around who had been at the treaty sessions. While everyone knew that something was wrong, fewer and fewer people understood exactly what it was.

With the completion of the irrigation project white settlers began pouring into the ceded lands of the Flatheads. The major influxes occurred in 1908 and 1910. Gradually, the Indians found themselves a smaller and smaller group in a raging sea of white settlers. The policy of forcing Indian lands out of Indian hands, practiced in the 1910–1930 period, contributed to the drastic loss of Indian lands.

By the time of the I.R.A. there was little left at Flathead to reorganize. Much of the land had been taken from the Indians in one guise or another and the allotments left in Indian hands were so scattered and fragmented into heirship tracts that it took a hardy tribal council to contemplate a revival of tribal prospects. Nevertheless, the reservation people determined to survive and saw the act as the best chance of preserving what few resources they had left. They voted to accept the act and on October 28, 1935, they adopted a constitution as the Confederated Salish and Kootenai Tribes of the Flathead Reservation.

In less than thirty years the Flatheads rebuilt their tribal land base to 554,240.44 acres of land and managed to hang on to some 62,875.72 acres of individual allotments, although many of these tracts were mired in complex heirship interests. Much of the tribal land had timber on it, and in 1966 the tribe received an income in excess of $1 million in stumpage payments. But with all of this apparent success real poverty problems continued to plague the tribe. Housing was very bad, educational problems remained a constant headache, and health care, especially for older Indians, was a continuing worry of the tribal members.

In 1946 Congress formed the Indian Claims Commission. For years the federal courts, particularly the United States Court of Claims, had been closed to Indian tribes by statute. Any claim that a tribe had against the United States could not be prosecuted unless the tribe was able to get special legislation passed by Congress admitting them to the court. Over the first decades of the twentieth century so many tribes had come knocking at the door of Congress that the weary senators and congressmen grew extremely wrought at the idea of spending their time listening to tribal delegations outlining past wrongs suffered at the hands of the United States.

Shortly before the passage of this act the Flatheads were successful in gaining legislation to prosecute their claims against the United States. The difference in the two forums is important. The Indian Claims Commission is forbidden from determining land titles except as a means of determining compensation. The United States Court of Claims is able to determine title although unable to return land, since the confirmation of title is considered a political act requiring the consent of Congress.

The Flathead jurisdictional act conferred jurisdiction on the court to "hear, examine, adjudicate, and render judgment in any and all legal and equitable claims to whatsoever nature." It was a broad mandate and the confederated tribes immediately retained an attorney, who filed a complaint pursuant to the provisions of the act. He set forth several causes of action, including claims that the surveys of the northern and southwestern boundaries of the reservation were erroneously made, thereby establishing a portion of the lands originally given by treaty outside the boundaries confirmed by the executive order establishing the reservation.

A hearing was held and evidence taken on whether or not the boundaries that had been surveyed were in fact those called for in the treaty. The court held, in *Confederated Salish and*

Kootenai Tribes v. *United States,* 173 Ct. Cl. 398 (1965), that the defendant's surveys were erroneous and that reserved treaty lands were outside the surveyed boundaries.

Armed with a judicial determination against the United States, the tribes began a thorough investigation of the status of excluded lands and discovered that while portions of the reserved lands had been patented to third parties or granted to railroads, 10,585.86 acres had been placed in various national forests by Theodore Roosevelt and his successors. The attorney filed a motion with the court seeking a determination that the lands still in federal hands had not been taken by the United States, by virtue of the erroneous survey, and that the beneficial title and ownership remained with the tribes. The Bureau of Indian Affairs had refused to acknowledge that the lands still belonged to the United States, thus fulfilling its historic role as defender of the Indian tribes in its traditional manner; without its support the Justice Department was able to argue from silence the position that the land had actually been taken at the time of the survey.

Establishment of the time of taking of land is vital to an Indian suit against the government. If the land was taken at the time of the survey, the value of the land at that time would be the measure of recovery available to the tribe. On the other hand, if the court finds that the land has not yet been taken, the tribe can seek congressional action to restore the lands or receive present prices for the lands. The difference is astounding.

The position of the Justice Department prevailed in the United States Court of Claims, and on July 3, 1968, the court held that the lands had been taken by the United States even though it had not known it was taking them at the time. A typical decision in an Indian case. A petition for a writ of certiorari was filed in the Supreme Court, but the court did not want a hot potato in its hands. The petition was turned down.

The tribe decided to go to Congress for redress. They secured introduction of a bill in the Ninety-first Congress that would have restored beneficial ownership (trust title) of the lands to them. The Indian Affairs Subcommittee of the Senate asked for reports on the legislation from the various government agencies that might be involved with the transfer of the land.

The comments of the respective departments were forwarded to the then Bureau of the Budget, which must comment on the fiscal impact on government budget policies of every bill. The Justice Department was predictably against the bill because it involved overturning by legislation a victory, albeit tainted, that they felt they had won in court. The Agriculture Department was against it because returning the lands to the Flatheads meant that the land would leave the environs of the department and journey to the Interior Department, actually a mere ledger entry but in bureaucratic-ego terms a career crisis of unimagined proportions.

The Interior Department, in a stunning report, actually supported the Flatheads, although from the criteria listed it was apparent that the tribe had had to perform a number of intellectual gymnastics of fantastic magnitude. The department stated that if the disputed land was contiguous to the reservation, if it had not been patented to third parties, if it was still in the public domain, and if there had been no firm intention by the government to take the land, it would support the legislation. The Flatheads miraculously cleared all hurdles, and so, the Interior Department felt bound to support the tribes.

The National Council on Indian Opportunity (NCIO), a coordinating council of department heads and appointed Indian members at large, received permission from the Bureau of the Budget to submit its comments before the Bureau released its own report on the proposed legislation. Copies of the departmental reports were sent to NCIO so that it could see the arguments the various departments were making. NCIO, after carefully digesting the various contentions, supported the tribe and the Interior Department position on the restoration of the land to the tribes.

The Bureau of the Budget was at an impasse, two departments were for the Flatheads, and two were against. A meeting was called to discuss the conflicting positions so that the administration could present a united front when the reports went to Congress for the hearings. The meeting was less a conference than an interrogation of the Interior representative by the Bureau of the Budget for the amusement of the people from the Justice and Agriculture departments. The Bureau of the Budget, instead of considering the respective reports and the issues they discussed, took the position that the Interior Department was wrong until proven right.

With the chips down the truth emerged. The Interior representative coolly informed the Bureau of the Budget people that he had seen a copy of a letter that the Justice Department had sent to the Interior Department in the early 1940's in which it discussed the claim for lands included in the erroneous survey. He related that it admitted that the Indians were correct but that the Justice Department instructed the Interior Department to say nothing to the Indians or their attorney about it. The silence was deafening. The meeting adjourned and the various participants scurried homeward quickly, the opponents to destroy the evidence and the proponents to locate the letter.

The tribal attorney immediately asked the Bureau of Indian Affairs for a copy of the letter, and bureau employees friendly to the tribes rushed to the files in search of the letter. The office of then Congressman Arnold Olson (a Democrat and the tribes' congressman, who was supporting them) requested a copy of the letter thinking that the bureaucrats would respond to the directives of a member of Congress. The Justice and Interior departments maintained a stony silence, broken only by terse denials that any such letter had ever existed.

Somewhat put off, Congressman Olson used his official prerogative to obtain interdepartmental correspondence files from the National Archives. But the opponents had covered that leak long before. He was told that the file was missing. Needless to say, the file has not reemerged and probably will not emerge unless Daniel Ellsberg becomes an employee of the Justice or Interior departments or the National Archives.

In effect, the case is now deadlocked. The legal theory remains constant: regarding the survey of the Flathead reservation, the United States intended to take an undetermined amount of Indian lands, of which 10,585.86 acres remains today in federal hands, because its surveying crew made a mistake. The intention, so articulately presented by the United States, was merely a tricky transit on the lake shore.

The Flatheads still demand a bill in Congress to give them finally the lands promised in the Treaty of Hell Gate in 1855. Senator Lee Metcalf, in opposing the restoration of the Blue

Lake area to the Taos Pueblo in 1970, vowed that if the Senate returned the lands to the New Mexico Pueblo, he would remain on the Senate floor until the Flatheads received their lands. Later, in a less heated state, he used his senatorial privilege and deleted the remarks from the Congressional Record, fearful that the tribes would remember his pledge at election time.

We would unhesitatingly recommend that the lands be restored to the Flathead tribe for a number of reasons. We believe that the United States Court of Claims made its decision without that missing file in the National Archives. Had the presence of the letter and its contents been known to the court, the decision almost certainly would have been different. Then, the generalities of treaty-breaking can be seen, in this case, not to be generalities at all but specific acts by specific people to subvert the laws and treaties of the United States for bureaucratic purposes.

We therefore call for immediate passage of the Flathead land restoration bill and project the following total acreage as the stabilized land base to be made a permanent Indian domain:

Tribal lands	39,663,412.09
Individual Indian allotments	10,697,621.58
Alaska native lands	40,000,000
Occupied Indian lands	4,723,017.2
Submarginal lands	344,811
Flathead lands restored	10,585.86
	95,439,477.73

7

The Forest Service Strikes Again, and Again— The Story of Warm Springs

JOEL PALMER, superintendent of Indian affairs of the Oregon Territory, had joined Isaac Stevens during Stevens's negotiations of the treaty with the Yakima tribe in early June 1855. Flushed with the heady success of Stevens's treaty negotiations, which would eventually divest the Indians of Washington, Idaho, and Montana of 64 million acres, Palmer scampered back to Oregon to try his hand at treaty-making. His treaty with Wascoes and Walla Wallas of middle Oregon was concluded on June 25, 1855. By June 23, 1855, Palmer and Stevens had published in the *Oregon Weekly Times* a premature notification of the opening of Indian lands ceded during Stevens's negotiations. The treaty signing took place at Wasco near The Dalles of the Columbia River in the Oregon Territory. The treaty states that Palmer acted "on the part of the United States" (12 Stat. 963), with the chiefs and headmen of the confederated tribes and bands of the Walla Walla and Wasco acting for their respective bands. With an eye to future challenges, Palmer's document notes that the chiefs were "duly authorized" to act for their people.

The middle Oregon tribes reserved to themselves an area

commencing in the middle of the channel of the De Chutes River opposite the eastern termination of a range of high lands usually known as the Mutton Mountains; thence westerly to the summit of said range, along the divide to its connection with the Cascade Mountains; thence to the summit of said mountains; thence southerly to Mount Jefferson; thence down the main branch of De Chutes River; heading in this peak, to its junction with De Chutes River; and thence down the middle of the channel of said river to the place of beginning. All place of which tract shall be set apart, and so far as necessary, surveyed and marked out for their exclusive use.

The treaty also provided that if the three principal bands (the Wascopam; the Tiah, or Upper De Chutes; and the Lower De Chutes) decided that they preferred another reservation to the reservation described in the treaty and if they could agree on an area, they could have the lands they preferred. The area set out in the treaty is known today as the Warm Springs Reservation.

As it turned out, the challenges against the Warm Springs treaty did not center on the authority of the chiefs to act. The objections centered on the correctness of the boundaries of the reservations. This is a difficulty that the Palmer-Warm Springs treaty has in common with the Stevens-Palmer-Yakima treaty and the Stevens-Flathead treaty. Each case involves thousands of acres of land, and in each case, land has been subtracted from the reservation boundaries. Further, each case involves imperfect knowledge of the land by the white negotiator for the United States who supplied a description written in English that was based on his faulty knowledge.

In 1944 the Senate was dealing with a definition for the boundaries of the Warm Springs Reservation. A report on legislation setting those boundaries quoted from a memorandum by Senator Holman of Oregon:

Under date of June 25, 1855, the Warm Springs Tribe of Indians entered into a treaty with the United States (12 Stat. 963), ceding all their rights to lands in Oregon and setting aside a reservation for their exclusive use and benefit. Indian wars were in progress at the time the treaty was negotiated and negotiations were conducted at a place about 75 miles distant from the nearest proposed reservation line. As the negotiators were not fully informed or advised as to landmarks and boundary lines, and a visit of inspection was impossible, the treaty boundary descriptions on the north, west, and south were ambiguous.

The "ambiguity" found by the United States Court of Claims amounted to 64,086 acres missing on the north and 14,525 acres missing on the west. The court also noted that at the time of the

treaty council there was "a sketch of the Warm Springs Reservation used by General Palmer when he negotiated the treaty with
the Indians" but added that "Palmer himself was but slightly
familiar with the country." As Stevens had done with the Yakima
treaty, Palmer included a sketch of what he believed the Warm
Spring cession area to look like. Little wonder then that boundary disputes should arise when the only recorded document describing the area apparently was based largely on Palmer's
imagination.

Two years after the Indians signed the treaty (the Senate had
not yet ratified the document), the leaders of the tribes joined
Agent R. R. Thompson for a tour of the reservation and a review
of its boundaries. In November 1941, 84 years later, the United
States Court of Claims noted that when "testimony in this case
was taken there was but one person living who had accompanied
the Indian Agent on this trip, one Albert Kuckup, 100 years old."
Albert Kuckup testified that the Indian Agent pointed out to
them, as the boundaries of their reservation, the lands "beginning at Little Dark Butte on the summit of the Cascade Range;
running thence southwardly through Olallie Butte, Mt. Jefferson, Three Fingered Jack, the Three Sisters, to Koo-SeeWah
Tum or Horse Lake, and thence south and east to the Paulina
Mountains; thence northwardly through Powell Butte, How-
Sash, and Shnip-Shee or Bake Oven; thence westwardly to the
point of beginning." It constituted an area three to four times
larger than that to which the whites had claimed the Indians
were entitled. It was two years after the reservation tour led by
Thompson that the Senate ratified the Warm Springs treaty.
The date was March 8, 1859. President Buchanan proclaimed
the treaty on April 18, 1859.

Before ratification, however, premature publication of the
opening of the treaty cession lands, the steady influx of settlers
into the Northwest, and the methods used by the treaty commissioners in their negotiations had escalated hostile feelings into
open warfare. The purpose of the treaties had been "to get the
Indians off the land wanted by settlers or needed for the building of railroads." When Stevens and Palmer announced the
opening of the Yakima lands (the Yakima treaty, like the Warm
Springs treaty, was not ratified until 1859), the Indians of the
area became acutely aware of what the results would be: "Land

hunters rushed in, and miners crisscrossed it on their way to new gold strikes in Canada and the Colville region of the upper Columbia." The general condition of the conduct of affairs with the Indians caused General John E. Wool, commander of the Department of the Pacific of the United States Army, to take a highly unpopular view. Repeatedly, Wool argued that "if the [Oregon] volunteers stopped provoking the Indians . . . the Indians would again become peaceful." His views were, of course, academic, for the general population of the whites, militiaman and farmer, had no intention of pursuing a course that would cease to provoke the Indians, as that would have restricted the selection of lands they wanted. Thus provoked, the Indians rebelled. It was not until a year after military defeat of the Indians that the Senate felt it safe to ratify the treaties.

In 1865 a supplemental treaty was concluded between J. W. Perit Huntington, superintendent of Indian affairs for Oregon, and the leaders of the confederated tribes on the Warm Springs Reservation. This treaty was not directed at the boundaries of the reservation. It had as its goal preventing the Indians from hunting, fishing, and living off of the reservation:

It having become evident from experience that the provision . . . of the treaty of the twenty-fifth of June, A.D. eighteen hundred and fifty-five, which permits said confederated tribes to fish, hunt, gather berries and roots, pasture stock, and erect houses on lands outside the reservation, and which have been ceded to the United States is often abused by the Indians to the extent of continuously residing away from the reservation, and is detrimental to the interests of both Indians and whites; therefore it is hereby stipulated . . . that all the rights enumerated . . . are hereby relinquished.

When we realize that where Indians can fish, hunt, pasture stock, and erect houses off the reservation, whites can too, and when we realize that when whites want Indian lands badly, Indians die, we can understand just how detrimental living off the reservation can be. The specter of the Oregon military lurking in the background ready to attack again can be quite an inducement to signing a treaty. The Senate ratified the treaty on March 2, 1867, and President Andrew Johnson proclaimed it on March 28, 1867.

The shape of the Warm Springs Reservation is roughly the shape of the lower right-hand segment of a circle divided into quarters. The curved edge represents the eastern and southern boundaries. Since the eastern line is formed by the De Chutes River and the southern boundary is composed of the Metolius River and Jefferson Creek, the curved edge is very irregular. The northern and western boundaries are more or less straight lines. The dispute that arose was whether or not those lines were far enough north and west. In 1943, Attorney General Francis Biddle summarized the issues in a letter to Senator Elmer Thomas, chairman of the Senate Committee on Indian Affairs:

Before 1859 practically all of the Indians who were parties to the treaty had been settled upon the reservation described in the treaty. The Indians, however, were dissatisfied with the size of the reservation, claiming that they were entitled to a much larger area of land than was included in the reservation. As a result of their claims several surveys were made of the area described in the treaty, but no two of these surveys were in agreement in all respects.

The first of these surveys came in 1871 and was conducted by a government surveyor named T. B. Handley. Handley's survey covered most of the northern boundary, but he stopped before he reached the western boundary. The treaty had described the northern boundary as "commencing in the middle of the channel of the De Chutes River opposite the eastern termination of a range of high lands usually known as the Mutton Mountains; thence westerly to the summit of said range, along the divide to its connection with the Cascade Mountains; thence to the summit of said mountains." Handley also had available to him General Palmer's sketch, which "shows a range of mountains on the north of the reservation, which runs in an almost due east and west direction from the De Chutes River to the Cascade Mountains." As a starting point at the eastern termination of the Mutton Mountains, Handley selected a point on the De Chutes River approximately midway between Antoken and Eagle Creek. However, heading west to the summit of the Mutton Mountains and along the divide that leads to the Cascades entails difficulties, for "if the divide or watershed is strictly followed, the northern boundary twice would dip far to the south, since the headwaters of Eagle Creek and Nena Creek are far to the south of the starting point." The result would be for the eastern half of the northern boundary to resemble the figure 3 turned on its right side. The 3 would be roughly fifteen miles in length. Handley chose not to follow the watershed strictly, and the result was an east-west line with a serrated appearance, running fifteen miles west of the river in a slightly north of west direction. The west end of the line terminated about a mile below a point even with Mt. Wilson. The line proceeded straight west for about six miles. Handley caused the line to make a peak after the straight line in an A-shape, four miles high and three miles wide at the base. The western leg of the A continued south for an additional four miles, making the A-shape into a kind of inverted check mark. Handley's survey never reached the summit of the Cascades. R. T. Campbell finished Handley's survey of the northern boundary. Campbell left out the peak, which began at milepost twenty-six and merely extended the line running straight west an additional ten miles to the summit of the Cascades. The western boundary was formed by running a line from this point south to Mt. Jefferson.

The Warm Springs tribes did not find the boundary line set up for the north or the west satisfactory. Their dissatisfaction was vocal enough so that on December 17, 1886, a new survey was ordered. It was conducted by John A. McQuinn the next year. McQuinn selected as the termination of the Mutton Mountains a point twenty chains south of Handley's starting point on the De Chutes River. Many years later, the United States Court of Claims noted that McQuinn selected a new point of beginning "only because the Indians were greatly dissatisfied with it and threatened to destroy all corners that he might establish, if it were adhered to." The thought probably occurred to McQuinn that the Indians might not stop with destroying just the corners, and he found it politic to accede to their wishes. Agent Thompson's tour of 1857 threatened to create problems. The Court of Claims found that "to meet this situation the Indian Agent was instructed by the Indian Office to undertake to arrive at an understanding with the Indians. They insisted that the beginning point was farther north between the mouths of Wapinitia and Nena Creeks and this was agreed to and adopted by McQuinn."

The difficulties then really began to surface. General Palmer's map showed a range of mountains running due east and west. The Mutton Mountains run in a northeast-southwest direction. The area McQuinn finally selected, six miles north of Handley's beginning, is in the Nena Hills, which have the same slant as the Mutton Mountains. Did Palmer believe the Nena Hills were part of the Mutton Mountains? If he did, the reservation gains about a township-sized area on the east. But what about the nonexistent east-west line of mountains? Does one follow the mountains or the compass?

The treaty called for the line to run from the beginning to the summit of the Mutton Mountains and "along the divide to its connection with the Cascade Mountains." From the starting point McQuinn settled on, he went southwest about eight miles to a point even with Mt. Wilson. From this point McQuinn went northwest in a straight line, approximately following the divide of the Cascades to Little Dark Butte. The western boundary was formed by running a straight line from Little Dark Butte to Mt. Jefferson. Despite Palmer's sketch, a straight line cannot be formed by following the mountains, whether one chooses the Mutton Mountains or substitutes the Nena Hills. One can follow the mountain divides or draw a straight line, but not both. On the eastern end of the northern boundary between the Muttons and the Nenas and their summits and divides, one can come up with several combinations of lines. However, the Warm Springs tribes were satisfied with the McQuinn survey primarily because it conformed to the two northern points Agent Thompson had pointed out to them in 1857, the final McQuinn starting point on the De Chutes and Little Dark Butte.

There was probably little joy over the new boundaries in Camp Polk, Cross Keys, or Bake Oven, those towns a couple of townships away that were, respectively, on the south, east, and northeast of the reservation. In the Tygh Valley on the northern and on the western boundaries of the reservation there was no joy at all. McQuinn had brought the reservation to the whites in the Tygh Valley and to their cattle on the west, along the summit of the Cascades and in Clackamas Meadows. As the United States Court of Claims succinctly reported, "The white settlers were dissatisfied with this survey."

It had taken the Indians of Warm Springs from 1871 to June 1887 to get a new survey. The whites were a little faster in their lobbying efforts. On October 7–8, 1887, the Department of the Interior directed H. B. Martin, special agent for the General Land Office, and George W. Gordon, United States special Indian agent, to investigate the northern boundary of Warm Springs Reservation and determine what line "would nearest conform to the treaty." Gordon and Martin reported they conducted their investigation by

carefully examining all the papers submitted to us touching the subject including Department letter the report of the Surveyor-general of Oregon dated July 22, 1887, the affidavits of the Indians taken in June last, Also the affidavits of certain white citizens taken in June 1887, the proceedings of a public meeting of white citizens at Tygh Valley, June 25, 1887, and the field notes and maps of the Handley and McQuinn surveys, we proceeded to the field and began a personal inspection of the respective lines run by Handley in 1871 and by McQuinn in June 1887, being accompanied by such whites and Indians as desired to be present, and whose verbal statements touching their knowledge of the lines and the topography of the country we heard at length, giving careful attention to both sides.

Their conclusions are summarized by the United States Court of Claims as follows:

They reported that the Handley line "more nearly conforms to the requirements and conditions of the treaty, but that at certain places he is materially at variance with its terms and intentions." They recommended a line which conformed in part with the Handley line and in part with the McQuinn line, but which was at variance with both in material respects.

This had the effect of straightening the first part of Handley's line and adopting most of the McQuinn line, which followed the divide of the Cascades but not all the way to Little Dark Butte. Gordon and Martin felt that the line they recommended would "not interfere with or encroach on the individual lands or rights of any white or Indian." They also recommended mileposts with monuments every quarter mile "in order that both whites and Indians may be enabled to see and trace the line without difficulty or mistake." They recommended the same for the western boundary and included their reason:

We make this recommendation in view of the information received that stockmen have been encroaching on the lands of the reservation from the west, and until this boundary is surveyed and defined they will probably continue to do so, claiming that there is nothing to show where the west boundary line is. The other two boundaries of the reservation, the south and east, are water-courses and are therefore sufficiently defined.

On July 19, 1889, the line surveyed by McQuinn was adopted by the Department of the Interior as the true northern boundary of the reservation.

Apparently, the whites of the area or the General Land Office in the Interior Department or, more probably, both were not to be outdone, for in 1890 Congress established a special commission by 26 Stat. 336, "whose duty it shall be to visit and thoroughly investigate and determine as to the correct location of the northern line of the Warm Springs Indian Reservation, in the State of Oregon, the same to be located according to the terms of the treaty of June twenty-fifth, eighteen hundred and fifty-five." This commission completed its work and filed a detailed report dated June 8, 1891. It was not designed to please the Warm Springs tribes. The report concluded

that the line known as the McQuinn line, as surveyed and run, in no respect conforms to the said treaty of 1855, and is not the line of the northern boundary of the Warm Springs Reservation or any part thereof. That the line known as the Handley line, as surveyed and run, substantially and practically conforms to the calls of the said treaty of 1855 from the initial point of said line up to and including the twenty-sixth mile thereof.

It is therefore considered and declared by the Commission that the northern boundary of the Warm Springs Indian Reservation, in the State of Oregon, is that part of the line run and surveyed by T. B. Handley in the year 1871, from the initial point up to and including the twenty-sixth mile thereof, thence in a due west course to the summit of the Cascade Mountains.

In other words, the report adopted the Handley beginning and the Campbell conclusion. The report provided the basis of the act of June 6, 1894 (28 Stat. 86), which stated

that the true north boundary line of the Warm Springs Indian Reservation . . . is hereby declared to be that part of the line run and surveyed by T. B. Handley in the year eighteen hundred and seventy-one, from the initial point up to and including the twenty-sixth mile thereof; thence in a due west course to the summit of the Cascade Mountains as found by the commissioners, Mark A. Fullerton, William H. H. Dufur, and James F. Payne.

One of the reasons given by the commission to justify setting the boundary by the 1894 act was that "since the Indians were wards of the Government and could not sue for a determination of the boundary lines, Congress itself . . . fixed and established the northern boundary." But the 1894 act did not settle the dispute —the boundary temporarily, perhaps, but certainly not the dispute.

The one really apparent characteristic of the Warm Springs boundary, equivocation, came forth again in 1917. Thus, the Appropriation Act of March 2 (39 Stat. 969) set aside $5,000 "for an investigation and report on the merits of the claim of the Indians of the Warm Springs Reservation in Oregon to additional land arising from alleged erroneous surveys of the north and west boundaries of their reservation . . . and the Secretary of the Interior is hereby authorized to make such surveys or resurveys as may be necessary to complete said investigation and report." United States surveyor Fred Mensch was appointed to conduct this investigation. His report was presented on January 16, 1919. It was characterized by three elements: (1) detail about the controversy, (2) criticism of the Handley survey, and (3) the conclusion that the McQuinn survey had set the proper northern boundary. The commissioner of the General Land Office fired back a detailed criticism of the Mensch report that touted the Handley-Campbell boundaries as proper for the north and west. With the whites and the Indians alternately gaining the upper hand, the only proper description of the status quo in 1917 is Ping-Pong diplomacy, in a quite literal sense.

Congress began to have an awareness that it was not having any luck with the Warm Springs Reservation boundaries. But someone had to decide where to set those mileposts. Why not give it to someone who has to make difficult judgments all the time, someone who settles claims against the United States all the time? Who else but the courts? But to sue the United States one must come within an existing statute that confers jurisdiction on a court or have a special jurisdictional act passed. The last part proved to be no problem at all, because by the act of December 23, 1930, "the Court of Claims of the United States was authorized to hear, determine, adjudicate, and render judgment on all legal and equitable claims of whatsoever nature of the Warm Springs Tribe of Indians" arising out of the treaties of 1855 or 1865, and this was "notwithstanding the provisions of the act of June 6, 1894," which adopted the Handley-Campbell line. The court rendered its decision on November 3, 1941.

One of the questions the court was asked to consider was the purpose of the 1857 tour by Agent Thompson. The Warm Springs natives contended that the purpose was to select the boundaries of a new reservation as provided under the treaty. This would have made the reservation approximately four times larger than everyone but the Indians and Agent Thompson had thought. The court dismissed the Thompson tour as being of little consequence. To consider it would have compounded the problems they had to deal with and would have allowed the tribe a tremendous money judgment. Therefore, the court concluded that the treaty procedures for altering the selection of the reservation had not been met: "There is no proof whatever in the records that the bands named in the proviso met in council and expressed a desire that some other reservation should be selected for them, as the treaty required." The court felt there was not satisfactory evidence, for the one living witness, Albert Kuckup, had testified that Agent Thompson had shown them their reservation lands. This could mean that the exploration was merely of the old reservation rather than a new selection by the Warm Springs tribes. The court based its opinion on strict interpretation of treaty wording, which called for the formal council. What the court overlooked was that the treaty had not yet been ratified at the time of the tour and was not to be ratified for another two years. Might not the boundaries set out by Thompson nonetheless have the effect of a novation, with the new boundaries being substituted for the old? The court concluded, "This trip was not for the purpose of selecting some other reservation but for the purpose of exploring the reservation described in the treaty."

Might not the boundaries set out by Thompson show just how far off Palmer's sketch was? The court then began consideration of the southern and eastern boundaries. Their conclusion was that the treaty clearly described the area with the words: "thence southerly to Mount Jefferson; thence down the main branch of De Chutes River; heading in this peak, to its junction with De Chutes River." The court decided that Mt. Jefferson was the southern boundary of the treaty and that although Jefferson Creek and the Metolius River were not branches of the De Chutes, they could have been thought of as such, and that that was what was intended in the treaty. The Indians had contended that the main branch of the De Chutes began in the

Three Sisters Mountains, which would have put the reservation farther south; it would have had the effect of creating a point in the southern boundary that the treaty speaks of and that more closely conforms to the tour the Indians took with Agent Thompson. The court decided that under the treaty it was clear that the eastern boundary is the De Chutes River, not the Paulina's, Powell Butte, and Bake Oven of Thompson.

The court then turned to the northern boundary. The first item to determine was the proper starting point. The Indians contended that it was the line set by McQuinn. The court disposed of that contention this way: "The Indians claimed that this was the proper beginning point because it was the point pointed out to them by Indian Agent Thompson, but we do not regard this as material since this was done two years after the treaty was signed." The moral would seem to be that one should never trust an Indian agent—he is liable to give the Indians exactly what is theirs by right. That left the Handley beginning point. It was, after all, at the eastern termination of the Mutton Mountains. To show that they were not alone in considering the Handley point, the court noted, "Everyone who has surveyed this northern boundary or investigated the surveys thereof agrees that this is approximately the proper beginning according to the treaty," at which point the court paused and ended sourly, "with the sole exception of Mensch." After wrestling with the surveys and the question of whether the Mutton Mountains could have included the Nena Hills, the court set out its decision: "After careful consideration of all the testimony, we are of the opinion that the starting point fixed by Handley is substantially correct."

That left the court to determine just what kind of irregular boundary it wanted on the eastern end of the northern boundary. It would have been possible to have the boundary dip, curve, curl, or zigzag, depending on just how imaginative the court was. "No survey has exactly followed the divide between the White River and Warm Springs River Systems from the Cascade Mountains to the end of its east-west course," the court began; but it then paused, for it was not certain what the effect of its conclusion would be since McQuinn's beginning point had been thrown out, and concluded, "but McQuinn's survey substantially does so." Since McQuinn had used a straight line instead of following the divide exactly as it winds northwestwardly, the court did not let McQuinn escape their disapproval: "He has erred both on the one side and the other." It must have been all for effect, because the court was as tired as everyone else of the controversy, and in the next sentence declared,

It, however, substantially conforms to the terms of the treaty, and we are of opinion that considerations of justice and equity, as well as of putting an end to uncertainty and further litigation, dictate that we adopt his line as the true northern boundary from his thirty-mile post at Little Dark Butte to his seven and a half mile post. From this point to the initial point as established by Handley we think the northern boundary should run in a straight line.

The northern boundary, then, was essentially a straight line running from Handley's beginning to Little Dark Butte.

Then came the determination of the western boundary. The court could run a straight line from Little Dark Butte to Mt. Jefferson or follow the meandering of the divide to Mt. Jefferson. Campbell and McQuinn had both gone straight south from the western end of the respective northern boundaries. A case could be made for following the divide. The lands ceded by the Indians were described as following the summit of the Cascades. The court was tired, and it may have had second thoughts about the meaning of the Thompson tour:

Although there is doubt that McQuinn's western boundary is in exact accord with the intention of the parties when the treaty was signed, we think it does substantial justice, and for this reason and to avoid another survey of these boundaries we adopt McQuinn's western boundary line as the true western boundary of the reservation.

As a result, the court concluded that the defendant, the United States government,

has appropriated to its own use all of the lands to the north of the Handley-Campbell line, and south of the true north boundary as herein defined, and the plaintiffs are entitled to recover the value thereof. The defendant has also appropriated to its own use all of the lands between the Campbell line on the west and the true western boundary as herein defined, and the plaintiff is entitled to recover the reasonable value thereof.

By November 1941 the dispute had not even lost inertia. The court still had to determine the value of the lands taken. Congress would have to appropriate monies to pay the judgment and to pass a distribution bill so that the money could be paid to the tribe. And all of this would take time.

In the interim Senator McNary and Congressman Stockman of Oregon had introduced a bill "to define the exterior boundaries of the Warm Springs Indian Reservation in Oregon, and for other purposes." The "for other purposes" satisfied the format for a bill title. The bill was designed to end the controversy by adopting the reservation boundaries set out in the United States Court of Claims opinion. Instead of giving the tribe monetary compensation as the court could have done because of the wording of the jurisdictional act, the bill proposed to return to the tribe the land still held by the government, some 64,000 acres, under the status of original treaty land. The tribe would then abandon any monetary claims before the court. Senator Elmer Thomas, chairman of the Committee on Indian Affairs, presented the report on S. 845, on April 28, 1944. In that report the committee mentioned certain difficulties:

The United States, under the jurisdictional act, may set up as offsets all expenditures made by the United States for said Indians, including gratuities, since the treaty of 1855. The report of the Comptroller General, filed some years after the suit was instituted, listed such expenditures and the attorneys for the Government advise that offsets to be claimed will equal or exceed 2½-million dollars. It is impossible to establish such value for the area awarded by the court to the Indians and the Indians, consequently, can expect to recover nothing in the court action.

The Warm Springs long-fought battle had all the potential for delivering a Pyrrhic victory. It was a result that the Indians and even Congress, judging by their actions subsequent to the court decision and the wording of the jurisdiction statute (46 Stat. 1033), had not contemplated, for the statute read "gratuities, if any."

The committee then noted that the departments of Agriculture, Justice, and Interior had also submitted reports on S. 845. The Department of Justice was consulted because it was defending the government in court; Agriculture, because the 64,000 acres were in Mt. Hood National Forest, which is administered by the department; and Interior, because it represented the Indian interests. The committee had this to say about the comments of the Agriculture Department:

Agriculture Department objections are that the area in question has been administered by the Forest Service and that it would be advantageous to continue such administration, and also that certain improvements have been made. The forest reserve has had these lands under its jurisdiction since about 1907 and has sold timber therefrom and leased grazing areas and wishes to continue its jurisdiction thereof and to make it a source of income. The court, on the other hand, finds that the Indians have been entitled to these lands from since 1855 and have consequently lost the use thereof for more than 80 years. The Forest Service has large areas of timberland under its control in the vicinity and there is not sound reason why the Indians should be deprived of the portions of the lands available for the benefit of some other government agency. The rights of grazing lessors are so protected under the last clause of section 2 of the proposed measure, as the lands in question "are to be added to and made a part of the existing Warm Springs Reservation subject to all valid existing rights."

The committee was not pleased that the United States, trustee of the Indians, would benefit by having the Department of Agriculture do the Indians in. Breach of trust was not one of the things the committee wanted the United States to commit.

The committee report then dealt with the Justice Department position:

The Department of Justice is concerned with the terms of the jurisdictional act that permit offsets of all sums spent by the United States for these Indians, including gratuities, since the treaty of 1855, and these as already stated will equal or exceed 2½-million dollars. These expenditures were not made by agreement with the Warm Springs Indians or under any treaty obligation. They were made at the instance of the United States, in carrying out its program or policy for all Indians, and to a considerable extent at least, to aid the Government in its administrative functions. Since the Indians cannot prove values for the additional areas as found by the court sufficient to overcome the large offsets of the Government, it is only fair and just that the lands to which they were entitled in 1855 before any such expenditures were made, so far as titles yet remain in the United States, be included in the Indian reservation, especially as the Indians lose about 17,000 acres which passed into private ownership in this area and no offset issue would have arisen had the lands been originally included in the said reservation as the treaty of 1855 intended, according to the findings of the Court of Claims.

The objections of Agriculture and Justice Departments, therefore, in the opinion of the committee should not be permitted to defeat the claims of the Indians. The measure will, in fact, cost the United States nothing in money at this time, will not injure the Forest Service with its large adjacent timberland holdings, and will render tardy justice to the Indians by restoring to them a portion of the lands originally intended for their exclusive use and benefit.

The issue of whether or not the United States government can offset money it has gratuitously spent on Indians when an Indian claim arises is one that is much discussed. In some instances the money has been spent in pursuit of a general public policy. For example, the United States government decides to support the education of children: funds are spent for children; some of the funds are spent on Indian children. If a tribe has a claim against the United States government for an unfilled obligation and a judgment is awarded, the tribe may find part of the school expenditures for their children deducted from the judgment in their favor. Felix Cohen, noted authority on Indian law, explained this principle and his objections to it very well during the hearings leading to the establishment of the Indian Claims Commission. The point at issue is whether or not gratuitous expenditures would be mandatory deductions from Indian claims against the government. In this excerpt of the discussion, Cohen expresses his belief that a court may consider the gratuitous expenditures if it wishes but that it is not required to deduct those expenditures:

If my understanding is correct, we have no objection. If I am not correct, if this means more than that, if it means that when an Indian has a valid claim against the United States, which may be a purely legal claim because the Indian made an agreement with the United States and the United States failed to live up to that agreement and make the payment it promised—if it means that the United States must then, under the decision of the Commission, deduct from what it owes to the Indians all the gratuities which it has spent on educating the Indian children, say, which is something it never does when a white man has a claim against the United States, then we would oppose it, because our conception is that this bill is designed to remove a lingering discrimination against the Indians which prevents them from being considered on the same basis as a white man; and if a white man has an agreement with the United States and the United States fails to live up to the agreement, the United States is suable in the Court of Claims, and the white man has a chance to collect what the United States promised to pay, and the United States does not deduct from such a payment sums that it may have given to the white man on relief or for the education of his children or anything else of that sort. That is entirely irrelevant to the claim.

Unfortunately, the wording of the jurisdictional bill of 1930 made it possible to deduct gratuities from the Warm Springs judgment. Congress may not have known the situation it was creating; if it did, it was malevolently farsighted. Since Congress was apparently trying to correct the injustice, we presume the former.

The report of the committee included letters from the departments involved. Abe Fortas, acting secretary of the interior, gave a hearty endorsement: "In view of the decision of the Court of Claims, I am strongly of the opinion that the Congress should restore the government-owned lands to the Indians. They have expressed their willingness to accept these lands in full settlement of their claims, and in return are willing to give up their adjudged rights to the lands now in private ownership." The letter concluded, however, "The Bureau of the Budget had advised me that the enactment of this proposed legislation, either in its present form or with the amendments suggested in this report, would not be in accord with the program of the President." When you are busy winning a war, you do not have time to help Indians, especially if it might cost money, assurances of the Senate committee report notwithstanding.

Attorney General Francis Biddle was of the same mind: "The effect of the proposed bill, if passed, would be to add to the reservation most of the lands found by the Court of Claims to have been erroneously withheld from the Indians regardless of whether the Indians have already been, in effect, fully compensated for the appropriated lands." He was not alone, for in the next paragraph he states, "The Director of the Bureau of the Budget advises me that there would be no objection to the presentation of this letter to the committee."

Once again, there was no danger of being crushed in the mad scramble to uphold the trust responsibilities of the United States to the American Indian. Biddle did not care whether Warm Springs had been compensated but merely whether it "looked as if" they had been compensated; and the Bureau of the Budget was right behind him. The Bureau of the Budget also backed up Acting Secretary of Agriculture Paul H. Appleby, whose letter opposing the bill has a tone of regret for lost revenues:

In the meantime non-Indian use of such lands has been quite extensive. For example, the change in the status of lands contemplated by the bill markedly would affect 3 range allotments upon which 22 permitees graze 666 head of cattle and 1,850 head of sheep, and on which $2,200 has been invested in range fences. Two very popular and important public camp grounds, which have been developed at Federal expense and are quite heavily used, would, through the bill, become the property of Indians.

The various types of physical improvements constructed by the Forest Service on the lands which would be affected represent a total cost of approximately $135,000. The lands involved support approximately 700,000,000 board feet of timber, of which a considerable proportion is of marketable species. The enactment of the bill S. 845 inevitably would necessitate some very considerable readjustment in the above-mentioned conditions, evidently to a degree greater than that contemplated or required by the decision of the Court of Claims of the United States.

Lindsay C. Warren, comptroller general of the United States, chimed in with the cheery news:

The report of this office on the said petition, which report was transmitted to the Department of Justice June 19, 1935, set forth such expenditures in the amounts of $2,622,660.41 and $47,408.59, plus amounts disbursed for the education of members of the Warm Springs Tribe of Indians in attendance at the Haskell Institute and the Salem Indian School, both being nonreservation schools. These amounts undoubtedly would offset the entire amount which may be found due the Indians as the value of the land.

That seemed to leave it to the Committee on Indian Affairs, Abe Fortas at the Interior Department, and the Indians, versus the bureacracy and the president. Things could have been worse; the Indians have had to face situations in which everybody, including the Interior Department, was working against them.

Then on May 7, 1945, the United States Court of Claims handed down its judgment on the land taken and the amount that should be paid the Warm Springs tribe. It is reported at 107 Ct. Cl. 741, and it found that the amount of land taken was

64,086 acres on the north of the reservation and 14,525 acres on the west. All of the acreage on the west and all but 17,251 acres on the north have been incorporated within national forests. Of the 17,251 acres on the north 3,672.58 acres thereof were patented under the Timber and Stone Act (20 Stat. 89) between November 18, 1897, and June 6, 1932; 715.86 acres in isolated tracts, not coming under the Timber and Stone Act, were disposed of at various dates from 1921 to 1932, and the balance are homestead acres, or have been otherwise disposed of for consideration other than cash.

The court then considered the value of the lands taken and concluded,

This totals $241,084.56.
Against this amount defendant claims offsets for gratuities totaling $2,622,660.41, as set out in the report of the General Accounting Office filed in this case.

Before dismissing the case, the court also noted the nature of the funds forming the offset:

Among the items set out in the report of the General Accounting Office is one of $252,089.72 for "care and protection of Indian timber lands." This expenditure was not required by treaty or other agreement with plaintiff and was a pure gratuity.

The case was a clear warning that the Bureau of the Budget, the Department of Justice, the Department of Agriculture, and the comptroller general would guarantee the violation of the trustee role of the United States with regard to Indian lands by allowing the encroachment on and taking of those lands with impunity and without compensation to the tribe involved. It looked as if Warm Springs was going down for the count.

Then, S. 1243 was introduced in 1947 in the first session of the Eightieth Congress. It was "an Act to provide for the payment of revenues from certain lands into the tribal funds of the Confederated Tribes of the Warm Springs Reservation of Oregon, and for other purposes." The wool had just been pulled over the Agriculture and Justice departments' collective eyes. Those "certain lands" were in the Mt. Hood National Forest and the bill read in part:

All money received by or on account of the Forest Service or other Agency of the United States after the dismissal of the proceeding in the Court of Claims entitled "The Warm Springs Tribe of Indians of Oregon versus the United States: numbered M-112, for timber (on a stumpage basis) grown on, the lease or rental of, or other rights in, the lands described shall be deposited to the credit of the Confederated Tribes of the Warm Springs Tribe of Oregon."

The reaction was not as thunderous as one would imagine, but it was what one would expect. Charles F. Brannan, assistant secretary of agriculture, fired off a letter to the Committee on Lands of the House of Representatives, which was holding hearings. Brannan opposed the Indians' new strategem on the basis of the Court of Claims decision. Nearing the conclusion of his letter, Brannan made the impolitic statement, "Enactment of S. 1243 would reopen a matter which Congress specifically authorized the United States Court of Claims to settle and which has been so handled." It was tantamount to telling the committee and Congress to keep their noses out of places where they were not appreciated.

Oscar L. Chapman, undersecretary of the interior, sent a letter to the committee that indicated that the Interior Department found itself very much on the side of the Indians. He began by recommending that lands held by the Forest Service be given to the Indians, and if the lands were not returned, the tribe should at the very least have the income from those lands. He also spoke out very strongly on the offset of gratuities:

I have never been able to see the fairness of the rule of law just mentioned, which permits the United States to evade its obligation for property taken by it from an Indian tribe by offsetting against those obligations expenditures which were appropriated by the Congress without any requirement for repayment. The Indians were not consulted at the time these expenditures were made. In fact these expenditures were made in accordance with a national policy carried out in the public interest. Yet the rule of law applied in this case has the effect of requiring the Indians to repay these expenditures which were made voluntarily by the Government. It also seems to me highly significant that this rule of law has since been greatly modified as to existing claims, and entirely abrogated as to future claims, by the Indian Claims Commission Act of August 13, 1946 (60 Stat. 1049).

The unfairness of charging the Warm Springs Indians for the protection of their forest lands is made even more evident when consideration is given to the fact that the Federal Government, under the act of June 7 (43 Stat. 653), spends large sums of money annually for fire protection, not only in Federal forests but also in State and privately owned forests, none of which is reimbursable. Whenever any State or individual who has received fire protection to his property under that act has a claim against the United States cognizable in the Court of Claims, the United States cannot offset against any judgment obtained the amount spent to protect the claimant's timber from fire. In 1944, the Federal Government spent in the State of Oregon alone the sum of $731,378 for fire protection under that act. This sum is nearly three times the total spent for the same purpose on the Warm Springs Reservation since the treaty of 1855 was signed. In view of the foregoing, there appears to be no adequate justification for withholding from the Warm Springs Indians lands which the Court of

Claims has found should rightfully belong to them, merely because Federal funds were used in protecting these lands from fire hazards.

Chapman then went on to note that there were 61,360 acres of land belonging to the Indians in Mt. Hood National Forest, with 17,251 acres in private ownership through the public land laws. He continued with an additional reason for returning the land to the Indians:

I am strongly of the opinion that a grant to the Indians of the future income from the unpatented lands would represent a very reasonable recompense to them, particularly when it is borne in mind that a substantial part of the merchantable timber on the lands has been sold, and that the future income from the property may therefore be rather limited.

Whether from Chapman's reasoning or Brannan's impolitic remarks we do not know, but the committee concluded the report in this fashion: "The Committee on Public Lands is unanimous in its recommendations for enactment of this bill." The Senate committee considering the bill also reported favorably, and S. 1243 became the Act of July 3, 1948 (62 Stat. 1237).

For almost any group of men that would have been enough. But if you are Indian and if you believe that as a people you are part of the land and the land is a part of yourself, to have the money is not enough, especially when you know the land is yours and the others know it also. And so in 1971, 100 years after the Handley survey and 116 years after the treaty was signed, the people of the Warm Springs Reservation caused to be introduced on December 8, 1971, H. R. 12114, a bill "to declare title to certain Federal lands in the State of Oregon to be in the United States trust for the use and benefit of the Confederated Tribes of the Warm Springs Reservation of Oregon."

H. R. 12114 provides the following:

(1) That the lands excluded on the north and west boundaries and known as the McQuinn Strip will be held in trust for the Confederated Tribes of Warm Springs and will be withdrawn from the Mt. Hood and Willamette National Forest.

(2) That any counties receiving receipts from the Forest Service timber sales shall not be affected by the withdrawal.

(3) That the timber in this area will be managed on a sustained-yield basis and will be sold by public oral auction until

January 1, 1992. Also, "during such period until January 1, 1992, the Confederated Tribes of the Warm Springs Reservation of Oregon shall not participate in the bidding and shall not purchase or cut and remove any of the timber from the McQuinn Strip."

(4) That existing livestock-grazing permits from the government are to be converted to leases with the Warm Springs tribes "on the same fee schedule, terms and conditions as existing permits, except that the leases shall continue until January 1, 1992."

(5) That the portion of the Pacific Crest Trail traversing the lands in the McQuinn Strip area to be managed by the tribe and open to the public in perpetuity like adjacent areas managed by the Forest Service.

(6) That lakes in the area are to be open to the public with means of access under tribal regulation.

(7) That the tribe is required to enter into an cooperative agreement with the Oregon State Game Commission for enforcement of state regulation and laws on hunting and fishing for the area for a period of ten years, with the state commission's having an option to renew for an additional ten years.

(8) That the Forest Service has the right to use, without charge, all fire-lookout stations.

(9) That all public campgrounds run by the Forest Service shall continue to be public campgrounds but managed and maintained by the tribe.

(10) That all public roads shall remain public roads in perpetuity.

(11) That the tribe is required to fence the north boundary of the McQuinn Strip to control livestock as soon as the bill is enacted. If fee land is crossed in fencing, the tribe is responsible for only 50 percent of the cost.

The following are facts pertinent to the bill: There are currently twelve campground sites in the McQuinn Strip, three of which are developed and nine of which are potential. Ten permittees currently have grazing privileges, which provides grazing for about 600 cattle. Sales of timber would go to the mills presently purchasing the timber. The twenty-year period would give the companies dependent on that timber adequate time to obtain other sources. The tribe currently has a company known as

Warm Springs Forest Products Industries. The area contains all, or portions of, ten lakes. There are thirteen miles of Skyline Trail in the area. There are eighty-one miles of forest roads in the area.

While the Forest Service may view this area as a loss, it should be borne in mind that the Forest Service became administrator of 525,000 acres when the Klamath tribe of Oregon, located south of Warm Springs, was terminated and that it may gain an additional 135,000 acres when Klamath affairs are wound up.

As one can see, the Warm Springs tribe has made many concessions, but in an effort to get legislation passed that will return their lands to them, they were required to neutralize as many potential opposing groups as possible prior to hearings on the bill. In this case, the historical pattern has been followed in regard to negotiated compromise by whites about Indian lands, an endemic pattern that defined a compromise on the basis of how much the Indians will give up in land or privileges. The attorney for the Warm Springs people, Owen M. Panner, of Bend, Oregon, in a November 23, 1971, letter to the Forest Division of the Bureau of Indian Affairs, characterized their feelings: "We want desperately to get this McQuinn Strip returned to reservation status and the sacrifice seems advisable."

The long history of the efforts of the Warm Springs people to effect return to their lands can leave no doubt as to how much they want to accomplish their goal. The terms and conditions surrounding the present bill seeking return of the McQuinn Strip leave little doubt that a sacrifice is involved. While the sacrifice seems required and advisable under the conditions necessary to pass legislation, it should shock the conscience of the citizens of the United States that such measures are required if the Warm Springs tribes are to receive a just return of their lands. In terms of the life of the tribe, the twenty-year limit is not long. The Warm Springs people will surely achieve their goal and pay a price that, while high, may be necessary. The question posed, however, is whether that price is too high for the American people, for American justice, and for the future of both.

With the restoration of the lands to the Warm Springs people, an additional 61,300 acres would become part of the national Indian land base, which would henceforth be inviolate from congressional confiscation or administrative waffling. It would most certainly place the Warm Springs tribe on a firmer basis for successful community development and void a gain of land by the Forest Service under such unjust conditions. The following total acreage would then constitute the national Indian land base:

Tribal lands	39,663,412.09
Individual Indian allotments	10,697,621.58
Alaska native lands	40,000,000
Occupied Indian lands	4,723,017.2
Submarginal lands restored	344,811
Flathead lands restored	10,585.86
Warm Springs lands restored	61,300
	95,500,747.73

❦ 8 ❦

Sick Transit Sorry'a

Iᴛ ᴡᴏᴜʟᴅ appear that Isaac Stevens was the only Indian negotiator who ever spawned mistakes, but such is not the case. Stevens was merely overeager to get the West settled; others compounded and benefited from his hasty treaties and confused descriptions of boundary lines. Stevens, if anything, personified the manifest-destiny bureaucrat who seeks justice in his own terms, letting the particularities fall where they may.

A perhaps more typical example of complexities in land titles is the controversy between the Northern Cheyennes and the Crow of Montana. Neither tribe is basically at fault, and yet each has been asked to assume the burden created by bureaucratic bungling and misinterpretation. The controversy is still under consideration by the various federal agencies at the writing of this book, and so hopefully the problem can be resolved in the near future.

Like other conflicts over Indian lands, the Crow-Northern Cheyenne dispute has a colorful history extending back at least a century. The two tribes occupied overlapping hunting areas at the start of the nineteenth century. The Crow had originally lived along the Missouri and were close relatives to the Hidatsa, the earthen lodge people who lived along the Missouri near Bismarck, North Dakota, and moved as far down the river as the Sioux would allow them to come. The tribe was consistently regarded as friends of the white man and of every other tribe except, of course, the Sioux, with whom the Crow waged a struggle to the death.

The Cheyenne, close allies to the Sioux during most of the last century, lived in the area directly east of the Black Hills of South Dakota and gradually drifted over into the Wyoming Powder River country by the middle of the century. Together with the Sioux and Arapaho, the Cheyenne formed a formidable hunting and war alliance, which lasted until the demise of General Custer. Then the three tribes sought their individual destinies and finally secured reservations for themselves in Wyoming, Montana, and the Dakotas.

The Crow and Cheyenne were never ardent foes, although the Crow obviously did not like the company the Cheyennes kept. Together at Fort Laramie in 1851 the tribes participated in what was probably the largest treaty session ever held. The government was very desirous of ensuring a safe passage for their wagon trains that were racing for the coast either to participate in the California gold rush or to assist in populating Oregon Territory to establish United States domination of the northwest.

The tribes assembled at Fort Laramie agreed to refrain from attacking the wagon trains along the Oregon Trail if the United States would give them certain annuities for a period of years and act as referee for the frequent quarrels over hunting grounds that broke out periodically between the tribes of the northern plains. In the treaty the hunting grounds of each tribe were carefully outlined, and each was allotted a territory within which it would have exclusive hunting rights. Some land was set aside as common hunting grounds with the provision that the tribes would consider the lands common ground and desist from lifting each other's scalps in the designated territory.

Each tribe was assigned a fort at which to receive their annuities. The Sioux and Cheyenne were to go to Fort Laramie for their annuities, while the Crow were expected to go to the upper Missouri for their supplies. Shortly after the treaty was signed, warfare broke out between the Crow and Sioux. The Crow had conformed to the regulations laid down by the treaty and stopped fighting, remaining close to Fort Ellis, Montana. Their traditional enemies, the Sioux, saw their peaceful retreat as a means of wiping them out now that the army had conveniently cornered the Crow for them. Thus, raids of increasing ferocity were carried on against the poor Crow.

The result of this one-sided combat was to create a division in the Crow nation. The more suspecting souls, wondering if the

army and the Sioux were not cooperating in this venture, perhaps as joint tort feasors, bolted the reservation and went hunting with the Blackfeet and Gros Ventres, who lived somewhat to
the northeast. Thus, it happened that the River Crow, as they
came to be called, signed a treaty several years later as part of a
confederation with the aforementioned tribes giving them a reservation in the vicinity of Camp Baker, several hundred miles
further northwest.

Over the years the River Crow came to visit the rest of the
Crow nation now designated as the Mountain Crow, and then
returned to their northern reservation, which they shared with
the other tribes. But the Bureau of Indian Affairs refused to
consider the break between the two bands of Crow as a permanent rupture and insisted that all River Crow receive their annuities at the agency of the Mountain Crow. After several
decades the two bands became merged, primarily as a result of
the refusal of the bureau to distribute rations to the River Crow
at the northern agency.

As tensions mounted on the Yellowstone River with Custer's
expedition in 1874, the Crow had little choice but to side with
the egotistical general. The Sioux would be after them in any
case, and defeating the Sioux was the only way that the tribe
could enjoy any peace. A number of Crow therefore signed up as
scouts for the army. They stayed as scouts until the end of the
Indian wars in Montana. Custer told them to leave the column
just prior to his entrance into the Little Big Horn valley, thus
reserving the credit for himself and saving a number of Crow
from the disaster.

Red Cloud waged an unceasing war against the forts that the
United States had built in the Big Horn valley to protect the
gold miners rushing to Bozeman along the Bozeman Trail.
Additional troubles broke out between the wave of whites entering Montana and the various tribes who had thought that their
hunting rights had been preserved by the treaties of 1851. Another conference was called, and the Montana tribes were assembled to discuss the problems they were having with white intruders. When the sessions began, however, it was apparent that
the United States wanted to talk about further land cessions and
not about enforcing the rights guaranteed to the Indians under
the previous series of treaties.

The tribes met at Fort Laramie beginning in April 1868, and eventually, all signed what were to become the famous 1868 series of treaties, later used by Indian activists to claim surplus government property. On May 7, 1868, the United States and the Crow nation signed a treaty, the second article of which described the boundaries of the Crow reservation as

commencing where the 107th degree of longitude west of Greenwich crosses the south boundary of Montana Territory; thence north along said 107th meridian to the mid-channel of the Yellowstone River; thence up said mid-channel of the Yellowstone to the point where it crosses the said southern boundary of Montana, being the 45th degree of north latitude; and thence east along said parallel of latitude to the place of beginning.

Following the Custer defeat the army rapidly rounded up all of the Sioux and Cheyenne bands and confined them to the agencies on the Missouri River hundreds of miles from their beloved Powder River hunting grounds. One would have supposed that the United States would have dealt kindly with the Crow because of their long alliance with the army in opposition to the Sioux and Cheyenne. Such was not the case. One need only recount the numerous land cessions forced upon the tribe to understand how the United States rewarded its Indian allies.

In the 1851 treaty the Crow reservation was established as 38,531,174 acres covering large parts of Montana and Wyoming. The treaty of 1868, to which the Crow had been invited as allies of the United States, reduced the reservation to 8,000,409.2 acres—a loss of over 30 million acres by a friendly tribe. In 1882, Congress took 1,559,000 acres from the Crow and paid them the magnificent sum of $30,000 for twenty-five years, but in the same year, at the request of the Northern Pacific Railroad, took 5,650 acres at a payment of $25,000. Five years later, in 1887, Congress took 700.52 acres for the Rocky Ford and Cook City Railroad, paying the tribe $875.64, surely a crucial step in settling the West. Two years later Congress took 1,377.8 acres for the Big Horn Southern Railroad, paying $4,133.40.

With the pressure for allotments and consequent opening of the Plains Indians' reservation to white settlers, Congress took 1,208,960 acres in 1891 and 1,082,960 acres in 1904. Thus, within a period of slightly over fifty years, the United States had stripped its most faithful Indian ally of over 34.3 million acres.

The Northern Cheyenne did not, however, suffer this relatively benign fate. After Little Big Horn the United States was
determined to punish the tribes that had inflicted upon it the
worst military disaster of its history. The Sioux bands were pursued throughout the unsettled northern plains until, in the
spring of 1877, Crazy Horse led the last of the hostile Oglalas
into the agency at Pine Ridge. Sitting Bull had fled to Canada,
where he was to remain almost ten years. The Cheyenne were
moved south to Oklahoma to be placed on a reservation with
their southern cousins. The Northern Arapaho were scheduled
to be moved, but they appealed for a reservation in the North
and were placed on the Wind River Reservation in western
Wyoming with their traditional enemies, the Shoshones.

Western Oklahoma was like another world to the people who
had roamed the beautiful Powder River country and Big Horn
mountains. The plains were hot, dry, dusty, malaria-ridden
deserts in which few people could exist. In a short time the
Cheyennes were greatly reduced in numbers through disease and
the near-starvation rations they were forced to accept.

Appeals to Washington were no more effective then than they
are now. Little Wolf, one of the Cheyenne chiefs, complained
that "since we have been in this country, we are dying every day.
This is not a good country for us, and we wish to return to our
home in the mountains." But the government refused to allow
them to return to Montana, fearful that they would combine
with the Sioux for one last shot at the army. The United States
was hesitant in those days about losing armies.

In desperation the Cheyennes decided to flee the reservation
and go north, confident that when they arrived in Montana, the
United States would be reasonable and allow them to stay.
Under cover of night the remnants of the northern band, led by
Dull Knife and Little Wolf, fled Oklahoma and made their
tragic and heroic "Cheyenne Autumn" flight to the north.

The army pursued them across hundreds of miles of plains,
aided by all the latest techniques in communications. Railroads
shifted the troops of cavalry back and forth to every town at
which the Indians were reported, and yet so skillful were the
Cheyennes that they had traveled through Oklahoma and Kansas before anyone knew they were going north. Like shadows in

the night they passed the settlements peacefully sleeping and got into northern Nebraska before they were surrounded.

The bands split, and Dull Knife's people were captured and placed in a stockade in Fort Robinson. So desperate were they to return north that they broke out into a hail of bullets and were virtually annihilated. Little Wolf's people were much luckier, and many of them survived the chase and made it to Montana. Once they arrived in the North, they discovered that a substantial number of Americans had been cheering them on. Newspapers had made the most of their heroic and daring flight, and the government was reluctant to fight public pressure, which demanded that they be allowed to remain in Montana. The government therefore gave the band, who now officially became the Northern Cheyenne, a reservation of 271,000 acres of land adjacent to the Crow reservation in southern Montana, in the Tongue River country. In 1884, President Chester A. Arthur issued an executive order setting aside the reservation for the Northern Cheyenne and recognizing the 107th meridian as the eastern border of the Crow reservation and the western border of the Northern Cheyenne reservation.

Then the trouble began. In 1889, five years after the two reservations had been established, a survey was begun by the United States government to chart the boundaries of the two reservations. The surveyor planted his transit, which must have been sick that day, at the intersection of 45° north latitude (the southern border of the Crow reservation as then constituted) and 107° west longitude.

Then, in the classic words of a Bureau of Indian Affairs report on the results of the survey, the line "extended northward by a course that diverged from the 107th degree line." It was like Noah admitting that "we've had a little rain." The boundary line staggered northward. It veered as much as a mile west of the meridian for as long as 53 miles. The result of this meandering was to leave approximately 30,000 acres of Crow land outside the boundary of the reservation.

In 1900, President William McKinley issued an executive order enlarging the Northern Cheyenne reservation by 400,000 acres. This order, carefully written as bureaucratic directives usually are, merely stated that the Northern Cheyenne reservation was to be extended to meet the eastern border of the Crow reservation. It continued to recognize President Arthur's determination of the 107th meridian as the valid boundary line. Why the two presidents felt they could add 400,000 acres to one reservation when it bordered another one, no one ventured to ask.

When allotment was forced upon the tribes, bureau officials went ahead and allotted the Northern Cheyenne in the area that was to be disputed because of the inaccurate survey. Because lands not allotted were considered open to entry for settlers, some of the lands in the disputed area were settled by whites entering upon what they regarded as public domain. Not all of the land was settled, and the United States retained title to some of it. Thus, by the early decades of this century the lands had a great variety of claimants: the United States, the Crow tribe, the Northern Cheyenne tribe, Northern Cheyenne tribal members, and white settlers. And yet no one had any inkling that anything was wrong with the title to the lands.

Although the surveying error was made in 1891, it was not discovered by the Crow until 1956. There was no reason to suppose that they or anyone else would have known about it. The government people simply came, set up their transits, and marked out a boundary for the reservation. The Crow had to accept the findings of the government, because the Bureau of Indian Affairs told them that they had to accept them. Questioning the deeds or determinations of an Indian agent in 1891 was a very unwise procedure.

But by 1956 the climate on the reservations had changed considerably. The Crow had seen the outside world and had picked up considerable skills. One Crow at least had become very adept at reading land descriptions and survey reports. So it happened that Joe Medicine Crow, a tribal member, had gotten a job assisting a government survey team that was busy plotting the Crow reservation to find a "perfect" site for another government dam. (By this time the Crow had learned to send someone along when one of the gallant bureaucrats set out to do them a favor.)

Every day Joe Medine Crow would pour over the day's work, hoping to learn more about surveying. It dawned upon him that the boundary line must be awfully crooked if it was the one 107th degree of longitude. He reported his finding to the tribal council, and they carefully went over the boundary, observing the meander with increasing suspicion.

The date of the discovery of the meander is vital to the understanding of the present situation. As you will recall, in 1946 the Congress had established the Indian Claims Commission to review, and if necessary to rehear, the numerous disputes involving land cessions of tribes at any time preceding 1946. Part of the provisions of the claims legislation was that every tribe was to have five years beginning in 1946 to file claims for causes for action arising before 1946. The problem at the Crow reservation was that the surveying error had certainly been committed prior to 1946, but it had not been discovered until 1956. Thus, the statute of limitations had already run on a claim that was not discovered until five years after the fact. The Crow were barred from entering the Indian Claims Commission by a quirk of fate. They had no legal remedy for a certain wrong committed against them.

The Bureau of Indian Affairs, following its long tradition of assisting Indian tribes to "protect" their rights, promptly put out the nasty rumor that the Crows had known about the surveying error all the time. They made it apparent that they thought that the Crows had hidden the discovery of the error so that they could avoid going into the Indian Claims Commission and thus seek legislative remedies that would include recapture of the lands remaining in federal hands.

If this had been a valid contention, it would have meant that Joe Medicine Crow had slipped out to the boundary line some ten years before the surveying crew, had determined by himself that the boundary line was in error, had waited for the government survey team to arrive a decade later to find a dam site, had ingratiated himself with the foreman and received a job, and had finally flashed the high sign to the tribal council, which had promptly demanded a return of the lands. Such a sequence is not possible in the ordinary world, but a highly likely occurrence in the view of the Bureau of Indian Affairs. For the rest of us, the fact remains that the error was not discovered until the government team came out to survey the reservation to look for a suitable dam site.

The tribe went to Congress in spite of the Bureau of Indian Affairs and sought legislation returning the lands that still remained in federal hands. Congress, fortunately, did not believe the Bureau of Indian Affairs mythological explanation of the turn of events. Congressman James Haley of Florida, chairman of the Indian Affairs Subcommittee of the House Interior Committee, made that quite clear. "Although the error was made many years ago," he related, "the tribe was not aware of the error until after the time of filing a claim under the Indian Claims Commission Act had expired."

The present status of the lands excluded by the survey is not as complicated as one might be led to believe. There are 15,360 acres presently considered to be a part of the Northern Cheyenne reservation. Of this amount 10,840 acres have been allotted to individual Indians under the act allotting that reservation. The tribe holds, through a repurchase land program, 4,520 acres in its own name. Originally 14,400 acres were erroneously considered public domain and 13,718 acres were patented to white settlers under homestead and other laws allowing entry on the lands. The federal government holds 618 acres that have never been settled, allotted, or given to their rightful owners, the Crow tribe.

The case of the Crows is somewhat different from other boundary disputes. The original error was an administrative field error and not really dependent upon an act of Congress, a treaty, or an executive order from the president. The United States has never contended that by the surveying error it "intended" to take the land away from the Crow.

The Crow did not want to go to the United States Court of Claims for a decision of what they feel is a simple matter of correcting the records. Bills were introduced in the Ninety-second Congress (S. 451 and H.R. 8288) to provide a compromise of the total land return. Realizing that much of the land has gone into private ownership and that other people love their homes as much as Indians love theirs, the tribe has not demanded a return of all the lands. They want only the 618 acres that still remain in government hands returned to them and made a part of their reservation, where, had there been no error, they certainly would be.

For the lands that have already been allocated, the Crow want today's market value and a fair rental value for the years in which it was wrongly withheld from them. They also want the reserved rights to oil and gas on the lands that they will not be able to recover. If this proposal seems unduly favorable to the Crow, picture what would happen if the same mistake had been made against ITT or another public-spirited corporation. They would certainly have the lands returned to them with interest and apologies. It would be, as everyone realizes, perfectly clear who the lands belonged to.

The proposed legislation that the Crow have had introduced would allow the secretary of the interior to appraise the lands not disclaimed under the legislation within ninety days of passage of the law. After that period the Crow would be able to go to federal court if the secretary had not acted to solve the problem within the scope of his powers.

The basic argument of the tribe is that they still have full and complete title to the lands involved. The surveying error did not mean that the United States intended to take their lands, since the boundaries of the two reservations were supposed to touch each other at the 107th meridian. Therefore, the government keeping the lands for a national park or forest is out of the question. The fact that the Northern Cheyenne tribal members were allotted within the disputed area simply means that within what the Bureau of Indian Affairs thought was Northern Cheyenne land, allotments were made.

The Interior Department has not destroyed any files as yet, but it has not supported the bill, because it has a policy that it will not support any land-restoration legislation unless that land is contiguous to land already owned by a tribe. The rule, if it is one, is designed for the administrative convenience of the bureaucrats rather than an affirmation of any federal statute. It is as if the government would not let you buy a car unless you had the kind of garage it thought you should have for that kind of car, not knowing what make of car you might wish to purchase, of course.

The administration has not, at this time, taken a firm stand on the Crow legislation. It has tended to take the contentions of the Interior Department as gospel in this instance, whereas it opposed the department on similar proposals to return lands to Taos Pueblo and Yakima under somewhat similar situations.

The Justice Department, which considers its mission to invent new legal theories to deprive Indians of lands and other rights, is very hesitant about the legislation. It fears that the United States may owe the Crow Indians a considerable amount of money. In thus undertaking to assume responsibilities of the Treasury Department, it has, of course, abandoned all pretense of being involved in anything legal.

It is probably just as well. What the Justice Department is really worried about is the fact that federal law as presently constituted stands solidly with the Crow position on the restoration and proposed payments that the legislation would require. The federal law reads:

Lands set apart as a reservation cease to be public lands, and until the Indian title is extinguished no one but Congress can initiate any preferential right on, or restrict the Nation's power to dispose of them. No private rights in the lands of the reservation can be acquired, nor can the United States give away to others lands granted to an Indian tribe or in any manner appropriate such lands without assuming the obligation to render just compensation thereof. As long as the reservation remains unextinguished, the United States holds the land in trust for the Indians rather than for a future state within the boundaries of which they may happen to be, and the state cannot on its admission convey title to any part of the lands within the reservation (42 CJS 692)

Another part of the federal law supports the treaty title of the Crow even stronger:

Vested treaty rights of the Indians in the land cannot be impaired by Congressional legislation or state court decisions. Lands reserved for the exclusive use and benefit of Indian tribes in a treaty ceding other lands to the United States are held in trust by the government for the sole benefit of such Indians, and their right of occupancy to lands within the legal boundaries of the reservation cannot be affected by an incorrect survey and the patenting to others of the lands thereby excluded.

It is apparent that if the Justice Department has to abide by the laws of the land, it will throw into jeopardy all of their positions on Indian rights. They would have no choice but to return to the Flatheads, Warm Springs, and other tribes lands illegally taken from them by erroneous surveys. People would lose respect for a government that did not fudge a little bit on the laws, and soon society would crumble as people began to obey the laws of the land. ITT might even have to go to trial in its antitrust cases.

When the tribe was discussing the merits of its case the sub-committee counsel on Indian affairs in the House, Louis Sigler, advanced a rather novel theory of law that stems from some mystical apprehension of eminent domain as practiced after the fact. He maintained that the United States now owns the land in question and that the only real question bothering him is which tribe should be given the land. The novelty of this approach is that history is somehow magically wiped away and that we have the rather confusing analysis that the United States, having suddenly discovered that the land existed, can give the land to whichever of the two tribes it feels is most deserving, thus completely avoiding the tedious references to treaties, surveys, and executive orders.

During hearings on the legislation, Sigler asked the Crow,

Do you see any reason why Congress should not now pass a bill deciding which of these two tribes own the land rather than paying one for it? What I'm saying is that the land is there, the United States is holding it in trust for someone, the question is for which tribe is it holding the land in trust; so that I was asking whether rather than pay one of the tribes and give the land to the other, why not make a decision on which tribe owns the land.

This happy theory ignores the origin of the controversy. Some 53,000 acres of land were taken from the Crow tribe by an erroneous survey. The Northern Cheyenne, through the process of allotting individual Indians, gained some of the benefits of that error unsuspectingly. But the land, by treaty and two executive orders, belongs to the Crow.

We would recommend that Congress review the case and pass the legislation requested by the Crow, thus compensating them in part and restoring the 618 acres that the government is still able to confirm to them from its holdings. It is true that 618 acres will not make an appreciable difference to the tribe as a great shifting of land ownership. The issue, here more than anyplace else, is the validity of federal law as it relates to the establishment of Indian title by treaty. If the sections of federal law cited above are not valid, they should be changed by act of Congress. But we do not believe that they should simply be ignored because of a quirk in the thinking of the Justice Department or because it may prove to be inconvenient to the bureaucrats of the Interior Department in administering tribal lands.

If we add the 618 acres of Crow land to our running total we find ourselves taking another step toward the final proposed figure of 100 million acres as the permanent Indian land base.

Tribal lands	39,663,412.09
Individual Indian allotments	10,697,621.58
Alaska native lands	40,000,000
Occupied Indian lands	4,723,017.2
Submarginal lands restored	344,811
Flathead lands restored	10,585.86
Warm Springs lands restored	61,300
Crow lands restored	618
	95,501,365.73

✤ 9 ✤

You Can Bank on Indians:
The Menominees

A MAJOR concern in establishing a new congressional policy on American Indian lands should be the restitution of the lands that have been illegally taken, whether deliberately or inadvertently. As we have seen in a number of cases, this change of policy would involve considerable revision of bureaucratic procedures and a major effort to make government agencies follow federal laws. The bureaucrats at the Interior, Agriculture, and Justice departments would rather twist laws than obey them; they evidently feel that protection of administrative ego is more important than following congressional directives.

Another major Indian land problem can be laid directly at the door of Congress for solution. In the 1950's Senator Arthur Watkins of Utah single-handedly pushed through Congress the policy of termination, in which he, with the consent of his colleagues in the Senate and House Interior committees, unilaterally severed the federal treaty rights and services of nearly a dozen Indian groups. The legislation was hasty, ill-advised, and founded upon Watkins's magical belief in the sanctity and healing power of individual property. The tribes that fell to Watkins's sword have been in a legal and economic limbo since their federal rights were terminated. In many cases the economic deprivation they have suffered has been so bad that it can rightly be said that the first war on poverty was conducted against these tribes in order to reduce them to poverty. We recommend total restoration of trust lands and federal rights for these tribes at the earliest possible time. In the next several chapters we will discuss how these tribes have suffered under this unjust policy and what we believe can be done to recompense them for the injuries they have sustained.

One of the tribes most drastically affected was the Menominee tribe of Wisconsin. The Menominee were a small woodland tribe living in the region around what is now Green Bay, Wisconsin, since time immemorial. Not as powerful as their neighbors to the east, the Ottawa and Pottawatomi, nor their neighbors to the west and north, the Chippewa, the Menominee nevertheless exerted some influence on the tribes of the Great Lakes area during the first period of European exploration of the region. They were visited fairly early by the Catholic French missionaries and enjoyed the benefits of the fur trade before the demise of French strength in North America.

After the American Revolution they became subject to the laws of the new country, and in a series of treaties beginning in 1827 and concluding in 1848 they were forced to cede some of their lands to the United States. They were, however, virtually neglected by the United States, so that there were rarely hostilities between the whites and the Menominees. The federal policy of removal of all Indians west of the Mississippi was the first federal Indian policy that had any effect on the tribe. Between 1848 and 1854 the tribe was forced to cede lands to other tribes that the United States was moving west as part of the general removal pattern. Thus, some of their land was taken for the Oneidas when they were moved to Wisconsin, and after the Menominee reservation was established in 1854, the tribe was forced to sell a part of it to the Stockbridge-Munsee, who had been moved into the state following their removal from the New York area.

The Menominees almost came under the removal policy themselves when the United States demanded that they move to Minnesota. But the tribe was adamant about remaining in their aboriginal homelands, and since their reservation was primarily woods and small lakes, which federal officials considered ill-suited for farming, the tribe was left alone in their wilderness area. The final acreage of the reservation after the sale to the Stockbridge-Munsee was approximately 230,000 acres of woodlands. Needless to say, the timber on this land came to the attention of the timber barons early in the game. Various efforts were made by the so-called Pine Ring to get the reservation, but the tribe resisted all efforts to get them to sell their lands.

The Stockbridge-Munsee and several other tribes were made early victims of the allotment process, and it was not until the passage of the General Allotment Act in 1887 that the Menominee tribe was put under any pressure to allot their lands. The Bureau of Indian Affairs, at the instigation of the timber companies, tried its best to get the Menominees to allot their reservation, but the tribe, realizing what was really behind the effort to divide their lands, refused to accept the provisions of the act in what was an almost unique action for an Indian tribe. It held its lands intact, and in the process developed one of the great conservation techniques of modern times.

The timber companies continued to pressure the tribe to allow them to cut timber on the reservation, but the tribe refused. It had seen how wasteful the companies had been and how they had virtually destroyed the other reservations in Wisconsin. The Menominees therefore designed what is known today as sustained-yield cutting of timber. "We will start at the east end of our reservation," they are reputed to have said, "and cut toward the setting sun, taking only the large trees and leaving the younger trees to grow. When we have completely traveled to the end of our reservation, the younger trees in the east will have grown. Then we will begin cutting in the east where the sun rises once again. In this way we will always have a forest."

Menominee timber-harvesting techniques were much more sophisticated than that, however, as they can be said to have invented custom cutting also. The method used by the tribe was to cut trees according to scale specifications. Most lumber companies cut trees by the weight, regardless of the market at the time. Thus, they are left with the necessity of tailoring the trees they have cut to the market available when they are ready to sell the lumber. The waste of good wood in this method of operation should be apparent.

By 1900 the tribe had built a sawmill to cut its own timber and was probably the first tribe to embark on a successful tribal business enterprise of this size. The remarkable thing about their development was that the Bureau of Indian Affairs worked steadily to destroy the authority of the old chiefs and supplant the tribal social customs with individualistic ideas of Western civilization. The traditional chiefs were frequently shifted from place to place in the reservation structures to undercut their authority and role in tribal affairs. At one time the bureau announced that they would no longer be considered chiefs but would be judges of the reservation. In spite of this tinkering with their customs the tribe managed to hold firm to its land and tribal enterprise.

In 1908 a large windstorm felled many of the trees growing on the reservation, and the tribe appeared to be in desperate straits. A federal law forbade excessive cutting on the reservation, and the tribe feared that it would lose a lot of the prime timber that was laying on the ground as a result of the storm. Consequently, they asked Senator Robert La Follette to introduce special legislation to allow them to cut the excess timber and manage the timber on a better sustained-yield basis. The legislation, unfortunately, allowed the United States Forest Service to manage the forest, and it promptly clear-cut the forest, causing untold damage and setting the tribe back a generation in its planning.

The Menominees continued in their persistence to survive, and by 1928 they had evolved their traditional customs into a fairly modern general-council type of government. The Meriam Report of that year indicated that the tribe was well on the way to a decent form of self-government and recommended that the Bureau of Indian Affairs allow them more freedom in decision-making on policies respecting the reservation. Almost coincidentally with the report the tribe established an advisory council elected by the general tribal council, which consisted of the whole tribe meeting in concert.

A constitution was established, and the tribe began to pursue various paths by which they could develop the reservation themselves. Resentment was still high against the stupid handling of the forest in 1908, and the tribe pressed for legislation to allow them to enter the United States Court of Claims to collect damages against the United States for the loss of their timber. In 1935 Congress passed an enabling act giving them access to the court, and they hired a lawyer who prepared what is now considered one of the most exhaustive cases in the history of Indian affairs.

In 1934, while the tribe was still attempting to get into the court, the I.R.A. was passed, allowing federal Indian tribes the right to organize constitutions and bylaws under federal law. The result of this act was to give many tribes as formal a governing structure as possible. The Menominees rejected the act, however, because they had developed a government more suited to their needs at the time and fiercely resisted any efforts by the Bureau of Indian Affairs to impose its ideas on them.

By 1934 the tribe had good reason to avoid bureau interference with its affairs. In the interim since the organization of its advisory council in 1928 it had managed to get veto power over the budget for the reservation. Cleverly using this power to support and oppose projects undertaken with either its own funds or federal money, the tribe had managed to set up its own telephone and electric companies. It paid most of the operating costs of the reservation administration from its tribal income and supported a hospital operated for it by Catholic nuns. With this record of progress it was no wonder that the tribe was suspicious of any intrusions from outside by the federal government, no matter how benign such efforts appeared.

In 1947 Acting Commissioner of Indian Affairs William Zimmerman was asked by the Senate Civil Service Committee to testify in its hearings to determine if federal expenditures could be reduced by cutting back on certain services then provided by the federal government. He was quizzed on what would be the net effect on the Bureau of Indian Affairs budget of allowing a number of tribes to conduct their own affairs and of reducing the personnel then assigned to those tribes. On the whole, the hearings had nothing to do with Indians but much to do with the impact on the federal budget of continuing programs at a certain level for the foreseeable future.

Zimmerman listed the tribes then receiving federal services in three major groups, according to his estimation on how long it would be before they could assume most of the administrative functions then being performed by the Bureau of Indian Affairs. The Menominees were listed in the most capable group. Zimmerman qualified his recommendations for severance from federal services so closely that the Senate committee concluded that the savings from cutting back bureau services would be negligible in comparison with the hampering effect it would have on the government's overall attempt to improve the conditions of Indians.

In 1948 the Hoover Commission, as part of its general survey of conditions in the federal government, recommended that states assume more responsibility for Indian people and that the federal government begin to require the states to take a more active role in Indian affairs. In 1950 the Bureau of Indian Affairs had a new commissioner, Dillon Myer, whose chief claim to fame was that he had managed the Japanese relocation camps during World War II. He was thus considered an expert on dark-skinned peoples.

Myer apparently believed his own press clippings, for he began a vigorous campaign to solve the "Indian problem." In a series of letters to his field personnel Myer emphasized the fact that he was ready to proceed with the severance of federal services to as many Indian tribes as the bureau could possibly convince to accept the program. He noted that where the tribe did not readily agree to such proposals the bureaucrats should proceed anyway, regardless of the tribe's feelings on the matter.

The following year, after sixteen years of litigation, the Menominee claim was decided in the United States Court of Claims. The tribe was awarded a judgment of $8.5 million. The money was put into the federal treasury to await a bill in Congress to authorize distribution of the award. With its other deposits, the tribe had in excess of $10 million in the federal treasury, and it had made plans for using the funds in what it considered the most sensible manner. It wanted to issue a payment of $1,000 per tribal member and invest some of the remainder in renovation of the sawmill. The tribe figured it had a balance in the treasury of somewhat over $2 million, which it considered the minimum amount needed to sustain the mill.

In late 1952 a bill was introduced in Congress to distribute the money in the way the tribe had visualized, but no action was taken, and so, the bill died with that Congress. In the next year the Republicans were in control in the new Congress, and Republican senators and congressmen assumed command of the various committees and subcommittees. Their first overt act against the Indian community was to pass a resolution expressing a "sense of Congress" that the object of federal Indian policy was to prepare Indians for what they characterized as "full citizenship" as quickly as possible.

The Republicans were a little late. Indians had been made full citizens in 1924 with the Indian Citizenship Act. This law had excluded tribal property as a special right due to members of Indian tribes. So there was no legal basis for the congressional resolution in 1953. Nevertheless, it passed without a dissenting vote on the consent calendar, and Watkins saw his chance to demand immediate change in federal policy. He had just taken over the Indian subcommittee of the Senate Interior Committee and thought that he had the answer to the "Indian problem."

When the bill to distribute the Menominee money reached the Senate after passing the House of Representatives, Watkins demanded that the Menominees accept immediate termination of federal services, in order to receive the money the United States owed them. He was outraged that they had won the claim against the United States and visualized a number of tribes suing the federal government for its mistakes and claiming millions of dollars. Therefore, instead of demanding that the Bureau of Indian Affairs follow federal laws and thus preclude any liabilities against the government, Watkins thought the better route was to do away with the Indians. After all, they were the ones complaining.

The bill died in 1953, and in the following winter Watkins began stalking Indian country after likely victims for his unique theory of federal justice. Combining with Representative E. Y. Berry, Republican South Dakota, joint hearings were set up between the Senate and House Indian subcommittees. It was the first time in history that such a procedure was used. It has never been used again. The genius of this setup was that it avoided any discussion of the legislation between two houses of Congress. The joint subcommittee would simply write up identical bills for each house of Congress and report them for the consent calendar. When the senators or congressmen answered roll call, the bills would pass and probably less than a dozen people would ever know what they had voted for.

Watkins had made a special trip to the Menominee reservation the previous fall after Congress had adjourned and had told the tribe that he was going to terminate it anyway and that it had better vote to accept the legislation since only then would it ever see any of its money. The tribe, lacking any knowledge of how the Congress functioned, assumed that Watkins had absolute control over their lives and voted to accept the "principle" of termination, thinking that they would be able to work out a sensible plan in the next Congress. The day after the meeting with Watkins other members of the tribe found out what had happened and called another meeting and reversed the vote, stating firmly that it opposed termination.

Watkins ignored the second vote and informed his colleagues in Congress that the Menominees were enthusiastic about the plan to terminate their treaty rights and federal services. In June 1954 Watkins managed to guide the Menominee termination bill through Congress, and it was signed into law. Neither the Menominees nor Watkins understood what the language really meant. Some fourteen years later the United States Supreme Court would hesitantly attempt to interpret the law, with a rather confused idea of what had really happened.

The law required the tribe to develop a termination plan and present it to Congress for approval. The final insult, however, was that the tribe had to use its own money to develop the plan. Thus, the United States government was forcing its Indian ward to use its own money to find a way for the government to avoid its responsibility. In contemporary terms the federal government had made the Menominees "an offer they could not refuse."

A period of intense turmoil then followed, with the tribe trying valiantly to develop a plan for the withdrawal of federal services and Congress continuing to impose irrational guidelines and limitations on the people. A number of amendments were made to the original legislation; they altered the conditions imposed on the tribe so severely that no one knew what was happening to them at any point. The Bureau of Indian Affairs steadfastly refused to assist the tribe in preparing for its venture into corporate America. It claimed that the intent of Congress was to force the tribe to do its own planning and that any help it might give would thwart the will of that body. The poor Menominees, who had never had the opportunity or need to deal with state governments, banks, insurance companies, corporations, or unions, had to plan within a very short time how to bring into existence a form of community life that would enable them to stay together as a people and yet enable them to face the complex modern world, which they had never known.

One of the problems in the whole planning procedure was that the senator had projected the successful termination of the Menominees on the fact that they had $10 million in the federal treasury. But he had to sweeten the pot a little to get the tribal delegates to accept the termination law, and so, instead of a per capita payment of $1,000, the legislation authorized a payment of $1,500 per member. Thus, the law that terminated the tribe was based upon the condition and financial position of the tribe absent the authorizing legislation.

The program was doomed from the very start, but since no one knew what the legislation was actually supposed to do, everyone assumed that it was only the reluctance of the Menominees to work hard that was blocking the success of the program. Thus, the congressional hearings on the Menominee termination bill and its various amendments and extensions are replete with senators demanding that the tribe try harder and with the Menominees trying to explain that the financial basis of the project had been destroyed from the beginning and that the deteriorating lumber market was making it virtually impossible for the tribe to remain solvent, regardless of what happened.

The state of Wisconsin was frightened at the thought that the tribe was going to be literally dumped on its doorstep without any indication on the state's part that it wanted the problem. During the various hearings, officials from the state continued to raise significant questions, which they wanted Watkins, Clinton Anderson, and later Frank Church to answer. They uniformly wondered why, after the federal government had taken over a century to reduce the Menominees to a condition of poverty unsurpassed in the state, they had to accept the problem in a few short years without consent on their part or any previous knowledge of managing Indian tribal affairs. The senators' reply was hardly rational. Almost unanimously they agreed that state governments were by definition more efficient than the federal government.

Doctrines of conservative philosophy were being applied to a real situation, without much tangible verification. Whenever a problem arose for either the state of Wisconsin or the Menominee tribe, the senators would lapse into a recital of every Horatio

Alger myth available to them. It made for a pitiful performance. The senators actually held a life-or-death legislative power over the fortunes of the little Indian community, and so, the experiment took on the aspect of a profound and senseless tragedy.

Finally, in 1961, the termination plan was completed, and Congress, in spite of overwhelming evidence that the whole affair was a disaster, refused further extensions of the period of federal supervision and services. The net effect of the deadline was that the tribe immediately came under all state laws and regulations, and no longer had a land base protected by federal laws. The tribe was finally set adrift to fend for itself.

As of 1961 the Menominees, in order to preserve some semblance of self-government, decided to become Wisconsin's seventy-second county—its smallest, poorest, worst educated, unhealthiest, and most undeveloped county. Each Menominee enrolled on the tribal rolls as of 1961 got a $3,000 bond that would mature in the year 2000, would pay 4 percent interest, and could be sold. This bond was to divide the capital assets of the reservation into a corporate structure. Since the land was the only asset of the tribe and the county, it meant that in effect the tribe was severed from its land by the bonds and that the people were further separated from the land by the fact that if they wanted to own the lands upon which many of their houses stood, they would have to trade in their bonds, thus disfranchising them from any future participation in the tribe.

In addition, the individual Menominees received 100 shares of stock in Menominee Enterprises Incorporated, a corporation set up to operate the sawmill. The First Wisconsin Trust Company was given the voting rights and shares of stock for minors and incompetents and thus had total control over the corporation. The board of directors of the corporation as it began its venture in private enterprise was made up of a majority of non-Menominees. The only way the Menominees could ever take over their own corporation would be when enough of the children had grown up and taken their stock away from the First Wisconsin Trust Company by reaching their majority. The trust still has control through its exercise of voting stock of children.

Several months before termination was final the tribal hospital closed for lack of funds and its inability to conform to state health standards. The utilities had been sold because the tribe

could not afford to operate them. The new county faced life
devoid of any of the common facilities every other county in
America enjoyed. It was the way in which Congress provided the
Menominees with first-class citizenship. They had been reduced
to helpless paupers.

Some of the tribal members began to fight back against the
law. Feeling that the new president, John Kennedy, would be
sympathetic toward Indians, a movement was begun to ask for
repeal of termination. A long petition was signed by several
hundred Menominees asking for repeal, but Kennedy was not
moved. Nor was Secretary of the Interior Stewart Udall. Perhaps
the most sympathetic listener on the federal level was the new
commissioner of Indian affairs, Philleo Nash.

Nash had been lieutenant governor of Wisconsin during the
years of planning for termination. He had opposed the plan
vigorously, but being the number-two man in the state had not
had the effect he had wished. When the board of trustees for
Menominee Enterprises had been set up, Nash was elected one
of the non-Indian members. He knew the situation of the Menominees too well from firsthand experience. Yet, Nash could do
little to help them, because he was but a minor figure in a
glamourous political honeymoon that had more important
things to do than bother about Indians.

Nash bided his time, and when Melvin Laird, then congress-
man from the Menominee congressional district, demanded to
know what the bureau was doing in Wisconsin, Nash appeared
to fumble a bit and happened to mention the Menominees.
Laird immediately requested a report to be submitted to the
House Appropriations Committee on the "status" of the tribe.
In early 1965 Nash handed the report to the committee, and
Washington got its first report on the progress of the tribe that
had been its glamour experiment in the new policy to assist
Indians. The situation was not pretty.

The basic question, as the Bureau of Indian Affairs saw it, was
whether or not a simple forest industry, subject to the fluctuations of the market, could support an Indian tribe-county government complex. The immediate impact of combining the
two ventures was the necessity of understanding the property-tax
situation. While still under federal supervision the tribal government had functioned in most instances needing municipal

exercise of powers. Where it had failed to act responsibly, the federal government exercised a veto power over expenditures and withdrawals of capital from the federal treasury.

After termination the forest enterprise was saddled with 90 percent of the taxes levied by Menominee County. In addition, it had the administrative expenses of its own operation. Thus, by severing the political life of the tribe from its economic life, costs had at least doubled. Property taxes in Menominee County for the first two years of operation never amounted to less than 40 percent of the new income of Menominee Enterprises. By 1965 the cost was $395,000 and increasing by $63,000 a year.

With rising taxes the corporation did not have enough current income to pay interests on the corporate bonds that had been issued to the tribal members. Consequently, it had to dip into the capital that had been reserved from the original amount on deposit in the federal treasury before termination that had been transferred by the law ending federal recognition of the tribe. In four years it had to take $239,000 from reserve funds, dropping the fund to $864,000. (It had been conservatively figured prior to termination that a minimum of $2 million was needed as reserve funds to make the sawmill economically feasible.)

The sawmill had to modernize to increase its efficiency to meet the expanding tax load of the county. Prior to termination the sawmill had provided employment for 410 Menominees. One of its primary purposes was to provide such employment to tribal members, and while still under federal supervision the tribe did not have to emphasize efficiency, because there was no need to generate large amounts of cash. After termination, with the modernization of the mill, the employment dropped to 230 people, with seasonal employment varying from 65 to 130.

Menominee County, upon its creation by the termination legislation, promptly became the Wisconsin county with the lowest assessed valuation for tax purposes, $16.7 million. Only fourteen of the seventy-two other Wisconsin counties had a valuation of less than $50 million. Total taxes to meet county needs skyrocketed from $296,700 in 1962 to $502,600 in 1965, an increase indicating a plunge toward bankruptcy as a result of termination. School costs, which had been covered by federal services prior to termination and which were cushioned somewhat by federal assistance after termination, jumped from $800

to $161,000. Sanatorium treatment expenses for the rising inci-
dence of tuberculosis in the county climbed from $300 a year to
$76,100 by 1965. For the whole state of Wisconsin the average
combined tax milleage rate in 1965 was 27.32, but for Menominee County it was 29.77. The people were paying more, and
receiving less, than almost every other group in the state.

The individual Menominees did not profit at all from termination as Watkins had envisioned. In 1959 the median family
income was $2,638 for the Menominees, and after two years of
"freedom," as the Senate Interior Committee had described it,
their median family income was $2,677. With inflation and the
new burden of taxes figured into the posttermination income,
one could only conclude that the Congress of the United States
had created a pocket of poverty.

In 1960 the Menominees had a reported median of 8.3 years of
school completed as against a statewide median of 9.9 years. The
dropout rate averaged between 46 and 51 percent, depending
upon which study one used to explain the educational problems
of the tribe. Not more than a quarter of the tribe had ever been
beyond the eighth grade. In housing, the tribe's condition was
described as a third in sound condition, a third in deteriorated
condition, and a third dilapidated. The average value of houses
in one of the two Indian villages was only $4,000—less than the
value of a summer cabin of the average white of Wisconsin.

Clearly, the new county and its people were not making the
spectacular progress that Clinton Anderson, Frank Church, and
Arthur Watkins had predicted they would once they were free of
the degrading effects of government services. In December 1963
the bonds of Menominee Enterprises became negotiable. Each
tribal member had received a bond of $3,000 that was to mature
in 2000, but the condition of the people made it necessary for
many to sell their bonds to maintain themselves. The Wisconsin
legislature established a special fund of $1 million to be admin-
istered by the State Department of Public Welfare for the benefit of the tribe. Grants and loans for welfare purposes could be
made from this fund on the basis of pledged Menominee income
bonds. A year later the fund was down to $200,000, many people
having pledged their bonds for immediate welfare assistance.
And the State Investment Board decided that it could no longer
pay the par value of $3,000 but had to discount the bonds to

$2,300, a loss of 30 percent of value in the three years since termination.

Considerable sentiment was rising in Menominee County against the desperate situation in which the people found themselves. The state of Wisconsin was equally baffled but virtually helpless to go into bankruptcy itself on behalf of a sidetracked federal experiment. Both Gaylord Nelson and Melvin Laird became concerned and sought some additional federal aid for the striken tribe. Finally, in desperation, the tribe leased its beloved Wolf River to the state for $250,000 a year to keep Menominee Enterprises solvent.

The end was in sight. Federal planning for termination had been, as we have seen, less than cogent. The tribe did everything it could to preserve its land base, but although it survived the Pine Ring, the General Allotment Act, the United States Forest Service, and the Bureau of Indian Affairs, it could not survive Watkins and the Senate Interior Committee. The lease of the Wolf River was the first crack in the solid front against loss of lands that the tribe suffered in its history of dealing with state and federal agencies.

In a related move the board of Menominee Enterprises decided that selective leasing of sites for summer cottages for whites might provide some income for the badly strapped corporation. As the tax situation grew worse, the decision was made to sell the lands instead of leasing them. The land sales had to be kept quiet, of course, and so, the tribal members did not know which lands were being sold and how much land was leaving tribal hands forever. They still do not know.

Once the decision was made to sell Menominee lands, the corporation considered selling a resort type of development in a selected area of the county on a more professional basis. Consequently, the Legend Lake project was created with the help of a white developer, who has not exactly lost any money on the deal.

The Menominees had a number of relatively small lakes where they used to hunt and fish. These small lakes were artificially linked together as Legend Lake, taking advantage of the white man's obeisance to the mystery of Indian culture. Some 5,000 acres of land afforded a maximum lake frontage for cottages, with a projected 2,500 lots for sale to whites. The argument used by Menominee Enterprises was that it was necessary to sell part of the lands in order to save the remainder. But it has not proven a popular idea with the tribe.

In 1967 Menominee Enterprises entered into a partnership with N. E. Isaacson of Reedsburg, Wisconsin, to develop Legend Lake. Isaacson got 5 percent off the top of all sales, expenses were deducted from the rest of the sales, and Isaacson and Menominee Enterprises split the remainder of sales income. The Menominee Enterprises put up the land, Isaacson the sales pitch to sell it. It proved to be a very expensive way of financing first-class citizenship.

By 1970 the situation in Menominee County was so complicated and tragic that it appeared as if a malevolent Keystone Cops drama was being enacted. The sawmill was operating at a loss, making it necessary for Menominee Enterprises to sell the lands at Legend Lake for funds to prop up the sawmill. Thus, the tribe was selling its lands upon which grew its timber supply in order to keep its mill running at a loss, and the annual cut of timber continued to climb as a result of efforts to cut the operating losses of the mill. Clearly, it was a vicious and rapidly accelerating cycle of financial disaster.

Then, the sawmill burned down.

In itself the sawmill represented the tribe's last chance to survive as a community, but the series of events during the burning indicate what a fragile existence the whole operation is. The fire engine would not start at the outbreak of the fire, thus allowing the flames to get a head start on the mill. When the fire engine finally got to the scene of the fire, the Menominees could not use the fire hoses. They were too rotten to spray water with. In their drastic cutting of expenses, the tribe was reduced to living simply on the faith that no drastic catastrophe would ever occur. Hoses simply did not have priority in the long list of needs of the county. While the Menominees stood by helplessly watching the drooping hoses futilely attempt to spray the fire, the flames reached two drums of oil, thus changing the fire from a mere catastrophe to a disaster.

Totally dependent upon the sales of lots at Legend Lake while the mill was being rebuilt, the Menominees discovered that the sale of lots was not as simple as promoters and well-wishers had predicted. Lots required additional police protection, fire protection, maintenance for the roads into the new subdivision, and other county services to provide for the white residents who wanted to live in their homes at Legend Lake year-round. As more lots were sold, problems in water systems and sewer facilities began to appear, adding to the already crushing tax load of the county.

In the interim Menominees began to realize that as more lots became year-round residence sites, the whites would soon outnumber them and take over the county government, thus placing them in total control of Menominee destiny. The First Wisconsin Trust Company, through its control of the stock of minors, already controlled the board of directors of the Menominee Enterprises Corporation. By the seemingly irreversible operation of inflexible state and federal laws the tribe was sent down the path of no return by the financial impossibility of managing a structure that the Congress had so casually created.

The Menominees began to organize to fight back. Prior to termination there had been a little band of dissidents who opposed the severance of federal rights, but they had not received any support of consequence. Part of the reason for the lack of fight prior to the passage of the law was that Watkins had bluntly told the Menominees that he would stop everything unless they agreed to his conditions. Most of the tribe could not understand how one man could have this much power, and so, a number of them assured the tribe that the United States, which had signed their treaties, would never allow this to happen. They did not reckon with the moral stance of the United States government, which has never achieved an exalted status in its dealings with anyone.

Throughout the years of planning, opposition to the termination grew but few people had the necessary organizational skills to crystallize the opposition. In 1965 a petition asking for repeal of the termination law and signed by some 788 people was sent to the president. President Johnson politely sent the petition to the Bureau of Indian Affairs for their form letter reply to Indian complaints. Nothing was done.

Finally, in late 1969 a Menominee college student, Ada Deer, went to the annual stockholders' meeting to find out what was happening with the development of Legend Lake. She asked for a more detailed statement of the financial transactions of the corporation. The board of directors nearly lost their minds. They had all retained their seats on the board by being obedient to the First Wisconsin Trust Company, which had taken a very conservative stance toward everything. The idea that a Menominee stockholder, particularly a woman college student, would ask questions about a corporation in which she had stock threatened the board of directors. They panicked and refused to supply her with any information on their activities.

The rejection of a mere college student enraged many Menominees who would otherwise have remained silent. Groups began to organize in many of the nearby cities to which a lot of the tribe had been forced to go following termination. Apparently, they figured that if the board of Menominee Enterprises could not fool a college girl, something drastic was going on in the county.

In the spring of 1970 a spontaneous demonstration against the Legend Lake project was sparked when some Menominees were made to leave an accustomed picnic spot by the new white owners of the land. The idea that whites now had the power to order Menominees off ancestral lands further infuriated the tribal members. Groups began to draw large crowds at their meetings and a new organization was born—DRUMS (Determination of Rights and Unity for Menominee Stockholders).

The more outraged the Menominees became, the more secretive the corporation became about what it was doing. Administrative employees of Menominee Enterprises began to speculate publicly about the possibility of Communist influence in the DRUMS organization—a typical response of frightened and ignorant people in the state that spawned Senator Joseph McCarthy. All the Menominees really wanted was information about what the corporation was doing. What they received were insults and implied threats, questions about their "Communist" activities, and denouncements. DRUMS began to expand its membership tremendously.

Under the conditions of the termination agreement the trust exercised over Menominee Enterprises consisted of four Menominees and three whites; they determined the policy of the corporation by voting for the board of directors. The trust could not be abolished except by votes to be taken every ten years following termination. Abolition of the trust would allow the tribal members to control the board of directors of the corporation without the necessity of having three non-Menominees, required by law in a voting trust, pick the board for them.

In December 1970 the DRUMS organization got out the Menominee stockholders, and the annual meeting brought out a number of things of which the tribal members had not previously been aware. In the summer of 1970 the corporation had filed a suit before the United States Court of Claims asking for damages for the losses suffered by termination. But they had somehow managed to keep the case secret. For what reason no one was able to determine.

DRUMS sued to prevent a vote from being taken until all of the Menominees had been located. Over the years since termination, a number of Menominees had simply vanished. No one knew where they were and with the vote to abolish the voting trust coming up, DRUMS wanted every tribal member to be able to cast a vote on the issue. All but 385 people were eventually located, and in April 1971 a vote was taken to determine if the voting trust should be continued.

Although the count was by shares and some of the shares had been shifted by births and deaths since termination, the practical result of the vote was that 1,190 Menominees voted to abolish the trust and 694 voted to keep it. Then, the First Wisconsin Trust voted its 486 votes to keep the voting trust, making the total for abolition fall short of the majority needed to do away with the stranglehold on the tribe. DRUMS filed a suit in court to prevent the voting of the shares in trust but lost the case. The point, however, was eloquently made: the Menominees had been beaten only by the intervention of whites who controlled their destiny, a situation that Watkins had promised would not occur with his new policy to "free" the Indians.

Since the victory, albeit moral victory, of April 1971, DRUMS has become the voice of an overwhelming majority of the Menominee people. In the spring of 1972 legislation was introduced to repeal the termination of the Menominee tribe and to repair the damages done by this hasty and ill-conceived act. The tribe is asking for full restoration of the federal trust, which would lift the incredibly brutal tax burden from the county and allow the county to once again become a federally recognized tribe thus eliminating the dual administrative burden forced upon them by termination.

In addition, the legislation calls for repurchase of lands that had to be sold by the Menominee Enterprises corporation to keep the sawmill afloat and restoration of all federal services. We believe that restoration of the Menominees to full federal rights and privileges is the very least that can be done by the federal government. The injury to the tribe was not of its choosing but was engineered by one United States senator who believed that the sanctity of private property was a magical formula for the solution of the "Indian problem." Once believing this, Senator Arthur Watkins promptly created a structure that was more oppressive and dictatorial than anything the tribe had ever experienced.

Things continued to break in favor of the Menominees. During the summer of 1972 Isaacson asked for a release of its contract. The vast majority of Menominees had demanded a cession of land sales and this tied up a considerable investment which Isaacson had made in the project. With no land sales authorized the investment was obviously a disaster. In addition the adverse publicity which the firm was drawing as a result of its involvement at Menominee County was becoming a definite liability. The Menominees now desperately need repeal of the termination act to remain solvent.

With passage of the Menominee restoration act the following total acreage would result:

Tribal lands	39,633,412.09
Individual Indian allotments	10,697,621.58
Alaska native lands	40,000,000
Occupied Indian lands	4,723,017.2
Submarginal lands restored	344,811
Flathead lands restored	10,585.86
Warm Springs lands restored	61,300
Crow lands restored	618
Menominee lands restored	230,000
	95,731,365.73

You Can Bank on Indians:
The Klamaths

Watkins scoured the nation looking for tribes to terminate. He found the Catawbas of South Carolina living in a remote area of that state without any apparent Bureau of Indian Affairs assistance and with no immediate prospect of bettering their situation. They came under his ax, and being defenseless and rather confused by the whole thing, agreed to sell their tiny reservation of some 600 acres, and dissolve their tribal government.

The demise of the Catawbas as a federally recognized tribe ended a long relationship with the United States of which Watkins was not aware. During the American Revolution many of the tribes on the frontier sided with the British. They had reason to believe that the king would win the struggle, and they felt that the regulations that the king of England had placed on the traders were generally beneficial to them. In the South, for example, there were continuing clashes between the eastern towns of the Cherokees and the settlers in the back country.

The eastern Cherokees formed a rather distinct grouping known as the Chickamauga. They were highly dissatisfied with the Americans because the settlers kept insisting that their land cessions had included much more land than the tribe had been willing to cede. They also were deeply resentful of the fraudulent practices in trading that were part of the South Carolina trade. The Catawbas remained loyal to the Americans during the war, risking not only the ire of the king of England but the very real depredations of the Chickamaugas.

Because the Catawbas had remained faithful to the Americans in the Revolution, they were not made to remove themselves to Oklahoma when the policy was put into effect by Andrew Jackson. Instead, they were given a small reservation of land and allowed to remain in South Carolina, where the state gave them support against the continuing fluctuations of government policy. Watkins rewarded their faithfulness as American allies by severing every right they had been given by the federal government as a reward for their services.

The same could be said for the Alabama-Coushattas of Texas. In the first days before the Mexican war, the Alabama-Coushattas occupied a rather extensive area of eastern Texas. They were very friendly to the American settlers who were coming in increasing numbers to the area. Among their good friends was Sam Houston, later to be the hero of the Texas revolution against Mexico. He lived with them for a number of years and always visited them when he felt like getting away from it all.

After the revolution started, Houston was a marked man in Texas. People were still not of one mind on the benefits of severing their ties with Mexico, and quite a few people thought that an independent nation was the best course of action. Thus, Houston was caught between the Mexican authorities, on one side, and those Americans who disagreed with him, on the other. A number of times he was in dire straits and had nowhere to hide from his pursuers. He hid out with the Alabama-Coushattas, who refused to give him up to his enemies.

When Texas finally entered the Union, it unleashed the infamous Texas Rangers against the tribes of the state. They swept from one end of the region to the other killing and burning Indian villages. The sole purpose of the series of raids was to clear the state of Indians. No one ever thought to reason with the tribes who lived there. They simply wanted the state free of Indians.

Houston, remembering the kindness of the Alabama-Coushattas when he was a fugitive from the Mexicans, spoke out against the removal of the tribe and defended them whenever people began to talk about doing away with them. Watkins, unfamiliar with this history and probably not caring to learn it, saw the tribe only as a drain on the taxpayers.

The Bureau of Indian Affairs was informed that Watkins

wanted to terminate the tribe and was instructed to get its approval on the legislation. Therefore, a bureaucrat visited the reservation ostensibly to get the tribe's approval on a new lease of tribal timberlands. When the people discovered what the bureau was actually trying to do, they were outraged. Representative John Dowdy of Texas spoke up for the tribe and demanded that the bureau stop its high-handed methods of getting tribal approval for the termination. But Watkins passed off the trickery as indicative of enthusiastic tribal approval of the plan.

The story, unlike so many Indian histories, had a happy ending. The tribe was transferred to the jurisdiction of the state of Texas and made, in effect, a "state" tribe, a category that is as yet undefined legally. Texas was sympathetic to the tribe's needs and set up a commission to help it with economic development. Since their termination the state has appropriated funds to assist the tribe, and it has made excellent progress in maintaining its lands and community intact.

Some of the other tribes that were terminated by Watkins were in the general situation as the Catawbas. The small Paiute bands in southern Utah were told that the proposed termination legislation was to approve their traditional tribal marriages. Instead, their lands were taken and placed under the trusteeship of a bank in Salt Lake City. The people still have no knowledge of the status of their lands. The bank will not give them adequate information on its role and trusteeship, and they do not have sufficient income to make the journey to Salt Lake City to do a thorough investigation of their situation.

Watkins was a firm racist. He believed that the infusion of white blood was sufficient to civilize a person and make him able to cope with the increasing complexity of the outside world. Thus, before he attacked the Menominees, he produced a plan to terminate the mixed-blood Utes of the Uintah and Ouray reservation in the northern part of the state. He indicated that if he terminated his own Indians (Watkins thought of Indians in terms of personal property), other senators would not raise a hand to help the Indians of their own states.

The northern Utah tribe was divided according to bloodlines: those with half degree of white blood or under were terminated from any further federal services, and their share of the tribal property was put into a corporation with the trust responsibility over the property vested in a bank in Salt Lake City. Recently, a series of law suits has shown the trustees derelict in their duty to protect the Indian lands and assets. Officers of the trust were implicated in a scheme to buy and sell shares of stock in the Indian corporation for virtually nothing. The case went to the Supreme Court, where it was decided that the activity had been less than aboveboard. But the court would not place ultimate responsibility on the secretary of the interior, who was supposed to be overseeing the situation. It decided that the responsibility of the United States stopped with the legislation that terminated the tribe.

The second large tribe that Watkins terminated was the Klamath tribe of southwestern Oregon. The Klamaths consisted of three distinct groups that had lived in the same vicinity since long before the whites came to the west coast, the Klamaths, the Modocs, and the Yahuskin band of Snakes. The Klamaths had occupied the area near Crater Lake that included mostly marsh and river country and generally supported themselves as fishermen. The Modocs lived to the south of them where the mountains trail off into the Great Basin desert area; they were mostly hunters. The Yahuskins were the westernmost band of Snakes and closely related to the Paiutes, who lived in the desert areas to the southeast.

The tribes were quite isolated until late in the days of western exploration. They were off the trails that led to early settlement of the coastal areas, being removed some distance from the Oregon Trail, which followed the Columbia and led into the Willamette Valley, and a great distance from the California Trail, which ended at Sacramento. It was not until the great gold rushes of California spread the news of riches to the settlers of the Oregon Territory that any significant number of whites came into contact with the Klamaths. The gold-crazed whites began coming down the Cascades looking for a way to California and ran into the Klamaths and Modocs, and sporadic fighting ensued.

The settlement of Oregon Territory did have a profound effect upon the tribes, however, in that for some strange reason they were generally included in the various scares that periodically erupted among the settlers following the so-called Whitman Massacre of 1847. The settlers generally regarded the

Klamath-Modoc confederation as excellent fighters and as a threat to the well-being of the territory. Thus, outbreaks of hostilities in northern Oregon between the whites and the river tribes generally brought the Klamaths into closer contact with the influential whites of the territory, as the whites wanted to neutralize the fighting strength of the Klamaths and prevent the tribes of Oregon from uniting on a broader front against them. Thus, the Klamaths were generally involved in policy-making, even if only as a constant threat that had to be dealt with.

By 1844 a subagent of the Indian affairs agency in Oregon had persuaded the Klamaths and Modocs to choose a chief for each band so that he would have someone to deal with on important matters. Two years later John Fremont led his expedition through the Klamath country on what was allegedly a friendly journey. He got into a skirmish with some Klamaths near present-day Klamath Falls and in retaliation slaughtered an innocent village of Klamaths some distance away. This initial hostility seems to have affected the attitude of the people toward the government, and throughout their days of reservation life until termination, they deeply resented directions from the federal officials sent to rule them.

The Modocs did not recognize the state line drawn between Oregon and California and rightly regarded the southern part of Oregon and northern part of California as their territory. They had signed no treaty ceding it and resented whites settling the area. Continuous warfare resulted between the Modocs and the invading settlers over hunting, fishing, and grazing of cattle on lands that belonged to the Modocs. The whites perpetrated a number of senseless massacres on Modoc villages, and hatred continued to increase between the Modocs and the new settlements of northern California.

The Klamath and Modoc confederation proved such a threat that the settlers asked for a special piece of legislation authorizing a commission to sign a treaty with the tribes, defining their reservation and ceding the remainder of their lands for the disposal of the government to new settlers. After years of negotiations a treaty was signed in 1864 that gave the Klamaths a rather generous territory. A subsequent treaty in 1869, ratified in 1870, reduced their reservation somewhat and had the distinction of being one of the last treaties the government would sign and ratify with an Indian tribe.

Under the 1869 treaty an agency was set up and education was made an integral part of the government services to be provided to the tribes. The treaty provisions of 1864 were designed to support a school for the Klamath, but they soon ran out and the school had to be closed. The first effort of the government to keep its end of the treaty contract had ended in ignominious failure. From 1860 to 1880 the Klamaths would experience a series of disappointments caused by the continual inability of the government to comprehend its role in respect of the Klamaths.

In 1870 a sawmill was built primarily to provide lumber for the Klamaths to use for building houses. The Bureau of Indian Affairs was insistent that they could not be civilized without adopting the housing patterns of the whites. By the next year the tribe had arranged for the bureau to buy its lumber from them, with the proceeds to be invested in livestock. They were planning a gradual transformation of their economic status from hunters and fishermen to cattlemen and lumbermen, but the change went virtually unnoticed by government officials.

In 1873 the Supreme Court had ruled that trees that had been felled to clear Indian lands might be sold as an incidental bonus for clearing the lands for farming but that timber cut for commercial purposes on Indian lands would be income to the government and not to the tribe that owned the timber. The Klamaths, promptly adopting the ruse that they were enthusiastically clearing lands for farming, developed a substantial lumbering industry on their lands. The people would run up large bills at the local stores, cut "fallen" logs on their lands into usable timber, sell it, and pay their bills. It was a novel way around illogical government regulations. By 1896 the Klamaths had expanded their illicit operations to a quarter of a million board feet a year, almost three-fourths of it green timber. It was a notable victory over the Bureau of Indian Affairs, but it marked the tribe as an "uncooperative" group destined for whatever the bureaucrats could devise to hamper it.

Things appeared to be going very well until the Modoc war broke out in 1869. The split on the reservation was between the liberal Klamaths and the conservative Modocs. Captain Jack, famous Modoc war chief, felt that his people were being subverted by Klamath ascendency to the political control of the reservation under the old treaty of 1864. He wanted a reservation of his own, where his people could govern themselves. His reward for his patriotic leadership of the Modocs in their heroic but hopeless battle against the army was a hangman's noose. Following the Modoc war, relations between the two groups worsened, and this split later proved to be fatal to any resistance to the termination policy.

The Klamaths (after 1870 all reservation people were referred to as Klamaths) fell victim to the allotment theory of Indian land tenure rather early in the game. In 1881 a bill was introduced in Congress to allot their lands, but the land was so rocky and volcanic that the agent made little attempt to survey and distribute the lands. Out of 933 members of the reservation, the agent was able to get the consent to allotment, albeit grudgingly, of 800 members of the tribe.

Almost ten years later, in 1891, the Klamath allotment act was amended to give each member 80 acres of farmland or 160 acres of grazing land. The government agent classified most of the land as grazing land on about a 25-to-1 basis over farmlands. He probably suffered considerable political pressure from the tribe, since the Klamaths had been turning lumber income into livestock holdings for nearly two decades prior to allotment. By 1897 most of the reservation had been allotted, but a dispute over boundaries with the California and Oregon Land Company slowed the process. There had been two surveys, in 1871 and 1888, and in 1903 Oregon had renewed its claim to swamplands in the Klamath Marsh, so that in addition to dividing the lands for allotment both the tribe and the government had to defend title to the reservation from outsiders.

Allotment was not completed until 1910, when the remaining Modocs, who had been sent to Oklahoma following the defeat of Captain Jack, returned to the reservation and claimed their lands. A few Modocs remained in Oklahoma Territory, but a number of families desiring to live in familiar surroundings returned to Oregon. Neither Klamaths nor Modocs felt a great need to ranch after allotment, however, since the division of lands into 160-acre parcels prohibited the increase of a herd to any significant number. Most of the Indians kept a few head of cattle and leased their lands to whites, who usually had the finances to consolidate large tracts of land for cattle operations of larger magnitude.

When allotment was over, the tribe somehow retained its surplus lands in its own name. Other tribes had been forced to sell their lands to the government for white settlers, but the Klamaths retained title to some 860,000 acres of land, nearly three-quarters of its prime ponderosa pine. By the late 1920's the tribal members were almost completely divorced from ranching activities and had unwisely sold their allotments, so that few allotments remained in Indian hands. Individuals therefore became increasingly dependent upon what the tribe did with its unallotted timberlands.

Somewhat like the Menominee the Klamaths evolved a form of tribal government well before other tribes conceived of the idea. They had originally required all adult males to sit in council before any decision could be reached concerning a change of the status of tribal lands or rights. Gradually this general council had to streamline its decision-making process in order to keep abreast of modern business developments. By 1908 an executive committee was formed to carry out the ongoing affairs of the tribe between general council meetings. Initially, the executive committee was made up of twelve men apportioned among the original bands of Indians who lived on the reservation. But a failure to make a quorum at meetings caused a reduction of the committee to eight men.

In 1927 a constitutional crisis occurred that eventually spelled the end of the Klamath tribe. A dissident group elected a new council and claimed that it had superseded the ruling council. There was great turmoil for a couple of years because the Klamaths had casually accepted a government on a gentlemen's agreement rather than a formal basis. This action struck at the heart of what had always been a rather tentative truce between Klamath and Modoc factions on the reservation.

The commissioner of Indian affairs had to intervene in the dispute. He forced the tribe to adopt a constitution and bylaws in order to end the dispute and forestall any further disruptions of the management of tribal business. The old eight-man executive committee was replaced by a six-man business committee.

But the people did not abolish the general council, which remained the supreme political organization of the reservation. Its powers remained basically unamended, and it was the power to appoint tribal delegations to deal with the government from outside the business committee that eventually resulted in the advocacy of termination by a small faction within the tribe.

Klamaths had always been partial to a quasi aristocracy in their prereservation days, and now this tendency toward stratification of tribal membership worked against the smooth operation of the new tribal constitution. In their former days of glory they had kept slaves, and a few families had been able to dominate the proceedings of the old general council. The new business committee was extremely vulnerable to such domination as pressures from the outside increased in the twentieth century. Thus, there came to be three basic factions that controlled political activities on the reservations, the Kirks, the Crawfords, and the Jacksons, all mixed-bloods and all more articulate and acculturated than the full-bloods of their respective bands.

Almost from the very beginning there were disputes between these three factions as to both use and possible disposal of tribal lands. Once the tribal lands had been preserved from the surplus category, and hence from distribution to white settlers, tribal politics revolved around allotment of the remaining lands and dissolution of the tribal entity. In 1929 Wade Crawford went to Washington, D.C., to propose a plan to establish a tribal corporation to take over complete management of tribal lands. No sooner had Crawford proposed incorporation than his opponents demanded total dissolution as a final settlement of Klamath interests and claims against the United States, of which several were then pending.

Crawford was no man to treat lightly when he set his mind to selling out his fellow Klamaths. He became acquainted with John Collier, destined to be commissioner of Indian affairs in the New Deal administration, and when Collier took office he appointed Wade Crawford to be superintendent of the Klamath reservation. It thus seemed that with his power consolidated at the highest level Crawford was in a position to dictate events at the reservation.

In one of his few humane acts, Crawford advocated the adoption of the I.R.A. But the tribe rejected it, primarily because he had advocated it; the tribe's suspicions of Crawford surpassed any faith it might have had in the act and its provisions. In suffering this major defeat in his effort to control the reservation, Crawford blamed the reservation people, and he began to build a political following among the Klamaths and Modocs who had moved away from the reservation but who still retained the right to vote in tribal elections.

Crawford's reign lasted from 1933 to 1937, when he was removed for cause. Once removed from his powerful position as superintendent, Crawford increased in bitterness against his people and became a loud advocate of per capita distribution of tribal assets and dissolution of tribal government. He carried on his fight for eight years, creating untold havoc among the political factions of the tribe and hampering development of a stable tribal government.

In 1945 he went to Washington as a tribal delegate and, while there, proposed, primarily on his own initiative, termination of the tribe. Crawford's proposal aimed at federal purchase of tribal timber tracts and liquidation of other tribal properties. When the business committee on the reservation learned of his plans, it was horrified and demanded that the proposal be dropped. The leaders of the other two factions, Boyd Jackson and Jesse Kirk, opposed the Crawford proposal, which was now being considered seriously as legislation in hearings both in Washington and on the reservation.

The superintendent of the reservation, a man named Courtright, prepared an alternative bill that would have permitted voluntary withdrawal of competent members as a means, allegedly, of settling the dispute. People failed to understand that the real alternative was no termination at all and became greatly concerned over which proposal would return them more money. Practically no one understood that if they sold the lands to the government, the reservation would cease to exist. They somehow were led to believe that they could terminate their tribal government and still remain on the lands as Indians.

Crawford had succeeded in raising the termination issue as a programmatic reality. Once the dissolution had been discussed in monetary terms, it would remain a hot political issue. The tribe had the finest stand of ponderosa pine on the west coast and was worth uncounted millions. Crawford gambled correctly that by inducing greed among a people unaccustomed to dealing with any large sums, he could have his way.

The demand for termination became so intense that Seldon Kirk, the highly respected chairman of the general council, tried to set up a committee to work for the preservation of the reservation. The committee was established, but it was very naive about the designs of both the Bureau of Indian Affairs, which had developed a hatred of the Klamaths, and of Wade Crawford, who was determined to destroy the tribe at his first opportunity. The committee felt that a better constitution would alleviate tribal dissatisfaction with conditions on the reservation and stop the pressure for liquidation.

Crawford cleverly blocked adoption of the constitution until 1950, when he was able to associate it with his voluntary withdrawal bill. Thus, the constitution was adopted, but instead of serving as an instrument of reform, as Seldon Kirk had envisioned, it became a stepping-stone to termination of the tribe. Crawford had now fought to terminate the tribe since 1927, and he was shortly to be allied with Watkins in dealing the fatal blow to his people. The original Crawford bill of 1945 continued to be introduced until 1953, when it was seen not as an attempt at vengeance by a spiteful tribal member but as an authentic call by an Indian tribe for rescue by a compassionate senator.

Suddenly, in 1953 an agreement was reached between Boyd Jackson and Wade Crawford on the creation of a tribal cooperative to handle the massive timber resources. For two long-standing enemies to appear as political allies advocating an apparently reasonable solution to the impasse was an event hardly credible in Klamath eyes. They rejected the proposal, figuring that something was rotten in the compromise. Jackson sincerely wanted to preserve the tribal lands and rights and felt that by coming halfway to meet Crawford a general settlement fair to all could be reached. Crawford saw it as the first breakthrough in the termination of the tribe. He zeroed in on the weakness and exploited the confusion of the people further.

In the closing days of the 1954 session of Congress the Bureau of Indian Affairs suddenly stepped in with a new proposal that appeared to satisfy the previous requirements of both factions. The Jackson forces were pressured to accept the draft, and it became Public Law 587 before anyone on the reservation knew what was happening.

Only later did the facts of the move come out. The Bureau of Indian Affairs had been secretly supporting Wade Crawford in his efforts to terminate his tribe. They helped him with travel money to get back and forth between the reservation and Washington. Every mention of the reservation was interpreted by the bureau officials through Crawford's ideology, and he was touted as the true representative of the tribe. Other tribal members, trying to prevent termination of tribal relations with the federal government, often found themselves without funds for travel or unaccountable lacking information on what was happening in the nation's capital.

Watkins was delighted with Wade Crawford, who exemplified everything that Watkins wanted to believe about Indians. The senator gave him sufficient performance time on the witness stand to make a record of strong protermination statements. Where the Menominees had been merely puzzled and betrayed by Watkins, the Klamaths were enthusiastically sold out by their own tribal member almost single-handedly, with Watkins simply conducting a performance thirty years in rehearsal.

The legislation was written without any indication that there might be complications. It simply provided that land and timber would be sold at the best possible prices to pay off those members who wished to withdraw from the tribe. The remaining tribal members would be placed in a trust to be managed by a bank in Oregon. This had not been anticipated in the discussions stemming from the original proposal in the late 1920's. No one had thought that they would be placed under a rigid trust operated by whites. Even those who supported withdrawal from the government envisioned some kind of cooperative venture by the people themselves.

The termination law required an appraisal of tribal assets and some indication of how much land would have to be sold to pay off the withdrawing members. The struggle to oppose termination had lasted from 1927 to 1954. It had been going on as long as most of the tribal members had been alive, and they were plainly exhausted contemplating it. Many families had been violently split between the various political camps. Relatives living off the reservation had become mortal enemies of people living on the reservation. No one wanted any more fighting, regardless of the rights and wrongs of the issue.

When the planning reports required by the law started to come in, it was apparent that Crawford had destroyed the last vestige of life in the Klamaths. Weary of the struggle and with no one they could trust to give them the correct facts, almost 70 percent of the tribe decided to withdraw and take their share of assets in cash. It then became apparent that Watkins had created a legislative monstrosity. The law simply called for sale of timber and lands to pay the remaining members but required that they receive maximum value consistent with state practices.

The state of Oregon, in hearings before Congress, rather shamefully admitted a number of things that had not previously been noticed. The state had received favorable publicity from its alleged model sustained-yield timber practices and was considered a leader in conservation law among the states. State officials and representatives in Congress had to admit that the state law, far from being a model, was a sham from start to finish and that the effect of the federal legislation when combined with state law would mean the clear-cutting of billions of board feet of timber.

State and local representatives rather tearfully told Watkins and Richard Neuberger, the senator from Oregon on the Interior Committee, that enforcement of the law would virtually destroy the timber industry in the area and drive the Klamath Falls region into a severe cycle of booms and busts that would be likely to cause the collapse of the local economy for years to come. Private groups alleged that they had not paid any attention to what had been happening among the Klamaths and that they now realized the extent of the disaster the Congress had authorized. From almost every quarter came cries for amendment of the legislation. All, that is, except Wade Crawford.

In the subsequent hearings in 1956, two years after the original bill had been passed, Crawford held out for full compliance with the original law, regardless of its impact on either state or federal governments. He knew he had won a bitter victory and feared that Congress would come to its senses about the whole thing if any amendments were allowed. Boyd Jackson and Jesse Kirk fought equally hard for amendments that would lessen the impact of the law on full-blooded members and older people who still did not understand what was happening to them. Elnathan Davis represented still another group that advocated no termination at all. Richard Neuberger might have been able to support this faction had not Watkins been always present to see that his pet project was not sidetracked.

The net result of the hearings was to amend the law to provide for the federal government to purchase the famous Klamath Marsh for the Fish and Wildlife Service and the remainder of the timberlands for the Winema National Forest. But the effort to reverse the trust that had been written into the termination law was a failure, and the Klamaths who chose to remain in the tribal entity became wards of an Oregon bank that regarded them as onerous increments to the land and not as people at all.

When the final decision was made as to tribal membership, it turned out that close to 78 percent of the tribe withdrew; took their share of the tribal estate, which amounted to nearly $43,500 per Indian; and virtually vanished, as the antiterminationists had predicted, from the face of the earth. The remaining Klamaths were to have their share of the property in lands, and the United States National Bank of Portland took over management of the property. Under the provisions of the law the trust could be abolished by a majority vote of the remaining members taken every five years after termination was final.

It is significant, at this point, to recount the state of the tribe immediately prior to termination. They had long since solved the problem of timber harvesting. Klamath timber, managed under a partial sustained-yield program by the Bureau of Indian Affairs, returned a payment of $800 per tribal member a year. The average family at Klamath had five people, and many families were not forced to hold a job when they were allowed to combine their timber per capita payments with the management of small farms and ranches and part-time seasonal work.

The educational achievement of the Klamaths was typical of Indian communities of the time, with an average school attendance of just over eight years per person. Of the approximately 1,050 adult Klamaths only a third were self-supporting, some 45 percent depended solely upon their per capita payments, and 22 percent had income supplemental to their timber payments. Over 800 minors held shares in the tribal estate, and their parents were allowed to determine whether or not they were to withdraw from the tribe. Many parents casually took their children's heritage away from them by indicating withdrawal.

Social problems of great magnitude came in the wake of termination. Young Klamath girls were quickly married to unscrupulous men, and their trust shares were rapidly dissipated. Klamaths who had never handled more than $800 before suddenly had thousands of dollars cash in hand. A famous story of the time relates how a Klamath appeared in a bar in Portland with his money in a papersack. He asked how much the bar cost, and when the bartender informed him that he had enough money, he handed over the sack and continued drinking, thinking that he had purchased the tavern. When he sobered up, they threw him out, pointing out that he had no paper indicating sale or purchase.

The contrast with the Menominees, before and after termination, is startling. The Menominees continued as a tribal entity, albeit a corporation turned over to an elite to operate. But the Menominees had always operated their sawmill to provide employment for tribal members. Thus, they had been able to soften the blow of termination. The Klamaths had always sold their timber to white sawmills in Klamath Falls and its vicinity, creating a tribal income but no employment for tribal members. Thus, Klamath termination almost immediately forced unemployment among those members who had lived on the per capita payments.

The United States National Bank turned out to be an extremely conservative trustee without any regard for the human aspects of its duty. The termination law provided a term of years before the tribal water rights would be forfeited, and as trustee, the bank simply neglected the whole water-rights issue thus crippling any chance of stability in any future development of the Klamath property. Over the years, the bank felt that its sole duty was to return audits and make payments to the remaining members without any acknowledgment of their social and other needs. It refused to keep white hunters off the remaining lands, and tribal members soon found themselves excluded from their own property during hunting season, as whites casually forced them from their lands. The bank rejected all efforts of the people to enforce its powers against intruding whites, thus cutting deeply at the Indian identity of the Klamaths.

The remaining members voted to continue the trust in 1964, when they were asked to vote on continuing it, but in 1969 abolition of the trust carried by a slight majority. Many Klamaths voted for the discontinuance of the trust in 1969 because they thought that by doing so the property would be turned over to them for management. They envisioned the formation of a corporation and true self-government after nearly a century of supervision by both government and private trustees.

Thus, it came as a surprise when the bank officials casually informed them that they had voted to liquidate their holdings. Confusion spread into panic. Some tribal members pointed out that the termination had not abolished the 1950 constitution, which required a certain number of Klamaths to vote in any general council meeting. Since only 474 Klamaths remained after termination, it was doubtful if any of the meetings of the past decade had actually been legal, let alone the two votes to abolish the trust. But no one seemed to know what the situation was.

Part of the problem in determining the validity of the tribal constitution was a result of the attitude of the remaining members. Many of them had not expressed their preference at the time of termination as to whether or not they intended to remain in the tribe. Thus no one ever knew the state of the Klamath tribe as a legal entity governed by a constitution because the membership only exerted itself sporadically. Of the remaining members whose property had been placed in trust with the United States National Bank, the majority simply did not return a ballot indicating their choice. Consequently it was ruled that no vote meant a desire to remain in the tribe. But did that constitute a real choice?

After the vote to abolish the trust a small group of Klamaths led by Elnathan Davis and Ed Chiloquin began to inquire into the possibility of taking their shares in land rather than having the lands all sold and the proceeds distributed. The bank panicked and sued the Klamaths, claiming that a question had been placed on the title of the lands the bank held. Consequently, turmoil erupted among the remaining members, who feared that

any questions would postpone distribution of the assets and result in further disruptions and unpleasantness in the community.

The action of the bank was rather curious and indicated that
something out of the ordinary may have been afoot. The bank,
although very conservative, had managed the timberlands so
that the Klamaths received over a ten-year period something in
excess of $50,000 and, upon liquidation, would receive in the
neighborhood of $110,000 per member. By merely holding out
for a decade the tribal members had in effect tripled their returns from the tribal forest. But the bank had figured distribution at the then-current depressed market price for timber. If
the distribution had been computed at the high price for the
timber during the three previous years, the per capita figure
would have been something in the neighborhood of $150,000 or
higher.

At this point complicated points previously neglected began to
be raised. The lands had become subject to federal taxes after
termination, and so, there was the matter of state and federal
taxes on the lands when they were sold. The federal tax would
be a capital-gains tax, but everyone who had tried to figure the
actual amount of net income from the sale had used a different
basis for figuring the original cost of the forest on a tax basis.

The argument on a purely fiscal basis of those members who
wanted to take their share of the distribution in land was sound.
If the lands were transferred to them, there would be no federal
tax since there would be no capital gain, only a distribution in
kind. On the other hand, if they merely received cash payments
with the right to meet the high bid, they would have to pay taxes
on the cash and have a greatly reduced sum to use for the repurchase of lands.

The conflict has grown extremely bitter on a number of fronts.
Many Klamaths are simply so tired of intratribal conflict that
they no longer care what happens so long as they do not have to
hear about it anymore. Others look enviously at the other tribes
in Oregon, which have created sparkling new projects under the
antipoverty program and have taken a major step in achieving
the self-government that the Klamaths wanted nearly a century
ago. The antiliquidation Klamaths point out the new resort
development at Warm Springs, the reservation to the north, and

encourage the protermination members to consider corporate development by all remaining members on their own terms.

In many other cases, the banks have appeared to have exerted too much influence in determining the fate of tribal property and lives. But the United States National Bank, while passively responsive to the needs of the remaining Klamaths, cannot be said to be maliciously using its trust capacity to harm the tribe. It may be morally wrong in its attitude toward the tribe, but it appears as possibly as great a victim of the termination act as do the Klamaths.

The Klamath movement has been gaining steam gradually. The Native American Rights Fund, a Ford Foundation-funded project in the field of Indian law, has offered to work with the remaining Klamaths to find a solution to the problem. It has been exploring the possibility of forming a management corporation for development of the lands of those who wish to remain in a communal relationship. The success of this venture, of course, is whether or not the bank will allow tribal members to take their share in land. At this writing the bank has not relented on its desire to liquidate the land and distribute in cash.

The Committee to Save the Remaining Klamath Lands has been formed and has continually petitioned the White House to allow government purchase of the remaining lands at approximately $55 million. The authority for doing so still exists under the old termination law: the government would be holding the lands until the social and political problems of the Klamaths can be resolved and a true indication of the desires of the people can be ascertained. It can be truly said that at no time before and after termination have the Klamath people ever been told what they were voting on and what its effect would be. We feel that the government owes at least this opportunity to a people who have been victimized by government and led astray by a Judas within their own ranks.

The remaining Klamaths own some 144,000 acres of prime timber and ranch lands. Even today after surviving the disaster of having some 78 percent of their members and assets taken away from them, they stand as the fifth richest Indian tribe in the United States. With their present assets they could purchase the lands of all of the tribes in South Dakota or New Mexico. Only some 500 Klamaths remain in the tribe today. They will surely fade away into poverty and despair if the bank is allowed to liquidate their holdings. No one can account for the 78 percent of the members who withdrew in 1959. They have simply vanished into a historical limbo.

We strongly urge that the federal government take immediate action to save the remaining Klamath lands for the present tribal group—that it refederalize the tribe as it is now constituted and that it make the tribe once again eligible for loan funds and economic development grants. After the economic situation is stabilized and the tribe has a chance to explore all alternatives, a gradual withdrawal program could be initiated that would allow those Klamaths who wish to remain to buy out the people who wish to finally sever their tribal relationships.

Today some 100 Indian tribes are smaller in membership than the Klamaths, and all of them have substantially less in assets than do the remaining members of the Klamaths. To sit by and watch the final destruction of this tribe would be the most unconscionable sin the government and the American public could commit.

We recommend that the remaining 144,000 acres of tribal lands be assured the tribe and that the remaining Klamaths be once again given treaty rights as federally recognized Indians. The 144,000 acres makes up a vital part of the 100 million acres of stabilized Indian lands.

Tribal lands	39,663,412.09
Individual Indian allotments	10,697,621.58
Alaska native lands	40,000,000
Occupied Indian lands	4,723,017.2
Submarginal lands restored	344,811
Flathead lands restored	10,585.86
Warm Springs lands restored	61,300
Crow lands restored	618
Menominee lands restored	230,000
Klamath lands restored	144,000
	95,875,365.73

✤ 11 ✤

A Beleaguered Little Band: The Nisquallys of Washington State

THE INCLINATION of the federal government, particularly of the departments of Justice and Interior, has been to protect Indian rights in direct proportion to the tribe's ability to protect its own rights. That is to say, if a tribe is large and powerful, the officials in the Interior Department will spend a great deal of time flattering tribal council members, will schedule the tribe for new programs, and will accommodate tribal politicians in their schemes. By allowing the largest and richest tribes to become the subject of pilot projects that America sees, the Bureau of Indian Affairs very cleverly submerges those instances in which it has refused to carry out its task of assisting Indians.

The Justice Department is similarly inclined. Tribes that have funds sufficient to hire capable legal counsel usually discover that the department has no objections to their proposed actions. Jursidictional problems are rapidly sorted out; treaty rights are carefully affirmed. Small tribes without money for legal services are treated as if they have committed an unpardonable sin in surviving. At the present time a valiant little group of Indians in western Washington is driving both departments crazy. They not only refuse to die, they claim to have rights to fish in their traditional fishing sites according to their treaty. And they have single-handedly forced the Justice and Interior departments to modify their flippant attitude toward Indians. This is their story.

We have encountered Isaac Stevens before in our tour of Indian history. His ambitions to forge a political career in the newly settled Northwest shaped his attitudes toward the Indian tribes of the area. In the mountain regions the large tribes such as the Flathead, the Umatilla, the Yakima, and the Warm Springs bands fought Stevens to a draw, and their very numbers forced the government to deal with them in a respectful manner until quite late in the nineteenth century.

The first treaties that Stevens signed in the Northwest, however, afforded him practice in his tedious task of bringing the Yakimas and Flatheads to bay by negotiating with the many small fishing villages in the Puget Sound area of what is now Washington State. In a series of treaties—Medicine Creek, Point Elliott, Point No Point, Makah, and Quinault—Stevens got the tribes of the western slope of the Cascades to cede him millions of acres of land for a mere pittance. The tribes were gathered at selected points along the inland waters of western Washington and induced to cede their lands to Stevens for the guarantee of reservations and the right to continue to hunt and fish in their traditional grounds and stations.

And why not, the tribes asked themselves? The whole concept of land ownership was unimportant to them. They had large prairies in which they pastured their horses, and the treaties guaranteed them the right to continue to do so. They also dug camas roots in the open spaces in the vast rain forest; the treaty guaranteed them the right to dig for roots and gather berries. But outside of the use of land in this manner the tribes were almost wholly unconcerned with land itself. They were fishermen and whalers. They were totally dependent upon the annual runs of salmon and steelhead trout. They ventured far into the ocean and up the coast of what is now British Columbia for whales and seals. The treaty guaranteed that they could continue to do so. Why, then, worry about land?

The problem, of course, was that the United States government had little understanding of Indian fishing as an economic and cultural unity. It considered that when the Indians saw the benefits of raising potatoes, they would stop fishing. The Indians immediately saw through the whole prospect of becoming farmers. The treaty signers refused to touch the pen until they were assured that they could continue fishing at all usual and accustomed places, that they could construct houses for curing their fish, and that they could continue the rather rigorous trade in fish that they had developed with the few settlers who had moved into Washington Territory prior to the treaties of cession.

Isaac Stevens took an optimistic view of the continued Indian trade in fish. He remarked that he was looking forward to the continuance of Indian fishing, because the Indians provided the settlers with food and would provide an important industry in the state that he envisioned arising from Washington Territory. Stevens therefore included in each of the treaties of the western Cascade area a special article in which the rights of Indians to continue as fishermen and whalers were spelled out.

The Nisqually Indian Reservation was authorized to be established by the Treaty of Medicine Creek in 1854. It was the first treaty with the Indians in Washington Territory and became a model for other treaties negotiated later with other tribes that Stevens would meet. The treaty provided that the Indians would cede and relinquish all their rights and claims and title to the territory held, used, or occupied by them. In its second major provision, however, it provided that certain reservations of land would be established for the several tribes that signed the treaty for their "exclusive use." Its third major provision was the preservation of fishing rights in all customary waters.

The sixth article of the Medicine Creek Treaty authorized the president of the United States to move the Indians from reserved lands to other areas or to consolidate the various bands of Indians on larger reservations if the need should arise. It incorporated the provisions of the Omaha Treaty of 1854 to govern the use of Indian lands and to govern the Indians' relationship with any state that might be formed in the newly created Washington Territory and that the treaty anticipated would be established.

The treaty designated an area of 1,280 acres to be set aside for the Nisqually Indians in the area of forested cliffs along the bayshore about two miles west of the mouth of the small Nisqually River, which ran from the Cascades into Puget Sound. The reserve was clearly away from the traditional fishing sites of the tribe, but the treaty provided for the protection of the fishing rights, and so, there appeared to be no conflict between the two provisions.

The federal government, however, failed to establish the reservation as provided by the treaty, which called for settlement upon the land so designated within a year's time of ratification of the treaty. Instead, the various bands of Indian fishermen were gathered from all over the Puget Sound area and resettled upon Fox Island in the Tacoma Narrows. A number of Indians, including Leschi, a leader of the Nisqually River area, resisted the government's breach of its treaty promise. They were dissatisfied with the selection of reservations made in the treaty and demanded that new reserves be set apart in the locations of their traditional homelands.

The government refused to abide by the treaty and refused to offer an alternative site acceptable to Leschi and other Indians. The result was that the Nisqually refused to move to Fox Island and the Leschi War of 1855–1856 ensued when the settlers aggravated the situation, forcing the Indians to fight for their lives.

The war ended tragically with the hanging of Leschi as a criminal under a modified form of legal lynching. Federal authorities, having been party to bloodshed, were moved to respond to the troubles in Washington Territory. On January 20, 1857, the president set aside lands and established a reservation as provided for in the Treaty of 1854 at Medicine Creek. In an executive order the president exercised his authority, under the sixth article of the treaty, to relocate the Nisqually Reservation from its previously designated site to the grassy meadow and forest areas along the Nisqually River in the general location once occupied by Leschi's band and their herds of horses.

A welcome gesture, but too late. Within a month Leschi was hanged at Fort Steilacoom as a murderer because of public outrage and agitation at his part in forcing the government to abide by its treaty. As much indignation was voiced toward Leschi's pyrrhic victory as toward his actual deeds against the settlers. The reservation remained intact until 1884, when it was divided into thirty family allotments under the Omaha treaty formula. The original reservation had contained 4,717.28 acres; this was divided into eighty-two different deeds for lands of varying sizes, which were given to the eighty-two Nisquallys living on the land.

The Nisqually families lived in relative peace and security for several decades after allotments were made. The Nisqually River continued to attract large runs of salmon, for which the Indians continued to fish. The transition from the old ways of life to new ways could probably only be detected by fence posts casually marking family gardens. Fishing remained the primary occupation, and fish continued to be the major food supply for the families gathered along the river.

As late as 1920, the Nisqually Indian families were found to be consuming annually as many as 500 salmon each. By curing their catch the people were able to maintain their traditional ways of life long after the nature of the territory had changed economically. A long-time Indian agency superintendent noted that government rations had never been supplied to the Nisqually Indians since "the Puget Sound Indian is self-supporting, because he is a fisherman."

Under virtually ideal conditions it was almost predictable that the United States government would do something to disrupt the Nisquallys. In the winter of 1917 the United States Army simply moved onto the lands of the Nisqually. The fact that it was an outrageous trespass upon the Indians never occurred to the soldiers. The army felt that it needed the land to train soldiers, and since it needed the land, it thought the quickest thing to do so was simply take it.

Indian families were summarily ordered to leave their homes and not return until advised of permission to do so. It was winter and cold and rainy, but some of the families were loaded on wagons with whatever household goods they could carry and transported to other parts of the Nisqually River valley and dumped. They were supposed to find shelter among the trees and cliffs along the river. Makeshift shelters kept them alive during the remainder of the winter. No one understood what had happened, but all realized that something had gone wrong with the vaunted American system of justice.

The tribe bitterly complained to the commissioner of Indian affairs, asking him to find out why they had been moved from their lands in the dead of winter. The findings of the commissioner of Indian affairs are rather enlightening. In December, nearly nine months after the forced removal, the commissioner sent a lame explanation to the local agency superintendent:

An investigation of the grounds in company with General Burr showed that the safety of the Indians during the hours of target practice would require the removal of the Indians from both the upland and the river bottom, to avoid ricocheting shells; that is, the entire reservation would have to be abandoned during those hours.

The General was advised as to the question of leasing the lands through the regular channel, which he has probably done.

The military requirements will undoubtedly force the War Department to make a demand for the permanent acquisition of the entire reservation. This as you are aware, will cause violent opposition on the part of the Indians; and, in view of the treaty relations, it will be impossible for them to entertain the idea unless adequate homes are provided for the Indians elsewhere, which should be done, if the lands are condemned, for military purposes.

The army had casually attached the Nisqually Reservation to the Fort Lewis army post without even informing the commissioner of Indian affairs!

A series of letters that ensued between the secretary of the interior and the secretary of war in the first three months of 1918 attempted to add some legalistic frills to what had been a naked power play and a blatant and unconstitutional act by the army. The secretary of the interior attempted to formulate an agreement for leasing or purchasing the reservation. The requirements of the Treaty of Medicine Creek were repeatedly stated and discussed during the negotiations.

The secretary of the army had a very weird idea of law. He initially advanced the idea that the lands could be obtained by condemnation proceedings being conducted by the local authorities of Pierce County. The reasoning he used was apparently novel in the extreme, because for county courts to hand over federal lands to the federal government would be a radical revision of the Constitution in procedural matters alone.

However, Interior Secretary Franklin K. Lane recommended that the matter be handled through the regular federal departments of War and Interior. He could not, apparently, subscribe to local governments as the real estate branch of the United States government. On February 23, 1918, nearly a year after the Nisquallys were driven from their lands, he wrote to the secretary of war: "I am still of the opinion that it would be unwise to obtain these lands by condemnation proceedings, and evict the Indians therefrom, who would no doubt object strongly to removing from their homes." No doubt.

On March 12, 1918, Secretary of the Interior Lane requested some immediate action from the attorney general of the United States to protect the interests of the Nisqually Indians, informing him that when the commanding officer at Camp Lewis had issued orders to restrain the trespasses of soldiers on the Nisqually Indian Reservation, a Colonel Ehrenbreck of the Army Engineers had retaliated by ordering the chairman of the Condemnation Board for Pierce County, Washington, to undertake condemnation proceedings. Ehrenbreck had demanded immediate possession of the reservation, and Pierce County had been happy to comply.

A few days later the attorney general responded positively to the interior secretary's request. He informed him that the United States attorney for the western district of Washington had been instructed by telegraph to "appear for said Indians and to fully protect their interests in the matter." The War Department quickly learned that it had run afoul of another bureaucracy and a couple of days later, on March 18, the acting secretary of war hastily accepted the interior secretary's "suggestion that the matter be handled by representatives of the two Departments concerned."

Secretary Lane telegraphed instructions to Agency Superintendent Hammond on March 25, 1918, informing him who the army's designated representative would be. He also directed him to arrange for the immediate withdrawal of the condemnation proceedings by the army and its ally, Pierce County, and to make arrangements for lease agreements that would be satisfactory to the Nisquallys. In a letter of response, Superintendent Hammond wrote that the county and local military authorities remained adamant that the Indian lands be condemned. He offered the surprising information that "I then consulted the District Attorney who advised me that it would be impossible to do anything with the case unless the Department of the Interior could place in his hands *before* April 19th, a statement from the War Department that they would purchase the lands."

But all was not calm in the state of Washington. A few days

later the governor, Ernest Lister, expressed his belief that the special state legislation that authorized Pierce County's condemnation proceedings did not anticipate nor provide for actions against the Nisqually lands. He strongly urged that the federal departments resolve the issue among themselves and advised them to provide the Nisquallys with land to replace any taken away from them for the Camp Lewis target area. He apparently did not want the state mixed up in the confusion over federal property.

The governor's benign intervention was rudely repulsed by the army and Pierce County, and they continued the condemnation proceedings. In the middle of April they forced the commissioner of Indian affairs to relinquish his defense of the Nisquallys. He proposed a compromise that was, in effect, a betrayal of the tribe:

In view of urgent need by War Department of Indian lands Nisqually Reservation you are hereby authorized to accept compromise offer seventy-five thousand eight hundred forty dollars. If this amount not sufficient to purchase other lands for Indians and equip them equal to their present holdings, Congress will be requested to supplement the amount of the compromise with a gratuity appropriation.

By telegram the commissioner had committed members of Congress to an appropriation to cover up an illegal theft of Indian lands by another government agency.

The United States attorney for western Washington was baffled at the change. Assistant United States Attorney G. P. Fishburne, who had earlier been instructed to represent the Nisquallys and "fully protect their interests in the matter," advised the attorney general of the United States of the outcome of the proceedings:

We settled for the Indian Reservation land today. This case was beset with many difficulties. The County strenuously opposed the Government leasing or purchasing this land. They had acquired, by condemnation, 33,000 acres of land and given it to the government. They had had hardly appreciable raises over their valuations. They maintained that if the Government, itself, purchased this land from the Indians and gave them a fancy figure for the land, it would absolutely ruin the County in the condemnation of the other 27,000 acres of land to be used for the Cantonment, and that the Government seemed to be trying to defeat the work of its gratuitous agent. I was of the opinion that, so long as the interests of the Indians did not suffer we should assist the County, which was really acting as the agent of the War Department.

But Fishburne realized that while the best interests of the Indians might be glossed over, he had better make some effort to appear a concerned federal official. He concluded by mentioning that

I am, today, filing with the Court, a claim for the money on behalf of the Indian Agent. We are taking the position that he is the trustee of the Indians, and is entitled to this money. I understand he will take steps to purchase these Indians homes elsewhere.

The $75,840 was not paid to the Indian agent, however, but was sent to the secretary of the treasury of the United States under the terms of a "Modified Order Awarding Proceeds of Indian Lands," filed by Pierce County Superior Court Judge W. O. Chapman. The court insisted that Superintendent Hammond furnish an equivalent cash bond to satisfy it that he could be trusted with Nisqually funds. After all, the federal government had not fulfilled its trusteeship for the Nisquallys when it gave in to the Pierce County court. This was an indication that it probably would not exercise any powers to preserve the Indians' money for their benefit. The county thus used its collaboration with the government to confiscate the Indian lands as the basis for denying the government the custody of the funds.

Superintendent Hammond, while not trustworthy enough to be given the Indian money, was yet able to be trusted to remove the remaining Indians from their lands. He advised the commissioner of Indian affairs on May 14, 1918,

Acting on the request of the Judge Advocate, the Nisqually Indians were removed from that part of the reservation which was condemned, within the two week limit set by the Judge Advocate.
The majority of the Indians preferred to move to the left bank of the Nisqually river, but five of the twelve families preferred homes elsewhere.
As the Commissioner is undoubtedly aware it is imperative that their homes be purchased for them without delay.

The judge advocate, Major George V. Strong, had been the person designated by the War Department to act with the Interior Department and United States Attorney Fishburne to arrange for the withdrawal of condemnation proceedings and the completion of a long-term lease on the Indian lands. Instead, he had conspired with Pierce County officials, shut out the interior officials completely, and expedited the condemnation proceedings of approximately 3,300 acres of Nisqually lands located in Pierce County. He concluded his impartial role in the matter by loudly demanding the immediate removal of the Nisquallys.

The Interior Department, somewhat shaken at the turn of events, began immediately to secure "lieu lands" for the dispossessed Nisqually Indians. The sixth article of the Treaty of Medicine Creek gave it ample authority to secure allotments for individual families or even to set aside additional reservation lands for the whole group. But few lands were found to be available in close proximity to the remnants of the Nisqually Indian Reservation in Thurston County, directly south of the Nisqually River and Pierce County. Lands were secured at locations as far removed as the Quinault reservation on the Pacific coast of the state, some 200 miles further west, and on the Lummi reservation in the extreme north of the state near the Canadian border. Other pieces of land were purchased on the Puyallup, Skokomish, and Chehalis reservations, and the displaced families were distributed to the new tracts of land.

In effect, the government, conspiring with state and local authorities, had not only deprived the Nisquallys of their lands but had deliberately scattered the Indian community, making cultural cohesiveness very difficult and political identity virtually impossible. A community had been ruthlessly destroyed for no good reason. The lands that Leschi had died to get for his people were casually distributed to the army officers at Camp Lewis as a backstop for their target practice. Some of the lands taken were never used by the army at all. It simply wanted breathing room where officers could camp and fish in their off-duty hours.

The loss of the Nisqually lands did not escape the attention of the men in Congress, however, and on June 30, 1919, the war fever having subsided, Congress directed the secretary of war and the secretary of the interior to report to them on the Nisqually removal. They were directed

immediately to investigate, and to report to Congress at its next session, the advisability and necessity of acquiring with a view to returning to the dispossessed Indians, from the authorities of Pierce County,

Washington, those several tracts of allotted Nisqually Indian lands, Nisqually Reservation, Washington.

The personnel had changed somewhat in the two departments, and the report submitted to Congress was exhaustive in its analysis of the incident. It was published as *Senate Document Number 243, Vol. 15, Senate Documents, Misc. 2, 66th Congress, Second Session* (1919–1920) (*March 2, 1920*). Several thousand documents, including exhibits, maps, and the correspondence involving the roles of the two departments, were sifted to compile the report. The data would have appeared to justify restoration to the Indians of the lands taken by the army during the frantic war years.

In spite of the overwhelming evidence in favor of the Nisquallys, the joint departmental recommendations to Congress advised that it was neither "necessary nor advisable to attempt to acquire the lands in question and return the Indians to their former homes." The report rationalized that inasmuch as "that in the cases where lieu lands had not been actually purchased, owing to delays caused in part by the Indians themselves, proper steps had been taken to acquire the same," and further, "when the improvements planned are completed the dispossessed Nisquallys will be comfortably located in their new homes."

It had been somewhat over two years since the Nisquallys had been rudely driven from their new homes, and yet the Interior Department was still in the process of helping the dispossessed Nisquallys to locate homes. An indication that problems still existed was clear, however, since the report did recommend that Congress act immediately to provide the Nisqually Indians with a supplemental appropriation of $85,000 for their benefit in recovery of losses sustained by them as a result of the condemnations.

The rationale for additional supplemental appropriations was provided by Special Supervisor C. L. Ellis, who had been assigned the responsibility of conducting the investigations and producing the report. His reasoning is quoted at length:

Before the Indian war of 1855 these Indians cultivated fields on what was afterwards set aside as their reservation. Their title, however, was clouded by the claim of the Agricultural Company until 1870, when the company surrendered its claim under provisions of a treaty between the United States and Great Britain.

Many earlier settlers claim that the unjust treaty of 1854 caused the Indians to go on the warpath because it deprived them of their homes and fields. In consideration of the cession of 2,000,000 acres, the Nisquallys were given only two sections of high, stony land covered with dense timber, where it was impossible for them to live and farm and where they never did live.

Realizing the injustice done by the treaty their present reservation of 4,717 acres was set aside for the Nisqually Indians in 1856 by Governor I. I. Stevens, and there they lived undisturbed and supported themselves from their live stock, farms, and fish from their river for over 60 years. Then the ambition of Tacoma to acquire one of the big Army posts, and the war necessity, caused Pierce County, Washington, in April, 1918, to condemn the best two-thirds of the Nisqually Reservation, being the part east of the Nisqually [river] where most of the Nisqually homes were. The Indians were scattered to seek homes elsewhere. Such is the fate of the little band whose fathers fought against an unjust treaty to make secure their homes.

It was not simply that the Nisquallys had lost their homes but that the whole incident had been rigged against them without the slightest indication that they had any protections under the law and treaties of the country. The report submitted by Ellis was particularly critical of the role played by Assistant United States Attorney G. P. Fishburne in the condemnation action. With information now available on the attitudes and actions taken by all parties of the government and state, Ellis was able to conclude with respect to the actions of Fishburne,

It has been suggested that the United States attorney's office would have been in a delicate position had it contested the inadequate award to the Indians; that that office's vigorous presentation of the Indians' suit to secure a fair award would have aroused charges in the press and elsewhere that the United States attorney was opposing the war and would thus encourage the dangerous element (all too numerous) into believing that disloyal acts would be treated leniently. I do not think that this idea prevailed in the least.

Necessarily the sentiments and interests of the county and the Army were mutual in this matter—both were very anxious to get 70,000 acres for the cantonment, and quickly. Fishburne's clients were the Indians, and if he leaned at all it should have been in their behalf. It is my opinion that a vigorous and thorough businesslike preparation of the case by an aggressive attorney of wide experience would have produced a different result for the Indians, and that they would have secured about the figure set by the Indian board appraisers. From the tone of his report one would think he held a brief for the Army, and not for the Indians, whose board of appraisers he belittles.

It was clear that the basic move against the Indian lands was one of simple confiscation by the whites in Tacoma. Indian lands had been taken by the United States for a number of purposes. Dams and highways had been run through Indian lands, railroads had been given reservation rights of way, and army posts had been created in reservation areas. This was the only case in which the federal government did not pass legislation and take the lands itself but allowed a county court to condemn the lands under state law and then transfer the lands to the federal government. In examining the deed on conveyance of the condemned Nisqually lands to the United States and the War Department, the reason for the action became clear. Pierce County had inserted a reversionary interest clause stating:

Subject, however, to the express condition that if the United States should ever cease to maintain the tract above described for the uses above named, *title to the lands above described will revert to said Pierce County without further act by it to be performed.* (Emphasis added.)

In other words the whole transaction had been simply to secure the lands for the establishment of an army post but with the idea that should the army ever leave or abandon its activities, the county would reap a rich harvest.

Special Supervisor Ellis was very concerned about a denial to the original Indian landowners of legitimate reversionary rights to the lands taken. He secured a legal opinion confirming his belief that "the reversionary clause in favor of Pierce County would not hold, but that the lands would revert to the original owners." He insisted that the Interior Department "keep informed of the progress of this Camp Lewis deed, so that in the event Congress refuses to accept the gift or establish a permanent post or cuts down materially in acreage the Indians can be properly represented and claim made for their reversionary interests in their condemned lands."

In summarizing the contents of the report for Congress, the departments of War and Interior concluded that the Indians had acted in extreme good faith in view of the circumstances and that only the conditions of fanaticism invoked by the war had caused the unusual procedures for taking the lands. It supported the special appropriation by Congress for the Nisquallys. The bill dragged on in Congress, but finally, on April 28, 1924, an appropriation for the benefit of the Nisquallys was authorized.

This unlawful destruction of the Nisqually Indian Reservation had an impact far beyond the simple loss of land, however, since the net result was to throw into some confusion the political status of the tribe. The officials of the state of Washington began to take the position that the tribe had been dissolved when the reservation was taken and that any treaty rights that the tribal members might have had prior to the loss of their lands had been extinguished with the taking of the lands. This curious doctrine coincided with the rise of state exercise of its police powers over the fish and game of the rivers of the state. It was totally without precedent in federal Indian law and directly contrary to the Constitution of the United States and a large number of Supreme Court decisions regarding the political existence of Indian tribes.

It comforted the quasi-educated state officials in the fish and game departments, however, and their desire was to expand their powers over all Indian lands within the state, thus achieving a virtual monopoly over the gigantic fish resource. The two departments existed because of a quirk in state law that categorized the various species of fish as either commercial or game fish. The posture of the state, as later fully developed, indicated that it would partially respect Indian fishing rights with respect to commercial fish, since most commercial fishing was done by large boats off the coast and the Indians were restricted to their traditional fishing sites. Thus, they would not be able to participate in commercial fishing to any significant degree. But with respect to fish classified as game the game department steadfastly refused to recognize any outstanding treaty rights because the game fish traveled in the inland waters, which the department intended for its large population of sports fishermen.

Following the assignment of in lieu allotments to the members of the Nisqually tribe, which according to law existed as lands with the same status as the original treaty lands, the state of Washington began a systematic campaign to prevent the Indians from exercising their treaty rights. Where the Nisquallys had been self-supporting and had maintained themselves by farming and fishing, they were now reduced to near starvation. The new allotments were so small as to preclude farming, and the shores of the Nisqually River were patrolled by game wardens to arrest any Indian who dared to fish.

Many tribal members grew discouraged and gave up the unequal struggle against the state officials. Fishing rights at usual and accustomed grounds and stations were attacked perennially by the fish and game departments, while the state revenue agency mounted its challenge against Indian tax immunities provided for in the Treaty of Medicine Creek. The struggle finally focused on a 6-acre tract of land situated on the Nisqually River a couple of miles below the remaining reduced Nisqually Indian Reservation. The property, commonly called Frank's Landing, had been purchased by the United States for Willie Frank in 1919 in lieu of the 205-acre allotment of the Frank family, which had been condemned in 1918.

For the last two decades the state of Washington has waged a continuous war against the people living at Frank's Landing. Numerous Indian fishermen have been cited and arrested for alleged violations of state fish and game statutes and regulations. Many of the Indians have been arrested many times without being once convicted. On occasion, as many as a hundred state police officers have overrun the property, making arrests and confiscating personal property and fishing gear. The average population of the landing is about twenty, four young adult men and the remainder women, children, and elderly Indians, including ninety-year-old Willie Frank, who continues to live on his land.

The Nisquallys at Frank's Landing fought back vigorously but with little effect. Federal officials frequently misled the state police and game wardens, with the net result that some of the attacks on the Indians occurred on federal property, over which the state has no jurisdiction. Finally, after much grief and the loss of one of the leading proponents of Indian treaty rights, Valerie Bridges, Willie Frank's granddaughter, the state lost an important point in its fight to deny the Indians their legal rights. Al Bridges, Valerie's father, was acquitted of criminal charges in connection with fishing, and Frank's Landing was ruled to be treaty-protected Indian property.

In the evidence submitted to the court, Hank Adams, the executive director of the Survival of American Indians, the organization created to protect fishing rights, introduced an excerpt from Governor I. I. Steven's letter to the federal officials in Washington, D.C., that spelled out the governor's intention in setting aside fishing rights as a federally protected right of the Nisquallys:

They catch most of our fish, supplying not only our people with clams and oysters but salmon to those who cure and export it. Their principal food is fish and roots and berries. The provisions as to reserves and as to taking fish, pasturing animals and gathering roots and berries had strict reference to their conditions as above, to their actual wants and to the part they play and ought to play in the labor and prosperity of the territory. It may be here observed that their mode of taking fish differs so essentially from that of the whites that it will not interfere with the latter.

Several years ago, the United States Army Corps of Engineers constructed a river development project on the northern bank of the Nisqually River about a thousand yards upstream from Frank's Landing. They reinforced the banks of the river so that the main current would curve sharply above the Indian property and head directly for Frank's Landing. In the spring of 1972 a sudden melt of snow combined with unusual rainfall to produce a raging Nisqually River, which cut away almost four of the six acres of the little allotment. The Indian homes were nearly washed away and college students from nearby state colleges worked as volunteers for a whole weekend without rest to prevent the total destruction of the landing.

Today, the little group at Frank's Landing is barely holding out against the river as it continually chips away the small part remaining of their in lieu allotment. Directly adjoining the Indian allotment is a much larger piece of land that, strangely enough, belongs to the Army. It was taken from the Indians in the event that if the need arose during another war to teach soldiers to build bridges, it would be available. It has been owned by the Army since 1917 and never through two world wars has the need arisen to teach soldiers to build bridges. But you never can tell.

Farther on down the river toward Puget Sound at an ideal place on the mouth of the Nisqually delta, a 1,300-acre farm is for sale. The Nisquallys have been asking the government to purchase it for them as a reservation under the authority granted the United States in the sixth article of the Treaty of

Medicine Creek. The farm would adjoin traditional fishing sites of the tribe and thus place all of the Nisqually fishing rights within a distinct geographical area, muting the continual harping of the state game wardens that the Indians are allowed to fish only in reservation land areas. Such a purchase would amount to a special appropriation of some $1.3 million dollars.

We would urge in the strongest terms possible that the United States make this special purchase and establish the farm as an additional tract of Nisqually tribal lands. We would also advocate that the Army cede to the Nisqually the small tract adjoining the present site of Frank's Landing and that, since it no longer has a great fear that the Indians will be harmed by its target practice across the river, it cede a strip of land extending 400 yards along the northern shore of the river for a length of 2 miles, to place the Nisqually River wholly within the Nisqually Indian Reservation as originally intended by the treaty. In these two moves the United States could regain some of the honor it has lost, make tangible amends to the Nisquallys, and clarify for the state of Washington for all time the nature of the Nisqually treaty right to fish. With this action the Indians could become self-supporting once again.

This land, restored to the Nisqually Indians of Washington, would mean a return of 1,375 acres to be added to the stabilized Indian land base. It would, in our opinion, be one of the most significant moves in the history of red-white relations.

Tribal lands	39,663,412.09
Individual Indian allotments	10,697,621.58
Alaska native lands	40,000,000
Occupied Indian lands	4,723,017.2
Submarginal lands restored	344,811
Flathead lands restored	10,585.86
Warm Springs lands restored	61,300
Crow lands restored	618
Menominee lands restored	230,000
Klamath lands restored	144,000
Nisqually lands purchased	1,375
	95,876,740.73

Those Whom Even Time Forgot

I N 1959 the Power Authority of New York State had a problem. It had big plans for expanding its Niagara facilities to increase its power output, but a tiny band of Indians stood in its way. The state needed 1,300 acres of land belonging to the Tuscarora Nation of Indians, a member of the Iroquois League. Its attempt to condemn the lands resulted in a lawsuit, the tribe charging that the state had no basis for breaking a federal treaty.

The case bounced back and forth in the federal courts, as the doctrines of law were twisted to prepare the way for an eventual Indian defeat. In order for the state to win, it was necessary to show that it had a license directly from Congress to break the treaty. In the course of the decision, however, the following doctrine, originally articulated in *United States* v. *Canderlaria,* was affirmed as primary law governing Indian tribes:

Not only does the Constitution expressly authorize Congress to regulate commerce with Indian tribes, but long-continued legislative and executive usage and an unbroken current of judicial decisions have attributed to the United States as a superior and civilized nation the power and the duty of exercising a fostering care and protection over all dependent Indian communities within its borders, whether within its original territory or territory subsequently acquired, and whether within or without the limits of state. . . . It is for that body [Congress], and not for the courts, to determine when the true interests of the Indian require his release from such condition of tutelage.

The doctrine sounds noble and uplifting, an example to the other nations of the world. In reality it has rarely been used to assist the "dependent" Indian communities within the United States. More often it is used as a means of taking land from tribes that the United States abandoned earlier but which have lands that the government suddenly needs. A consistent use of this doctrine would force the federal government into admissions concerning its historical treatment of Indian tribes that it would not like to make. Therefore, few people ever mention this total responsibility, for fear that the liability of the United States might be established in a new area—the unrecognized tribes. No conception of federal responsibility to American Indians, and certainly no solution to the problems of Indians, can be adequately understood without mentioning those tribes that history and the federal government have forgotten.

Western expansion pushed rapidly into the interior in the decades following the revolutionary war. The Ohio Valley was the scene of bitter conflict between whites and Indians until after the War of 1812. By the conclusion of that war, it was evident that Great Britain had plans to abandon its Indian allies within the drainage of the Mississippi-Ohio complex and consolidate its Canadian possessions. A series of treaties beginning in 1817 and ending in 1834 swept the Ohio Valley free of Indians and pushed the Five Civilized Tribes out of the deep South.

The tide of settlement continued on into the Great Plains, Rocky Mountains, Pacific coast, and Southwest. In many places, tribes with sufficient ability to wage war fought back, creating the legends of the settlement of the West. In other regions, tribes allied with the United States against their traditional enemies and helped to defeat the still independent tribes. Members of a number of small tribes in the Southwest, for example, signed up as Indian scouts to help the Army track and capture the Apache war heroes, such as Victorio, Geromino, and Cochise.

When the reservations were set up, tribes were gathered and held in various states according to their ability to threaten the United States with further warfare. The tribes fishing on the Puget Sound, for example, were gathered at a couple of small reservations, where the government made desperate attempts to change them into farmers. In the Southwest, the various Apache bands were gathered at the San Carlos Reservation and the western Arizona tribes were collected at what is now the Colorado River Reservation. In Wyoming, a tribe of Northern Arapaho were hustled onto the reservation of the Shoshone and kept there. In all, reservations were set up haphazardly and without concern as to which tribes actually owned what lands. If a tribe was strong enough to cause trouble, it was forced onto a reservation.

But what of the tribes so small, so peaceful, or so isolated that they posed no threat to white settlement? In most cases, they were simply forgotten. Decades passed in which the government policy gradually evolved to a sophisticated understanding of social reality. Sophisticated, that is, for the bureaucrats and congressmen who made Indian policy.

In 1934 the I.R.A. was passed; it allowed the various tribes to organize business committees and tribal councils to govern the reservations. Part of the legislation authorized the secretary of the interior to purchase lands for homeless Indians, to organize groups that had never had a formal structure, and to provide federally recognized self-government for the dependent Indian communities of the nation.

In large measure, the government during the early years of the I.R.A. made efforts in good faith to accomplish the task set before it. Land was purchased, particularly in California, and new Indian groups were organized out of groups that had been neglected. Almost every place that the federal government went, it developed Indian reservations and new tribal councils. Some tribes that had previously been dissolved were given new rights to organize, to reconstitute themselves, and to share in the federal programs being developed under the New Deal.

As a new generation of bureaucrats began to inhabit the halls of the Interior Department, a curious, although tacit, understanding developed that the I.R.A. was no longer in force and that its provisions were not to be carried out. Mere passage of time was considered sufficient to negate the rights that Indians were intended to have under the law. That attitude is entrenched in the Interior Department and the Bureau of Indian Affairs today. They refuse to use the law to assist Indians, and they consider the I.R.A. as effectively vetoed by the passage of time, even though it has never been legally repealed or amended.

Thus, shortly after 1940, all efforts to enforce the organizing provisions of the I.R.A. were considered fruitless, in spite of the secretary of interior's unlimited discretion to do so, as defined by the act. Whenever the Bureau of Indian Affairs was contacted by tribes eligible to organize under the act, it would refuse to have anything to do with them. They would be rather brusquely dismissed, with the advice to take their problem to Congress. Needless to say, Congress was not at all sympathetic. If the secretary of the interior did not want to recognize the petitioners under his authority—given by Congress—then, congressmen felt, perhaps rightly so, that they had no business overriding an administrative decision.

Congress, when passing the I.R.A., should have made provisions for the insertion of either a brain or a backbone in the secretary of the interior and the commissioner of Indian affairs. That probably would have solved the problem. But no such provision has been written into law at this date. So an administrative "Catch-22" has come into existence. A tribe has to prove that it has always received federal services and federal recognition in order to get a constitution, that is, to be organized under the act. But, of course, if it had really received those services it would naturally have had a constitution approved by the secretary of the interior.

The tribes without formal federal recognition, although apparently having rights according to the doctrine expressed in both the *Candelaria* and *Tuscarora* cases, are scattered primarily along the eastern seacoast, where the tide of white settlement rushed by them so swiftly that they had no opportunity to sign a treaty or fight a war against the United States. Others, however, like the Tonto Apaches and the Little Shell band of Chippewa, have rather unique stories.

The Tonto Apaches once occupied an extensive land area that extended in several directions along the Mogollon Rim and into the Tonto Basin of Arizona, including parts of what is now known as the Tonto National Forest. Around 1863, gold was discovered in the Black Mountains of Arizona, and prospectors began to enter the area, which had previously been the exclusive domain of the Tonto Apaches. The Apaches proved to be a most formidable enemy, and it is said of them that they prevented the settlement of Arizona by a generation, by their resistance to intruders.

In 1871, the Tonto Apaches and the Yavapai Apaches were given a large reservation at Camp Verde, Arizona, known as the Rio Verde Reserve. However, four years later this reservation was dissolved at the instigation of the Tucson Ring, a notorious political group that subcontracted the supplies due the Indians of the area by treaty. The Tucson Ring wanted all the Indians gathered in one place, where they could be more easily swindled. Thus, the War Department moved the Tonto and Yavapai to San Carlos, where they were unceremoniously dumped. The reservation held the remnants of the other Apache bands who had fought against the United States.

The stay at San Carlos was heartbreaking for a people who had been accustomed to the clean mountain air. San Carlos was mostly desert land, hot and miserable. When the Army needed scouts to chase the bands of Victorio and Geronimo, the Tontos volunteered, thinking that if they proved themselves to be allies of the United States, they would be allowed to return to their homeland. But the United States showed no such gratitude; it kept a watchful eye on all the Apache bands, intending to keep them forever prisoners of war at San Carlos.

After the surrender of Geronimo in 1886, the warfare between the whites and Apaches generally ceased and the reservations were no longer guarded as carefully. Although they had lived at San Carlos for twenty years, the Tontos still remembered their homelands along the Tonto Rim, and in 1895 they made a dash for freedom. Returning to their old campsites, they discovered that whites had moved into many of their most sacred places, and so, they simply kept out of sight and lived in those parts where there was no settlement.

The Tontos returned quickly to their traditional life. They spent the winters in camps along the Tonto Basin and moved to summer camps in the mountains. They cultivated gardens along the streams in the valley, gathered the wild plants that had always been part of their diet, and hunted food for drying for the winter. Occasionally, they worked for whites who owned mines and ranches in the neighborhood.

Knowing very little about the laws of the United States, the Tontos felt no compulsion to claim formally lands that they had owned since before the memory of man. Consequently, when the Tonto National Forest was established in 1905, they were totally unaware that the federal government was setting aside the lands for another purpose. The Forest Service made no attempt to move the Apaches, although it did prevent whites from using the lands without special range permits. Thus, well into the present century there was no indication by the government that it did not regard the lands occupied by the Tontos as their own lands.

When the Apaches did come to the attention of the Forest Service, Chief Forest Inspector Bronson recommended that free, special-use permits be issued to them for their permanent use. A permit issued in 1909 was finally canceled in 1965, following the death of the old scout and medicine man of the band, Silver Allen.

The record of government dealing with the Tontos is muddled, to say the least. While the lands were still public domain in 1896, an Apache named Charley Nockey filed a homestead on lands now within the forest area. An application for homestead by George Randall, a white man, was turned down in 1908 because of Nockey's prior claim, so there is an indication that the title of the Tontos was recognized by the land office.

In 1919, Delia Chapman, a Tonto who lived in the East Verde region, filed and received a homestead allotment with the understanding that this allotment should serve as the communal land of the tribe. The lots that were developed from the trust allotment were sold for $500 in 1943 and are now worth thousands of times as much as the selling price since they make up a subdivision of the present-day town of Payson.

Until the 1950's the Tontos remained living on what was called Indian Hill, a high piece of ground northwest of the town of Payson. In 1954 land developers discovered that the Tontos has no title to the lands (that is, none that would be defended by the federal government), so they saw to it that the Tontos were evicted from their houses. In one significant episode, a building contractor ran a bulldozer through an Indian house before the Indian family could get its personal effects from the building.

Pushed out of the Payson area in 1954, the Tontos moved onto Forest Service lands southwest of Payson. They appealed to the Bureau of Indian Affairs for assistance but were told that they must move to San Carlos in order to receive services. They were apparently regarded as San Carlos Apaches by the bureau. In 1962, the Public Health Service, Division of Indian Health, extended contract medical services and hospital care to them. They were thus recognized as Indians eligible for federal services by one agency but not by another.

Representative Sam Steiger attempted to get them eighty-five acres of land in the Tonto National Forest as a reservation in 1971, but at this point the traditional Bureau of Indian Affairs attitude intervened to stop the legislation. Supported by Harrison Loesch, assistant secretary of the interior for land management, who oversees the Bureau of Indian Affairs, the official Interior Department testimony on the legislation was designed to deny the Tontos any rights as Indians and to set up a corporation that would oversee fifteen acres of land for them. With the cost of developing sewers and water facilities being extremely high and with taxes placed upon lands producing no income whatsoever, the legislation, if passed, would be merely a variation of the termination schemes developed by the Republicans in the 1950's—schemes, as we have seen, that proved incredibly disastrous.

The case of the Tonto Apaches is typical of the fate of the small Indian bands that live in a legal no-man's-land across the nation, untouched apparently by the pious words of the *Tuscarora* and *Candelaria* decisions, which make it clear that it is the duty of the United States to care for and protect the dependent Indian communities within the United States.

In addition to the Tontos in central Arizona, a number of tribes occupy a nebulous legal status and are apparently under the watchful eye of the federal government, should it need anything from them. The 100 million acres of stabilized Indian land base should certainly include the lands of these isolated communities, and the tribes should be granted full recognition by the federal government and reservation status for their communities.

The Burns Paiutes live in Oregon. They are a small community that lingered in central Oregon while the wars of the Northwest were taking place. Eastern Oregon is very desolate, probably among the least developed regions of the nation. Consequently, little was done to track down the Paiutes, and they were left to their own devices until the Depression. At that time, they gathered near the town of Burns, and land was purchased for them to live on But the Bureau of Indian Affairs never got around to organizing them under the I.R.A. Instead, it merely held the lands, submarginal in nature, and allowed the people to live on them and to work in town.

With the passing of the years, as we have indicated above, the bureaucrats grew afraid of the presence of the Paiute band on government lands. They tried to pretend that in fact the tribe did not exist, even though land had been purchased by the government for them to live on. During the late 1960's, legislation was introduced to give the Paiutes the lands and allow them to organize as a tribe under the I.R.A. When the legislation was heard in the Senate, the recommendation was that the lands be given to the tribe in fee simple and thus be put on the county tax roll. What was conveniently overlooked was that the lands produced some $1,700 in income a year, but had an annual tax of $1,900. The whole proposal was simply one to take the lands away from the tribe by getting them out of Indian and government hands.

Perhaps the point that must be made "perfectly clear," as the administration has been fond of saying, is that the Department of the Interior has authority under existing laws to establish the lands of the various tribes as reservations now. It was commanded to do so, in fact, by the Congress in the I.R.A. But, by making the whole matter a bothersome thing for Congress, an excuse exists not to recognize the groups administratively.

In Montana lives a group known as the Little Shell band of Chippewa. Originally, they lived in western Minnesota and North Dakota. The Chippewas waged no wars with the United States, and thus, the tribe was not prominently known to the American public outside of Longfellow's romantic poem about Hiawatha. In 1882, a reservation was established in North Dakota known as the Turtle Mountain Reservation, which consisted of twenty-two townships made up of the lands claimed by the Chippewa at that time. It was an easy way to forestall the Chippewas joining Sitting Bull, who was just across the border in Canada at the time.

The Indians of Chief Little Shell's band moved onto the reservation, established homes, planted gardens, and began new lives as farmers in conjunction with the policies of the government. In 1884, barely two years later, at the instigation of the Bureau of Indian Affairs, the president issued an executive order

reducing the size of the reservation to two townships and opening the rest of the former reservation lands to white settlers.

A new tribal roll was prepared. All Indians not living on the
lands within the two remaining townships were told to select
homestead lands instead. They were simply pushed out of the
tribe. In desperation Chief Little Shell appealed to the government for justice, but the federal officials simply refused to talk to
him.

The remnants of the tribe, under Chief Little Shell, started
for Montana, where they hoped to get a reservation, being aware
that some Chippewas were settling with the Cree Indians on the
Rocky Boy Reservation. But no reservation was given to the
Little Shell band, and eventually, they drifted to an area near
Great Falls and simply camped outside of town. All across North
Dakota and Montana are little allotments of land taken up by
discouraged members of the band who had dropped out of the
exodus. Strangely enough, the Bureau of Indian Affairs has insisted on keeping these lands in trust but has denied federal
rights to those Indians who completed the trip to Montana.

In 1910, a former superintendent of the Turtle Mountain
Reservation encouraged the band members, who by this time
were aptly called the Abandoned Chippewas, to file on public
domain in North Dakota and Montana. The remaining members were heartened at this show of interest and spent a great
deal of time and money getting applications prepared under the
General Allotment Act. But, once again, the Interior Department showed its true colors. When the applications were forwarded to Washington, the department insisted that the Indians
were really Canadian Indians who had crossed the international
line to get land in the United States.

In 1924, the Indian office again encouraged the Little Shell
people to establish their federal rights. It advised the group to
apply for reenrollment at Turtle Mountain, their original reservation. In compliance with this request—from the Bureau of
Indian Affairs, mind you—the band members prepared statements and affidavits and sent in their application forms for enrollment. When the application forms were received, the Bureau
of Indian Affairs notified the people that it could not reenroll
them after all.

Thus, once again the peculiar logic of the Interior Department intervened to deprive an Indian group of its right to land and tribal recognition. The arbitrary disfranchisement of the group in 1884 should be sufficient to establish beyond doubt the wrong that has been done to the Little Shell band, but the bureaucrats insist that the group does not have, and never has had, any federal rights.

Senators Mansfield and Metcalf of Montana made sporadic and hålfhearted attempts to help the tribe, but it has been apparent that they have done so only to quiet the group and not actually to help them. The inactivity of the two senators must stand as one of the more heartless acts of American politicians. Mansfield, for example, has been majority leader of the Senate since Lyndon Johnson left that body in 1960. If he really wanted to help the Indian, he could put the law establishing a reservation for them through Congress in a morning. Mansfield's concern, however, has been more for the Vietnamese than for his own constituents.

On the outskirts of the town of Marksville, Louisiana, lives a group of Indians with a history perhaps more unique than any other group in the nation. They are the Tunicas. Historians debate whether this group was responsible for the sudden demise of De Soto or whether it was a related group. At any rate, the Tunicas are one of the oldest tribes still living on their original homeland.

In the 1830's the major tribes of the South—the Cherokee, Chickasaw, Choctaw, Creek, and Seminole—were forced to move to Oklahoma. They were the largest and most powerful tribes with whom the invading whites had to deal. Some of the Seminoles broke away and retreated into the swamps of Florida; a few Creeks settled near Atmore, Alabama; the Cherokees fled to the hills of North Carolina; and a small group of Choctaws stayed near Philadelphia, Mississippi. The Chickasaws moved almost totally.

Outside of these stragglers of the Five Civilized Tribes, no one seemed to question the existence of Indians in the South. People knew that there were probably some groups that defied the removal policy, but since no one was sure who they were or where they were located, no one made any inquiries.

The Tunicas were one of these groups. They lived peacefully near Marksville until the early 1870's. At that time there was a dispute between a woman of apparently dubious character and "some Indians," who turned out to be the remnants of the Tunica tribe. The only evidence introduced at the trial as to ownership was a scrap of paper written in French that apparently made some reference to the Tunicas.

We do not have the results of the action since the records have been lost. We can safely assume, however, that the Tunicas won the right to remain on the property and cut wood, perhaps to continue living on it, since they presently occupy the land in question.

The tribe was visited by field workers from the Smithsonian Institution in 1908 in an effort to gather data on the tribes still remaining in the lower Mississippi Valley. Unfortunately, the Smithsonian people, like most scholars, did nothing to see if these Indians had any rights as Indians. They merely recorded their observations and returned to Washington. The data was written up as *Report 43* of the Bureau of American Ethnology Series.

Apparently, the Tunicas and other tribes that settled the river area under French direction received grants from the king of France to certain lands. Indications are that the Tunicas, for example, originally had 4,000 acres confirmed to them. Today, they have less than 127 acres left of this original grant.

Because the tribes of the delta area had different languages, they had to adopt French as a means of understanding each other. Since the 1700's, French has come to predominate, and only certain Indian words are still left in the respective tribal vocabularies. But the traditions survive, the ancient medicines and herbs are still used, and arts and crafts of an earlier time are relatively intact.

The Tunica children were not allowed to attend school in Marksville until 1946, and then they were forced into the segregated schools used for blacks of Avoyelles Parish. The Indian parents rebelled at this treatment, and rather than lose their identity they kept their children at home. Their educational level is thus very low, and few know how to read or write English. They do mostly farm work and common labor to keep some kind of income for themselves. The younger people often leave the vicinity and go to Texas or other places in the South to find work.

The Tunicas were apparently doomed to drift unnoticed through American history until 1967. At that time, the state of Louisiana was building its portion of the interstate highway system from New Orleans and came to Marksville's section of the system. To broaden the highway, it happened to need some lands belonging to the Tunicas. A court case ensued, and some of the land was condemned. While the Tunicas were uncertain as to the papers needed to prove their ownership of the lands, no one else had a better claim to it.

The strange thing about the Tunicas is that they could have had federal recognition. In the first few years of the I.R.A., field workers from the Bureau of Indian Affairs went into the state of Louisiana and began to organize the small Indian communities under the provisions of that act. They went south into the bayou country and visited the Chitimacha tribe in the delta. The Chitimachas agreed to draw up and approve a constitution under the act. They did so, and received some lands held in trust by the Bureau of Indian Affairs for them.

But with war clouds gathering, travel funds were cut back by the Bureau of Indian Affairs, and so, the remainder of the small identified Indian communities of Louisiana were not visited. They consequently became legal nonentities in the eyes of the federal government. The rights to federal services and recognition in the case of the Louisiana tribes rested on the availability of federal officials to carry out their jobs and nothing more.

The Tunicas are only a clearly identified version of the many groups of Indian people scattered in the backlands of the South. They have been clearly mentioned in accounts of travelers and explorers, government reports, and literature for some time. Many groups have not been as clearly and consistently identified but remain Indians nevertheless. In Virginia and North Carolina, isolated groups live without any apparent contact with modern civilization at all. They are discernible only by the traces that they leave behind them. A few scraps of garbage, a burned-out fire, a run-down hut, remnants of a gathering on an isolated beach are all that mark the existence of these peoples. Yet, the Indians in the neighborhood know that they are there in the swamps and woods.

In southern Louisiana, in addition to the Tunicas and Chitimachas previously mentioned, live the Houmas and bands of

Coushattas. The Houmas have approximately 3,500 members, most of whom live in the swamps and tiny villages in the back country. The Houmas have attracted to themselves remnants of the other early tribes that refused to leave the South for Oklahoma. The Aoclapissa, Bayougoula, Washa, Chawasha, Biloxi, and scattered Choctaws live with, and near, the Houmas. The Koasati, a group related to the Coushatta (the spelling of the name being the primary difference between them), number about 350 people.

The state of Louisiana has the second largest concentration of Indian people in the South, outside of North Carolina. But few people know that Indians still live there, and since fewer Indians emerge from the bayous and swamps to plead their case, the situation remains unnoticed. As we have seen, the federal government established, through gifts of land and special field work, the Indians of Florida as federally recognized Indians. It could do as much for these isolated groups in Louisiana.

Florida itself has a great many more Indians than are presently receiving federal recognition and services. The Appalachiacola Indians live around Eastpoint, Florida. They signed two treaties with the United States in the 1830's, when the government was forcing the Indians out of the South. The Appalachiacolas were to have received six sections of land if they decided to remain in Florida and not remove to Oklahoma. When the main body of Creeks, of whom the Appalachiacolas were apparently the southernmost group, left for Oklahoma, the Appalachiacolas refused to leave Florida. Since they lived in an isolated spot and caused no one any trouble, they were simply forgotten. What ever happened to their six sections of land no one seems to know. It would seem that the United States is at least six sections short in its treaty provisions in Florida.

North Carolina, as noted, has the most substantial Indian population in the South. The Eastern Cherokee band has a federal reservation in western North Carolina, and the Lumbees live in the eastern part, in Robeson County, but without any federal recognition for services. They currently have a bill in Congress to give them full federal status; a weaker version passed more than a decade ago recognized them as Indians but prevented them from receiving any federal assistance. In Rockingham County lives a group of Indians that apparently is a remnant of the Cheraw tribe. And in Halifax and Warren counties lives a large group of Indians that has adopted the name Haliwa, a combination of the two county names. The Waccamaw and Machapunga tribes also live in the Carolina region. They are mentioned in scholarly journals as extinct, because no one has bothered to leave the library long enough to visit thm.

Virginia has a number of Indian tribes still recognized by the state as having reservation status. In King William County, the Pamunkey and Mattaponi people live. They have a very small land base, and so, the children simply move away from the reservation to live and only return at the end of their lives to spend their declining days at home. The Indians are remnants of a tribe that was early affiliated with the Powhatan Confederacy. As early as 1658 these Indian lands were confirmed to them by the governor, the council, and the grand assembly of Virginia. Henning's *Statutes at Large, 1657–1658*, records the acts confirming the Indian title. In spite of the virtually impeccable title, these Indians have never received any notice or services from the federal government. The Chickahominy, Potomac, Nottaway, Nansemond, Wesort, Wicocomoco, and Rappahannock tribes also live in the state but without any recognition from either state or federal government.

All these groups fully qualify as dependent Indian communities under the doctrine articulated in the *Tuscarora* and *Candelaria* cases. They are people who should have the same rights as other Indian tribes. But they are people who were never powerful militarily and thus able to force the United States to deal with them by treaty. Consequently, there was no need to recognize them or to move them to Oklahoma. It may seem strange to realize that Indian legal rights depend upon the ease with which the United States can abuse Indian communities, but such appears to be the case.

A full investigation of the status and current condition of the federally unrecognized Indian tribes is imperative and has been promised by the staff of the White House. Its objective, however, at this writing, was to postpone the necessity of taking a position prior to the national elections on the Menominee restoration bill. Thus, the Nixon administration is carrying the "benign neglect" theory to its ultimate conclusion in its treatment of Indian people.

The nonfederal Indian people offer an outstanding opportunity for the United States to create a progressive alternative to its present Indian policy. Each administration is caught between cries for complete termination of Indian rights and solid resistance against such a move. No middle ground has ever been offered. By giving federally recognized land bases to these groups and allowing them the corporate status of federal tribal governments, the United States could create a middle ground in which the whole administrative apparatus of the Bureau of Indian Affairs would be absent, while the federal protections for the land base would be present. It would combine the best of both worlds.

We believe that some fifty groups can be clearly identified as Indian tribes by a careful survey of existing Indian communities in the South and East. We believe that these peoples should have the rights and privileges of other Indian peoples. We would recommend that a land acquisition program be started to provide a land base for them according to their present needs. In some cases this would mean the purchase of lands in the immediate neighborhood of their local communities. Some tribes would need more than 1,000 acres, others would need less. We estimate that with the purchase or transfer of federal forest lands in the amount of 200,000 acres, all of these communities could be placed on a solid economic basis.

Restoration of lands to nonfederal groups would be an important part of our proposed permanent Indian land base. To recap:

Tribal lands	39,663,412.09
Individual Indian allotments	10,697,621.58
Alaska native lands	40,000,000
Occupied Indian lands	4,723,017.2
Submarginal lands restored	344,811
Flathead lands restored	10,585.86
Warm Springs lands restored	61,300
Crow lands restored	618
Menominee lands restored	230,000
Klamath lands restored	144,000
Nisqually lands—purchased and restored	1,375
Nonfederal tribes—purchased	200,000
	96,076,740.73

❧ 13 ❧

The Rocking of America: Alcatraz and Beyond

FEW EVENTS have so captured the attention of the American public as did the landing of the Indian activists on Alcatraz. From a relatively unknown "other" minority group, Indians suddenly emerged as a force to be noted in the ongoing social movement of the present. While other groups had used massive demonstrations and sweeping legislative measures to achieve their ends, the young Indian college students of the late 1960's gambled on spectacular invasions of federal property to illustrate their claim for social and legal justice and public support.

The background to the Alcatraz landing is as fascinating as the actual invasion. In the sedate years of the Eisenhower administration, the Interior Department began to develop programs to move Indians from their reservations into the cities of the Midwest and the Pacific coast. It felt that forced assimilation into the urban ghettos of the nation was the final solution to the "Indian problem." We can be thankful at this late date that there was no large gas lobby pressing for a different final solution at the time. The result was nearly the same, however.

By bringing Indians into the mainstream of American life and unceremoniously dumping them in the slums of Chicago, St. Louis, San Francisco, Los Angeles, Cleveland, and Dallas, the bureaucrats hoped that their failure to assist Indians would not be discovered. Over the years a large number of Indian people became concentrated on the west coast. Los Angeles and San Francisco Indian immigrants developed their own Indian centers to provide services and counseling to the hundreds of families that were being stranded in the city by the Bureau of Indian Affairs.

A generation of Indian children eventually grew up in these areas. They were well aware of their Indian blood because of the large-scale discrimination practiced against Indians in the cities of the west coast. Only the worst housing was available, jobs were scarce or nonexistent, and Indians were the first fired if hired at all. Medical services were refused because city officials believed that the Indians should go back to the reservations, where medical care was assumed to be available to them. Federal officials studiously avoided any contact with the people once they had brought them to the cities.

In many instances the only experiences of Indian communal life that these young people had were occasional powwows on the small California reservations or summer trips back home to visit relatives. But, for the most part, they had been very young when their parents had left the reservations, and outside of a hazy memory or two of rolling hills and desert mountains, they had few experiences to which they could relate the endlessly recited stories of their parents concerning the reservation.

Sporadic efforts had been made by churches and urban Indian clubs to develop programs for the people in the cities. Hampered by a lack of funds, by the consistently shifting membership of the Indian organizations of the cities, and the general apathy of non-Indians toward Indian needs, few urban Indian centers were able to survive. Resentful of their treatment in the cities, furious at the callous attitude of the federal government, the urban Indian people were a curious mixture of assimilated, economically secure families who had been able to adjust to the new environment and a very large group of families who had never adjusted to urban life and who frequently traveled back and forth to the reservations in search of a better life.

By 1964 the situation was very tense and Indian people were restless about their rejection by the social and economic power structures. They looked for a dramatic means of calling the public's attention to their suffering. In the back of their minds was the thought that the government relocation program, which had forced them into the cities a decade earlier, could be reorganized to provide direct funding of the programs they were developing in their urban centers. The government's abandonment of Alcatraz Island as a federal prison in 1964 provided the key to the problem.

In midyear Dick McKenzie and Allen Cottier, Sioux Indians from South Dakota who had moved to the San Francisco Bay area some years before, made their way to the island and claimed it as Indian land under the Sioux treaty of 1868. While the claim was uncertain, the judges and federal marshals did not know the treaty as well as the Indians, and so, the situation remained deadlocked for some time. Eventually, it went to court, where the judge gave a brief statement that the treaty could not be used for such a purpose, and the case was dropped.

It was a valiant attempt to bring attention to the state of Indian affairs but a little too early. America's attention was focused on the struggles of the black community in the South. A couple of Indians landing on an abandoned prison island meant nothing to the communications media, which were having a great time recording the police dogs and cattle prods of the forces of law and order in the South. But the idea was planted in the minds of the younger urban Indians that the island was a potential symbol that could be used forcefully to catch the eyes of the world should the American people again begin to question the existence of Indians on the continent.

Time passed and the civil rights movement changed into the black-power movement. The media began to get interested in other minority groups. The public got tired of the continual reports on the black community and began to feel that other groups should get some attention also. In late October 1969 the San Francisco Indian Center was host to a national convention of urban Indians. The Officers of the American Indians United, a rather premature grouping of urban centers of the various cities of the Midwest and the Pacific coast, held the organizing session of the organization in the bay area.

Meeting at the San Francisco Indian Center for three days, the urban Indians from nearly sixty cities and small towns struggled to define a constitution and bylaws that could be used to hold the independent groups' loyalty and yet focus efforts on national concerns. In spite of brilliant speeches and the admonitions of elder statesmen to remain "until the business is done" and to "keep out of smoke-filled rooms," the convention broke up late

on Sunday night without haved resolved any issues and most of
the delegates left for home.

One notable thing happened during the convention. College
students from the schools in the bay area had come to the convention and tried to participate in the proceedings, but they
were rejected as being too young and without any practical experience in Indian affairs. The students left in a state of firm
disagreement with the older urban Indians and determined that
they would show the old-timers how to get things moving if it
was the last thing they ever did.

That night, the Indian center burned down. The cause is still
unknown. The Indians of the bay area had been having some
trouble with the Samoan community, whose members also had
become expatriates in a foreign city. Some people blamed the
Samoans for the fire. Others thought that a cigarette had been
carelessly thrown into some trash that was piled against the rear
wall of the building. Whatever the cause, by the next morning
the center had been totally gutted. Three stories of equipment
and records were destroyed, and the Indians of the area were
without any building in which to meet and operate their programs. Funds were practically nonexistent for repurchase of
equipment.

The Indians of the bay area were heartbroken. The center
had served them for almost twenty years. It had been the focal
point of the activities and programs of Indians for nearly a
hundred miles around. The work of decades of lonely struggle
for identity in the strange city was lost. Some means had to be
found to attract large amounts of money immediately to rebuild
the center. Then came the remembrance of 1964 and Alcatraz.

Several days later a group of Indian college students from the
bay area, mostly from Berkeley and San Francisco State, pushed
around to the backside of the island in a Canadian boat and
swam ashore. The guards chased them all night, and the next
day, they were escorted off the island. But they had learned an
important fact, their sparsity of numbers had made their removal inevitable. If more Indians were landed on the island,
they could not be gotten off so easily. On November 19 nearly
250 Indians landed on the island and announced that it was now
Indian land under the treaty of 1868 and a number of other
land and allotment laws.

The press and television rushed to the aid of the Indians. Publicity sprang from the rock until one almost believed that all the Indians in the world were gathering there. Movie stars and celebrities made pilgrimages to Alcatraz, and Jess Unruh, then campaigning for the governorship of California, introduced a resolution in the California legislature to give Alcatraz to the Indians. It got him the Indian vote, although the Alcatraz occupants failed to realize that a resolution of the California legislature has little impact on the General Services Administration in Washington in the handing out of surplus federal lands.

The subsequent story of Alcatraz was both profound and silly, tragic and glorious. The major problem was that the students could not take too many days away from the classroom and with Indians rushing to Alcatraz from every part of the nation, the movement turned from a student movement to a general Indian uprising without much of a sense of direction. Eventually, in the summer of 1971, the scattered little group of Indians remaining on the island, numbering not more than twenty, was taken by surprise by federal marshals and taken off the rock. The island was once again secured in federal hands. Most of the original invaders had long since left the island to set about other business. The survivors were simply people who had nowhere else to go.

But Alcatraz was not a failure. Its primary significance lay in awakening the Indian people, particularly the urban Indians, to what was happening on the national scene. It focused the concern of various city administrations on the problems of the Indian community as no other event could have done. And it gave birth to numerous other invasions of federal property in areas in which there was a desperate need by the local Indian people for services and programs. Most of all, Alcatraz gave birth to the idea among Indian people that no more Indian lands should be surrendered to the federal government. In this sense, Alcatraz became the most important event in the twentieth century for American Indian people.

The original group of Indians at Alcatraz had styled themselves the "Indians of All Tribes." This name was chosen to encompass all Indian groups and tribes and to use the invasion as a device for bringing all the tribes together. The name was taken up by urban Indians in other areas, and soon a number of groups in different parts of the nation were calling themselves Indians of All Tribes and making their own forays into federal lands. The most successful was probably the group at Seattle under the leadership of Bernie White Bear.

Seattle had been quietly dickering with the federal government for some lands at Fort Lawton, an army post that was being partially deactivated and that occupied a prominent point on the Puget Sound in the northwest portion of the city. The lands were within the original occupancy area of the Duwamish tribe, whose chief, the famous Sealth, was the leading negotiator of the treaty ceding the Seattle area to the United States. Needless to say, the city of Seattle was named after the old chief in lieu of giving his tribe a reservation of their own.

An old statute gave the secretary of the army the discretionary power to use abandoned army posts for Indian educational needs, and the Indians of the Seattle area, desperately in need of services and training for vocational skills, wanted the statute used to create an Indian service and cultural center on the 440 acres of land comprising the excess fort grounds. But the city of Seattle, backed by Senator Henry Jackson, refused to acquiesce to the Indians' application for the lands. Although already overburdened by numerous parks, which it could not support in its budget, the city insisted that it needed all the lands for a new city park. In fact, word had already been sent out on the grapevine from both the mayor's office and Jackson's office that neither would have "an Indian reservation in the middle of Seattle." It was not a matter of land title or need at all. Rather it was a case of pure racial prejudice, for which the good people of Washington are famous. They simply did not want any Indians in Seattle.

One spring morning the guards at Fort Lawton awoke to find themselves invaded by a strong contingent of Indians led by Bernie White Bear and spectacularly supported by actress Jane Fonda, who was herself somewhat disgruntled with the military. With her presence and the contingent of reporters covering her activities, police brutality was held to a minimum. Washington State is notorious for its brutal treatment of Indians, and generally uses snipers hiding in ambush to keep the Indians cowed. There is no doubt that again Jane Fonda's presence saved some Indian lives.

At any rate, the invasion force, while repulsed, had indicated that it would return as many times as necessary to force the issue. The city, in order to forestall an escalating series of invasions, agreed to negotiate with the Indians on the establishment of an Indian training and cultural center on the fort grounds. Bernie White Bear and a team of Indian negotiators then began the tedious task of conferring with the city for use of part of the grounds for the Indians of Seattle. The negotiations lasted over a year, the city negotiators continually twisting words and phrases, rarely giving the good faith that the Indians were giving in the sessions.

Every dirty trick in the book was used by Mayor Wes Ullman's city negotiating team to break up the Indian coalition of urban organizations and small tribes that demanded the use of the fort. Programs that had been providing services for Indians in the city were hampered, threatened with loss of funds, harassed, and bribed in an effort to break the united front developed by the Indian of All Tribes council. The strategy of the city was to give the various organizations a chance for programs that were badly needed, with the implication that they would receive support from the mayor's office. Then, suddenly, the Indians would be told that nothing could be done unless the group disclaimed Bernie White Bear. But the Indians held firm, and no group that was authentically Indian broke ranks. Whenever city officials tried to pry loose an Indian organization from the coalition, they were politely told that they would take whatever the city was offering and Fort Lawton.

The Indians of All Tribes were not simply negotiating with the city, however. They organized a team and went to the convention of the National Congress of American Indians (NCAI) in Anchorage, Alaska, and pushed through a top-priority resolution binding that organization to support their drive for an Indian center in Seattle. With the NCAI behind them, they toured the regional Indian organizations and got their support, so that every major force in national Indian Affairs was solidly committed to back up the Seattle contingent.

Then the climate began to change. Friendly people in the Department of Health, Education, and Welfare, cognizant of the Indians' need for social services, agreed to place a request for the land with the General Services Administration on behalf of the Fort Lawton Indians. This request tied up the transfer of the lands to the city and forced the city to justify its proposed use for the lands on the same basis as the Indians. With this variety of forces mustered behind the Seattle Indian community and growing stronger, fate appeared to intervene.

Senator Henry M. ("Scoop") Jackson, long regarded as the contemporary archenemy of American Indians, had a change of heart. He met with the Indians of All Tribes delegation and listened to their story. Realizing that they had come so far against such odds and were determined to continue, perhaps escalating their activism if the city continued to refuse to deal in good faith, Jackson stepped into the picture in an effort to reconcile the two parties. Eventually, a use permit was worked out giving the Indians eleven acres for a cultural center on a ninety-nine year lease. Of all the claims on federal property, the claim to Fort Lawton was perhaps best grounded in legal doctrines and best supported by the Indian people themselves.

The success of the negotiations, however, was probably owing more to the stubbornness and ability of Bernie White Bear than to any change of heart by the Seattle city administration. One can only conclude that Seattle has strong prejudices against Indians. Other cities in the West have had themselves named as relocation centers for reservation Indians. As such, they receive the benefit of federal payrolls and programs for the relocated Indians amounting to many millions of dollars a year. The negotiations in Seattle occurred at a time when Boeing had lost its contracts for the SST, when unemployment was skyrocketing, and when the hunger situation got so desperate that Seattle's sister city, Kobe, Japan, had to send rice to the starving people of Seattle.

When the city desperately needed an infusion of federal funds and programs, when Indian unemployment could have been resolved by having the city named as a relocation city, and when a superior funding package could have been brought to the city, the city administration refused to budge on any compromise, preferring no federal assistance to assistance that would go to Indian people. Fortunately, Jackson saved the day.

The activist movement triggered by Alcatraz spread rapidly to other cities. Lighthouses, abandoned air bases, several radar stations, and eventually Mount Rushmore were invaded, held briefly, and then surrendered. From beneath all of the confusion and apparent disarray of events, one fact stood out clearly. Indian people wanted a chance to reclaim the lands illegally taken from them.

Perhaps the most humorous incident of these disparate events was the proposed capture of Ellis Island, the former isolation ward for new immigrants in New York Harbor. With the major events of Indian activism happening thousands of miles from the center of the communications industry in New York City, Indian college students in the East recognized that they would have to bring the impact of the movement to the sophisticated and secure citizens of New York City before anything meaningful could be achieved in the eyes of eastern whites, who had traditionally been good allies of Indian people.

The plan to capture Ellis Island was therefore worked out so that Indians would hold the two most famous islands in the major cities on each coast. Jokes were made about using Ellis Island as a deportation port for dissident whites and Alcatraz for those who refused to leave—jokes that would have outraged the rednecks of Oklahoma and Washington beyond belief had they heard them.

Early one morning in April 1970, a strange contingent of cars left the Indian center in Brooklyn, heading for the Jersey shore. Six cars, each loaded with a canoe or boat on the roof, drove silently through the deserted city streets toward the launching place on the New Jersey side of the harbor. Needless to say, such a caravan attracted the attention of everyone who was awake at that hour, and a goodly crew followed to watch the fun.

Instructions had been given to the Indians remaining at the center to call the press within two hours of the departure of the caravan and to announce that Ellis Island had been freed from white oppression and that the situation was well in hand. Everything went according to plan, at least as far as the people at the Indian center were concerned. At the appointed hour, the newspapers were solemnly called and told that an Indian contingent sat on Ellis Island.

On the Jersey shore, however, things were not quite functioning. Arriving at a predesignated landing, the students unlashed their boats and put them into the water. Carefully attaching the outboard motors, they made fierce departure statements to the assembled multitude, got into the boats, and tried to start the motors. Alas, no one knew how to start the outboards. After much debate, many additional departure speeches, and considerable delay, the landing was postponed until the students regrouped to learn how the infernal machine of the white man actually worked. Such incidents speak more of the humanity of the Indian than of his alleged savagery, since the students repaired to a friendly bar, laughed and joked at their misadventure, and promptly began making plans for the invasion of Plymouth Rock, an undertaking that was to prove much more successful.

An activist invasion that proved quite successful was the takeover of surplus government lands near Davis, California, for an Indian-Chicano university. A combined force landed on the piece of property, which was to be turned over to the state university system in the summer of 1970. Plans had been drawn for the creation of D-Q (Deganiwidah-Quetzalcoatl) University, which would present a curriculum of American Indian and Mexican American studies. The invasion was followed promptly by a concerted lobbying effort in Sacramento and in Washington, D.C., with the proper government agencies. Funds were obtained for the programs, and the new university was launched. While encountering some difficulty in getting underway, the program, it is generally agreed, is good and attractive to Indians and Chicanos and is filling a great need.

The Indian activists have raised a number of interesting questions in their adventures that indicate a change in thinking by Indians about Indian lands. Many of the controversies have swirled around land use as well as the title to the land itself. The primary goal of the Alcatraz invasion was to establish a center where the philosophy and traditions of Indian ecology could be studied. This center would have combined scientific studies with Indian religious traditions and would thus have been uniquely Indian and contemporary at the same time.

Although the Alcatraz invasion was successful, some older Indians in the bay area had predicted that it would fail, primarily because the rock itself had been defiled by its former use as a prison. The spirits of the dead, criminal and innocent alike, remained on the rock, the old-timers said, and the rock could not divest itself of them. The prediction proved to be true, even though the younger Indians had hoped that the establishment of a religious center would be sufficient to cleanse the island of its evil connotations and vibrations.

Mount Rushmore was the scene of demonstrations in the summers of 1970 and 1971. The Black Hills had long been regarded as sacred by a number of tribes. The famous Bear Butte, scene of many Indian ceremonials, is located just northeast of the Black Hills and may be regarded as one of the spiritual centers of the Sioux and Northern Cheyenne. Thus, to capture Mount Rushmore, a "shrine of democracy" as the local chamber of commerce has so aptly described it, was a way of serving notice that the Indian conception of land, its sacredness and spiritual value, cannot be disregarded in favor of simple commercial development.

Of such concern is the land issue among American Indians that it was made the subject of a minority report to the platform committee of the Democratic party in 1972. Several Indians had testified on various proposals that they felt should be part of the policy of the Democrats for 1972. The proposal to give priority to Indian tribes for all surplus federal property was rejected as being too vague. The Indian delegates to the convention promptly organized and wrote a minority report and put it on the agenda. They had to organize the seventeen Indian delegates who were at the convention in Miami and work most of the night so that when the time came to give their report, they would have sufficient strength to get it through.

The Indian report was given by Leon Cook, Chippewa from Minnesota and president of the NCIA, and Shirley Daley, a Menominee from Wisconsin and a key figure in DRUMS, which, as we have seen, is spearheading the move to restore the lands of the Menominees. A white man from Louisiana opposed the move to support Indians on surplus lands for reasons all his own, and then the vote was taken. By a loud margin the delegates put priority to Indian tribes on surplus federal lands into the Democratic platform.

We hope that both parties make the return of surplus federal lands part of their Indian policy for the future. In many instances federal property is becoming surplus in the urban areas and in areas adjoining those in which a great many Indian people live. Transfer of parts of these lands to Indian groups for the creation of all-purpose service and cultural centers would be a very valuable investment for the federal and state governments. Educational problems and employment needs of Indian people could be handled by special centers developed on these lands. In the long run, solving these basic problems will return in responsible citizenship and earned taxable income everything that the government invests and then some.

We are not advocating the simple restoration of all federal lands that could conceivably become vacant some time in the future. Many of the surplus lands will be situated far from Indian people. There is no reason therefore for giving them to Indians. However, when lands are situated such that they could support a small resident population, some housing, and an educational or cultural center, we believe that a very good investment would be to deed them to an Indian center, tribe, or intertribal council for its use.

We would urge that a minimum of 30,000 acres be set aside as a goal for restoration of select sites of federal surplus lands for use by Indian people. We would still include in this total the whole 440 acres surplus at Fort Lawton, the 19 acres at Alcatraz, and the lands in Minneapolis and Milwaukee now in dispute between the two cities and their resident Indian groups. All of these lands obviously have commercial value, some very small and others very great. But these lands should not be judged on commercial value alone. Rather they should be considered as lands upon which true communities can be built.

We urge the General Service Administration to convene a general meeting with Indian organizations. This meeting should openly discuss the lands that are, and may in the immediate future become, surplus to the needs of the federal government. The possible uses for such lands with a minimum investment should be outlined for everyone's benefit. And those pieces of land that appear to have some relationship to the needs of identifiable Indian communities should be marked out with the notation that planning should be done to determine if programs, housing, or cultural centers can be built upon them for use by Indian people.

With the Indian population now expanding rapidly and future opportunities for rural people becoming fewer and fewer, it is apparent that some new form of collective, cooperative, or communal economic forms will have to be developed for rural people. The present Indian land base will not support the populations of the tribes at present even if the restoration that we have suggested in previous chapters are all made immediately. Therefore, there has to be some means of expanding the land base of those tribes that have a large population and small tribal lands.

We believe that tribes presently lacking an adequate land base should be given preference in loan funds to rebuild an adequate land base for themselves. Many tribes have lost land through procedures that were questionable at best, scandalous at worst. The Nisqually story may be retold many times, changing only the tribal name to Seneca, Pottawatomi, Sac and Fox, and so on.

In order to compensate the tribes that have been victimized at some time in the past and to help them to maintain themselves, we advocate changes in the present federal laws regarding lands of Indian tribes. First, we recommend that any time an Indian tribe purchases land within or contiguous to presently owned reservation lands and boundaries, it be allowed to take such lands into federal trust and hold them in the same status as lands they presently own under treaties and statutes.

We recommend that a special fund be established to loan interest-free funds to small Indian tribes for the purchase of such lands so as to increase tribal income until the tribe can support its own governmental service functions and so as to provide sites for economic development and housing programs. Such a fund should receive appropriations in the amount of $5 million a year for twenty years. The funds would be taken from the vast amounts now made available to scholars, bureaucrats, study centers, research agencies, and other groups that have received tremendous amounts of money in the past to study why Indians are poor, uneducated, economically disadvantaged, hungry, sick, and discontented. The taxpayer and the Indian would thus be assured that the funds were accomplishing something.

We recommend that the Department of Agriculture and the National Parks System cede to Indian tribes lands that are adjacent to those of small tribes lacking sufficient lands. These additional lands would be attached to the existing reservations to make them economically viable for the Indian community concerned. The Badlands National Monument, for example, could be ceded to the Oglala Sioux tribe, which would receive a regular contract to operate the monument for tourism and recreation.

We anticipate that this program would involve the restoration of some 2.5 million acres of land to nearly a hundred tribes. It would almost immediately reduce the rate of unemployment on some reservations by a substantial amount and would increase the income of smaller tribes rapidly so that they could support governmental functions with their own funds instead of being individually dependent upon welfare and unemployment doles from the federal government.

With the addition of these lands we estimate that a restoration of 2,530,000 acres of land would be added to the national Indian land base. Adding that to the total to this point gives the following:

Tribal lands	39,663,412.09
Individual Indian allotments	10,697,621.58
Alaska native lands	40,000,000
Occupied Indian lands	4,723,017.2
Submarginal lands restored	344,811
Flathead lands restored	10,585.86
Warm Springs lands restored	61,300
Crow lands restored	618
Menominee lands restored	230,000
Klamath lands restored	144,000
Nisqually lands purchased and restored	1,375
Nonfederal tribal lands purchased	200,000
Surplus federal property ceded	30,000
Agriculture and park lands ceded	2,500,00
	98,606,740.73

❦ 14 ❦

One Hundred Million Acres:
A New Federal Policy for
Indians and Indian Lands

THROUGHOUT THE summer of 1972 the tensions began to build in Indian country. A series of killings of Indian people around the nation took place which culminated in the shooting death of Richard Oakes, leader of the Alcatraz movement. Oakes had gone to a YMCA camp in search of a young Indian boy who had apparently gone there to look for horses. The caretaker of the camp killed Oakes claiming that he had jumped out from behind a tree in an effort to scare him. Apparently there had been some previous trouble between Oakes and the caretaker.

As fall approached, the Indian activists began planning a giant march on Washington to coincide with the national presidential elections. They hoped to highlight the precarious state of Indian reservations and the oppressed life which many Indian people live. In a meeting in Denver in mid-September, the young Indians decided to call their march the "Trail of Broken Treaties." Beginning in early October, a number of caravans began to cross the country. One caravan left Los Angeles and traveled the southern route across Arizona and New Mexico, visiting the large southwestern reservations en route.

From the Northwest the Survival of American Indians group, which had fought out the desperate fishing-rights struggle during the previous decade, started another caravan of Indians. Among their complaints was the failure of the Justice Department to move forward on the case the group had filed some two years earlier, a case that would determine the extent of Indian fishing rights. As we have seen with the Nisquallys, the fishing tribes of the Pacific Northwest had not only been deprived of fishing rights, but in many cases their reservations had been taken for government installations and other projects. The SAI group hoped to regain both lands for their families and a measure of protection from the federal government in the exercise of their treaty fishing rights.

As the caravan moved across the United States it was joined by numerous reservation people. Youngsters left their high schools and colleges and moved forward toward the nation's capital. Older reservation Indians, some in their seventies and eighties and tired of a lifetime of neglect, became the most ardent supporters of the movement and, even though too old for extensive travel, packed their bags and chose the most comfortable automobiles for the long trip.

Part of the caravan began in Canada and included descendants of some of the tribes that had been pushed across the border in wars fought nearly two centuries ago. Both Canadian and American Indians had been having trouble with border crossings (in violation of the Jay Treaty between the United States and Great Britian to which the tribes of North America were third-party beneficiaries). With respect to the international border between the United States and Canada, the people maintained, there was no border for Indians; they were free to come and go as if the two larger nations had never come into being.

As the caravan toured the nation picking up participants, the people had the cooperation of state police, local officials, church and civic groups, and private citizens. They stopped at the twin cities of Minnesota briefly and held a general workshop on how to present their demands. As a result of the workshop a list of Twenty Points was drawn up to present to Congress, and the two presidential candidates. The Twenty Points covered a variety of problems which all Indians shared. Almost half of the points were concerned with reestabishment of the traditional treaty relationship between the United States and the respective tribes.

A return to treaty-making as a basic procedural format for defining the relationship between the United States and Indian tribes would appear to be a novelty. As we have seen previously, the treaties involved a general concept of land cession in which the tribes had traded their aboriginal homelands for certain rights, privileges, and services given to them by the federal government. Renewing the treaty relationship would appear, then, to reaffirm the concept of land cession. But the tenth point of the Twenty Points covered the question of land problems. The people of the Trail of Broken Treaties asked that a permanent land base of 110 million acres be established for Indian tribes by congressional action in the coming Congress:

The next Congress and Administration should commit themselves and effect a national commitment, implemented by statutes of executive and administrative actions, to restore a permanent non-diminishing Native American land base of not less than 110 million acres by July 4, 1976. This land base, and its separate parts, should be vested with the recognized rights and conditions of being perpetually non-taxable, except by autonomous and sovereign Indian authority, and should never again be permitted to be alienated from Native American or Indian ownership and control.

The Trail of Broken Treaties thus advocated precisely what we have advocated in this book with respect to the establishment of a permanent land base for American Indian communities. The distinction, if one can be said to exist, lies in the formulation of the figure at which the land base is to be maintained.

During a workshop at Minneapolis the people of the Trail of Broken Treaties developed a formula by which they arrived at the figure of 110 million acres:

When Congress acted to delimit the President's authority and the Indian Nations' powers for making treaties in 1871, approximately 135,000,000 acres of land and territory had been secured to Indian ownership against cession of relinquishment. This acreage did not include the 1867 treaty-secured recognition of land title and rights of Alaska Natives, nor millions of acres otherwise retained by Indians in what were to become "unratified" treaties of Indian land cession, as in California, nor other land areas authorized to be set aside for Indian nations contracted by, but never benefitting from, their treaties. When the Congress in 1887, under the General Allotment Act and other measures of the period and "single system of legislation," delegated treaty-assigned Presidential responsibilities to the Secretary of the Interior and his Commissioner of Indian Affairs relating to the government of Indian relations under the treaties, the 135 million acres, collectively held, immediately became subject to loss. The 1887

Act provided for the sale of "surplus" Indian lands, and contained a formula for the assignment of allocation of land tracts to Indian individuals, dependent partly on family size, which would have allowed for a average-sized allotment of 135 acres to *one million Indians*—at a time when the number of tribally-related Indians was less than a quarter million or fewer than 200,000.

The Interior Department efficiently managed the loss of 90 million acres of Indian land, and its transfer to non-Indian ownership (frequently by homestead, not direct purchase), in little more than the next quarter-century. When Congress prohibited further allotments to Indian individuals by its 1934 Indian Reorganization Act, it effectively determined that future generations of Indian people would be "landless Indians," except by heirship and inheritance. [One hundred ten million acres, including 40 million acres in Alaska, would approximate an average 135 acres multiplied by .8 million Native Americans, a number indicated by the 1970 U.S. census.]

Simple justice would seem to demand that priorities in restoration of land bases be granted to those Indian nations who are landless by fault of unratifield and unfulfilled treaty provisions; Indian nations, landless because of congressional and administrative actions reflective of criminal abuse of trust responsibilities; and other groupings of landless Indians, particularly of the landless generations, including many urban Indians and non-reservation Indian people—many of whom have been forced to pay, in forms of deprivations, loss of rights and entitlements, and other extreme costs upon their lives, an "emigration-migration-education-training" tax for their unfulfilled pursuit of opportunity in America—a tax as unwarranted and unjustified as it is unprecedented in the history of human rights in mature nations possessed of a modern conscience.

The contention of the participants of the Trail of Broken Treaties, therefore, is simply a formula attempting to restore the ratio of Indians-to-acreage that existed in 1887. It is fair in its conception and simple enough for the dullest mind. We are highly gratified to discover that a figure in the neighborhood of 100 million acres of land as a permanent American Indian land base is accepted by so much of the national Indian community.

As we have seen, the dice were loaded in favor of the white man and against the Indian from the very beginning. Under the doctrine of discovery, the only title to land that the European nations would have recognized would have been a piece of paper written in Heaven and given directly to the pope along with a divine restraining order forbidding trespass. Since the various Indian tribes were not Christian and had no chance of becoming Christians or of entering into the European political scheme prior to Columbus's voyage, the place of Indian nations in world affairs was preempted from the very beginning.

Times have certainly changed. The doctrine of discovery is no longer applicable, and as pointed out, the claim of the United States and its entire scheme of political relationships with Indian tribes is dependent upon this ancient and obsolete doctrine that has no place in the modern world.

We therefore recommend that Congress by legislation disclaim the doctrine of discovery and announce that all lands now held by Indian tribes or to be acquired by Indian tribes shall be placed in a new legal category to be called Indian lands. They will be held, as are all lands of Indians at present, in a legal status that makes them immune from all forms of taxation, state and federal, on all forms of income derived from them or from activities conducted by license from the tribal governments that have control over them.

Tribal governments shall have complete control of all hunting and fishing, gathering of berries, wild ricing, cutting of timber and mining of minerals thereon. Tribal governments shall have complete power of zoning, and they shall never be subjected to condemnation by state or local governments or by federal agencies for any purpose whatsoever. Any change in the title of these lands shall be by congressional action, with full and open hearings in each house of Congress on every aspect of the proposed legislation. The tribal governments of the respective reservations shall have first-priority water rights on all streams arising on or passing through the lands, as they do now, but in any proposed use of the water on any river or drainage system that would affect the Indian rights to water, the full potential use of the Indian tribe shall be determined prior to the determination of any other rights to the water.

We additionally recommend that it be the policy of Congress that if any lands are hereafter taken from any Indian tribe by any action of the United States government or any of its constituent agencies, the amount of acres taken from the tribe shall be replaced, so that the tribe does not suffer a loss of its lands; it shall be the duty and responsibility of Congress to purchase sufficient acreage contiguous to existing tribal lands and make it a part of the reservation from which the lands were taken. It shall be the additional duty and responsibility of Congress to pay compensation to the tribe from which the lands have been taken for the dislocation of its community and for expenses incurred in its loss of lands.

Indian lands would not be subjected to the control of the Bureau of Indian Affairs or the Department of the Interior. It would be under the control of the Indian tribe to which the lands belonged. Such lands could be sold by the Indian tribe only after any plan to sell lands was presented to the whole membership of the tribe meeting in a general council and was discussed for a period of three consecutive years in open council in its identical and original form. After the three-year period of presentation the matter of the sale of the land would be placed on a special referendum vote of the entire tribal membership. Such a proposal would have to be approved by a two-thirds majority of all members of the tribe, eighteen years and older. Approval by a majority of the people voting in the special referendum would be insufficient to approve the sale. Leases of tribal lands in tracts exceeding twenty acres would be subject to the same conditions as the sale of lands. Leases of tribal lands for periods extending beyond five years would also be subject to the above conditions.

Any distribution of funds derived from the sale of tribal lands to a tribal member would not be subjected to income tax at ordinary income rates. Retention of funds by tribal governments would be immune from any taxation by any state or federal revenue agency.

We additionally recommend that the occupied lands and submarginal lands now held or previously purchased for Indian use or for purposes of the administration of any function of government relating to Indians be deeded to the Indian tribe concerned, the government to have rent-free use of the lands so long as it maintains its present use of such lands. When the present government use of such lands changes, negotiations for rentals and leases shall be made with the tribe to whom the lands belong.

We additionally recommend that the lands of the Flatheads, Warm Springs, Crow, and other tribes that are presently and illegally held by the United States Forest Service or departments of Agriculture or Interior be ceded to those tribes to be added to their reservations.

We additionally recommend that bills repealing the terminations of the Menominee Indians of Wisconsin, the Klamath Indians of Oregon, the Siletz and Grande Ronde Indians of Oregon, the Affiliated Utes of Utah, and the bands of Paiutes of southern Utah be introduced in Congress and that these tribes be restored to full federal Indian status, with their lands placed in the new category of Indian lands.

We further recommend that two special funds be created for use by tribal governments. One fund of low-interest loans in the amount of $100 million to be made available to Indian tribes to purchase the allotments and interests in allotments of individual Indian allottees, the lands thus purchased to be added to the existing tribal estates. The other fund should be a no-interest fund to be made available to small tribes for the purchase of lands not now under Indian ownership for the expansion of their existing tribal land base consistent with their needs.

We further recommend that a special appropriation be made to purchase lands for the nonfederal Indian tribes now without land. These tribes shall be given full federal rights and status as Indian tribes, and the lands purchased for them shall be placed in the category of Indian lands.

We further recommend that the lands of the Nisqually tribe of Indians be expanded as recommended in the chapter discussing their land needs and that any additional traditional fishing sites, grounds, or stations of the tribes of the Treaty of Medicine Creek be purchased and made a part of the reservation of the tribe concerned.

We further recommend that the Indian Claims Commission be made a permanent court for litigation of cases and controversies involving Indian lands and uses of Indian lands.

We additionally recommend that the General Services Administration be authorized to convene a general meeting and inform the Indian tribes and organizations concerned about land currently surplus or soon to be surplus that may be made available to them. We advocate priority to be given to those Indian tribes or groups that present adequate use-plans for the lands that are or may become surplus to federal needs.

We realize that such a program appears to be frightfully expensive. It is not. A great deal of money is now spent to pay bureaucrats to keep records on heirship lands owned by individual Indians. Incredible amounts of money are being spent by bureaucrats traveling hither and yon to visit Inidian tribes to prevent them from using their lands. Literally millions of dollars are being spent by colleges and universities, research and consultant groups, and government agencies trying to discover what Indians are doing. We advocate that these scandalously wasteful and perenial budget items be abolished and that the funds now wasted in these futile efforts be placed in the special funds we have advocated above to be used for land purchase by Indian tribes.

The proposals we have made with respect to Indian lands and their sale and leasing, if carried out, would result in gigantic reduction in the number of anonymous bureaucrats who toil in hidden offices, creating problems for the Indians and the American taxpayer alike. The proposal for the establishment of hunting and fishing rights in the new Indian lands would save the state of Washington a great deal of money in its continual harassment of the people at Frank's Landing and would probably enable the state to balance its budget.

As continually pointed out in this book, all previous proposals for improving the condition of American Indian people has revolved around the confiscation of their lands and pious admonitions for them to stop being Indians. We truly believe that motivational programs of any ilk are demeaning and serve merely to perpetuate problems, not to solve them. The federal government is now spending in excess of a half a billion dollars a year trying to confiscate Indian lands and water rights, while motivating Indians to become something they are not, do not wish to become, and have steadfastly resisted becoming for four centuries.

In the name of justice, mercy, sanity, common sense, fiscal responsibility, and rationality we present this program to place Indian communities on a solid legal and economic basis once and for all. We appeal to the American people to demand of their senators and congressmen a new day for American Indian people, without any hidden agendas in the legislation or any shifting of concepts and programs to confiscate Indian lands in the name of progress, patriotism, or religion.

Index

Index